D1102735

THE *Hillier* GARDENER'S GUIDES
SHRUBS

Andrew McIndoe

D&C
David and Charles

A DAVID & CHARLES BOOK

David & Charles is a subsidiary of F+W (UK) Ltd.,
an F+W Publications Inc. company

First published in the UK in 2005
Text Copyright © Andrew McIndoe 2005
Copyright © David & Charles 2005

Andrew McIndoe has asserted his right to be identified as author of this
work in accordance with the Copyright, Designs and Patents Act, 1988.

All rights reserved. No part of this publication may be reproduced, stored
in a retrieval system, or transmitted, in any form or by any means,
electronic or mechanical, by photocopying, recording or otherwise,
without prior permission in writing from the publisher.

A catalogue record for this book is available from the British Library.
ISBN: UK 0 7153 2022 X

Printed in Singapore by KHL Printing Co Pte Ltd
for David & Charles
Brunel House   Newton Abbot   Devon

Commissioning Editor Mic Cady
Art Editor Sue Cleave
Production Director Roger Lane

Series Editor Sue Gordon, OutHouse Publishing
   Winchester, Hampshire SO22 5DS
Copy Editors Polly Boyd, Sue Gordon
Proofreader Alison Shakspeare
Indexer June Wilkins

Visit our website at www.davidandcharles.co.uk

David & Charles books are available from all good bookshops;
alternatively you can contact our Orderline on (0)1626 334555 or write
to us at FREEPOST EX2 110, David & Charles Direct, Newton Abbot,
TQ12 4ZZ (no stamp required UK mainland).

ORNAMENTAL PLANT OR PERNICIOUS WEED?

In certain circumstances ornamental garden plants can be
undesirable when introduced into natural habitats, either
because they compete with native flora, or because they act
as hosts to fungal and insect pests. Plants that are popular
in one part of the world may be considered undesirable in
another. Horticulturists have learned to be wary of the effect
that cultivated plants may have on native habitats and, as a
rule, any plant likely to be a problem in a particular area if it
escapes from cultivation is restricted and therefore is not
offered for sale.

PHOTOGRAPHIC CREDITS

The publishers would like to acknowledge with thanks all those whose
gardens are pictured in this book.

**ALL PHOTOGRAPHS WERE TAKEN BY ANDREW MCINDOE AND
JOHN HILLIER WITH THE EXCEPTION OF:**

David Austin® Roses: 113(Good Companions 3, 5), 115(Good
   Companions 3)
Eric Crichton: p14(lft)
Duncan & Davies: 51(*Acer palmatum* 'Burgundy Lace')
Garden Picture Library: pp (GC=Good Companions) 29(top lft)/J S Sira;
   49(GC 1) & back cover(top)/John Beedle; 49(GC 4)/Clive Nichols;
   52(top lft)/Philippe Bonduel; 52(top rt)/Mark Bolton; 56 & back
   flap/Clive Nichols; 63(GC 2)/J S Sira; 63(GC 5)/Sunniva Harte
   79(lft)/Mark Bolton; 85(GC 1)/Neil Holmes; 85(GC 3)/Jerry Pavia;
   90(top lft)/Vaughan Fleming; 93(GC 5) Neil Homes; 98(GC 3)/David
   Askham; 133(GC 1)/J S Sira; 136(top lft)/Neil Holmes; 154(GC 4)/
   J S Sira; 157(top ctre)/Didier Willery; 165(top rt)/Neil Holmes;
   175(btm rt)/Sunniva Harte; 177(ctre rt)/John Glover
New Leaf Plants: 43(Good Companions 4), 55(Good Companions 4)
Osberton Nurseries: 101(Good Companions 3), 105(Good
   Companions 3)

Contents

Introduction

In writing this book I have borne in mind the questions I am most often asked. I have also drawn on advice from other gardeners and on experience gained from successes and failures in gardens with which I have been involved.

This is not intended to be a definitive work on woody plants. That has already been written by the late Sir Harold Hillier, revised and updated by John Hillier VMH and Allen Coombes – *The Hillier Manual of Trees & Shrubs*. This book is a practical guide to choosing and using shrubs.

Thirty years of garden centre experience has taught me that most of us look at the individual plant, when what we should be doing is looking at the overall picture. We concentrate our efforts on assessing whether or not we like a particular plant, without considering how it will fit into our garden and what it will contribute.

Shrubs are the backbone of the British garden, and sometimes it is easy to forget the significance of their contribution. Some of our best shrubs are not glamorous, nor are they the plants of the moment, yet we have come to rely upon them and perhaps take their presence for granted.

The recent upsurge of interest in herbaceous perennials, and the ongoing increase in the popularity of bedding plants, sometimes diverts our attention from getting the basics right.

A few years ago I moved from a small garden to a much larger plot, and I determined to garden accordingly: big, bold planting from the start, and no more messing about with little treasures that need close scrutiny to be admired. Yet I have to admit that I struggled – I was just as reluctant to make those bold decisions as the gardeners whom I have so often advised.

Interest in gardening is fostered and encouraged by success. This book is about helping you to attain success. A good garden has variety, and it has continuity of interest through the seasons. With container-grown plants now being the norm, we are able to select plants by season, at the time of year when they are performing at their best. As most of us are fair-weather gardeners, it is no wonder that our gardens tend to be at their most prolific in spring. With a little planning and thought, however, the interest can be spread over the whole year.

Most shrubs are good-value plants that will give many years of pleasure for a relatively small outlay. Because they may well be with us for a very long time, and are not plants that we choose every year, it is crucial that we select our shrubs wisely and grow them well. I hope this book helps you to achieve this.

Andrew McIndoe

Cornus kousa 'Gold Star'

WHAT IS A SHRUB?

A shrub is a woody plant that has more than one stem arising from ground level, whereas a tree has a single stem arising from ground level. Size is irrelevant; there are large shrubs and small trees, and the former can be bigger than the latter.

Shrubs are deciduous or evergreen. Deciduous means that they shed their leaves and have a dormant season. This is an adaptation to an environment where light, water and warmth are insufficient to sustain the plant in full leaf. Evergreen shrubs have adapted their foliage to conserve moisture and stand up to temperature variation. Growth slows during periods of lower temperature. Some shrubs are semi-evergreen and go half way, reducing their leaf numbers during a semi-dormant period.

The production of woody tissue is a means of perennation, or survival. Woody stems enable plants to grow larger, to spread their leaves further apart by branching and to grow taller than low plants, so competing more efficiently for air and light.

And here lies the difference between trees and shrubs on the one hand and herbaceous plants on the other. Both may be perennial, but the size of the herbaceous plant is limited. The stems can grow only to a height that can support the leaves and flowers. Any further growth would result in their collapse. If the herbaceous plant is to have a dormant period, then it must die down to ground level and perennate in some way: through fleshy roots, bulbs, corms, tubers, or any of the other ingenious methods that plants have devised for storing water and nutrients.

Woody plants have devised a means whereby they support the growth made in one season and build on it in the following season. The key to this is secondary thickening, which involves lignin. Lignin is a substance laid down in the old vessels that carried water and nutrients up the plant; it thickens the vessel walls and blocks them, thus forming reinforcing rods that permanently strengthen the stem. These vessels are replaced by new ones on the outside of the stem in what is called the cambium layer, under the bark and epidermis. This may happen year after year, making the stem thicker and thicker and enabling the plant to grow taller and taller, as happens with some trees.

Man has been dependent upon lignin through all stages of his evolution. The deposition of lignin results in the production of the wood that is used for fuel, building, ships, paper and so much else on which mankind relies.

INTRODUCING SHRUBS

Shrubs: woody plants with several branches arising from ground level. Some have showy flowers, others variegated or colourful foliage; some have attractive stems and bark, others aromatic leaves. Shrubs contribute to the garden picture at all levels, from the ground level to way above eye-level. Some of the most important shrubs are just plain green but retain their foliage throughout the seasons. For centuries man has planted them, shaped them and used them to create the structural framework of the garden.

Right: Le Jardin d'Angélique, Normandy, France

Shrubs in the English garden: a history

Ornamental horticulture has evolved over two millennia, with the most dramatic part of that evolution taking place in the past two centuries. Early gardeners had to choose from native plant material and a limited number of introductions from overseas. Since the golden age of plant hunting, instigated by the Victorians, gardeners have had a far greater wealth of plant material to work with. Since the very beginning, shrubs have played a vital role as structure plants in gardens. Today, their diversity of shape, form, colour and texture takes centre stage.

The earliest-known gardens in Britain are those planted by the Romans during the 1st century AD, attached to large villas and palaces such as Fishbourne, near Chichester in Sussex. It seems likely that these gardens consisted of a symmetrical planting of box hedges, divided by gravel walks, alongside an open, landscaped space. There may well have been kitchen gardens too, growing vegetables and fruits brought from the Continent. Sweet chestnut and walnut are thought to have reached Britain at this time.

Early gardens attached to monasteries cultivated a variety of trees and plants in orchards, kitchen gardens and recreational areas. Most plants were aromatic or had medicinal properties.

IN A MONASTERY GARDEN

In the Anglo-Saxon period that followed the end of the Roman era in Britain, the record becomes blurred, and little is known about horticulture at that time. During the Middle Ages, however, the spread of Christianity from continental Europe saw the establishment of monastic houses in Britain and, with them, a fostering of the tradition of cultivating plants. Aromatic plants and plants with medicinal uses – rosemary, thyme, sage, lavender – as well as any fruiting plants of food value, were brought over to be grown by the monks in their physic and kitchen gardens. The covered walks of the cloister surrounded an open green space, often with a central well.

Some medieval castles, too, had courtyard gardens, with paths criss-crossing flower beds in which native plants probably grew alongside those collected on religious crusades and missions abroad. Linking the garden with the surrounding landscape were mounds that provided views over the castle walls.

THE PLANT SHAPERS

As the need for fortification became less intense and the medieval manor replaced the castle, gardens became a place for pastimes such as bowls or tennis. Attached to the house, gardens were generally enclosed by a hedge, often of box or yew.

After the dissolution of the monasteries and the sale of monastic properties in the 16th century, the new landowners enclosed tracts of land for keeping deer or

Topiary and trimmed hedges at Cliveden, in Buckinghamshire. For many years trimming and shaping was the only way in which gardeners could enhance the variety of hardy plant material.

cattle and created formal gardens and terraces near the house, sheltered by hedges or walls, in which they grew ornamental flowers and herbs.

By now, the influence of the Italian Renaissance was beginning to show itself in the gardens of grand English palaces and houses. Geometrical layouts mirrored the alignment of the house, featuring sundials, fountains and statues. To this period belongs the Tudor knot garden – an intricate pattern of low hedges, usually box.

In the 1600s wealthy Stuarts took inspiration from the French, rather than the Italians, and introduced broad avenues of trees, often in conjunction with rectangular ornamental parterres of formal low hedges, best viewed from a mount, raised terraces or the upper floors of the house. The spaces between the hedges were often filled with herbs, low shrubs or annual flowers. King James I's head gardener, Mollet, used topiary extensively, thus making it very fashionable. It was also popular in the Dutch style of garden, along with water features, trees and bulbs including, of course, tulips.

THE LANDSCAPERS

The formality of the Italian Renaissance garden gave way to a more natural look in the 18th century. William Kent's garden for Lord Burlington at Chiswick House, with its temples, statues and classical ornaments in open parkland with trees, became hugely influential. Kent's pupil and son-in-law Lancelot 'Capability' Brown

continued his work, making the house an integral part of the landscape. Formality was taking a break: no hedges, no clipping and a different type of control of the plant material. Humphry Repton followed in Brown's footsteps as a landscape gardener, but re-introduced terraces and flower gardens adjoining the house.

ACROSS THE ATLANTIC

The 17th-century British colonists in America took the gardening tradition with them. Their first priority was growing food, but before long New England cottage gardens were flourishing with the seeds and bulbs of favourite plants from home. In the New York area the Huguenots too brought their love of gardening, and by the late 1660s clipped evergreens were found alongside the roses, tulips and crown imperials of Dutch and French gardens. The first commercial nurseries began importing trees, shrubs and herbaceous plants from Europe. When William Penn founded Pennsylvania he envisaged a 'greene towne', with each house having a good-sized garden. His own property was later to become the site of the world-famous Longwood Gardens.

The expansion of trading in the 18th and 19th centuries brought great wealth to America as well as to places along the trade routes, such as Madeira. Shipbuilders,

The gardens of Quinta do Palheiro, Madeira, originally laid out in the 18th century. Gardens on international trade routes, such as these, became rich in plant material from all over the world.

merchants and sea captains built houses in fashionable Continental styles, and gardens followed suit. As cargoes moved across the seas, so too did plants. The wealthy liked the variety that the new plants brought to their gardens; gardeners enjoyed greater prestige.

THE PLANT HUNTERS

The Victorian era saw the emergence of a new passion for plants. Bedding plants made their debut in a big way, raised in greenhouses and planted out for exotic summer colour. Public gardens, parks and open spaces brought horticulture to the masses in styles varying

This magnificent plant is the original specimen of *Rhododendron maccabeanum*, collected by Frank Kingdon-Ward in the far east and planted at Trewithen Gardens, near Truro, in Cornwall.

from formal to wild. The fruits of the labours of plant hunters and collectors started to make their impact.

Plants from China, Japan, the Himalayas and the Americas swelled the nursery catalogues manyfold. British gardens could not have been better placed to appreciate this influx of new plant material. A wealthy population, a long gardening history and a love of plants were contributory factors, but most significant was the country's climate: temperate, with plenty of rainfall – broadly similar to that of the main regions of the world that were so rich in good garden plants.

Plant hunting was nothing new. The John Tradescants, elder and younger, had brought plants back from Europe and Virginia, USA, in the 17th century. However, it was during the late 18th and early 19th centuries that collecting began in earnest, with hunters such as John Fraser and David Douglas seeking

out plants in North America, Philipp von Siebold in Japan, and William Lobb in Chile and California.

The late 19th century and early 20th century proved to be the golden age of plant hunting. Wealthy private gardeners and the nurseries that served them sponsored expeditions: Robert Fortune in China and Japan, John Gould Veitch in Japan, William Hooker in the Himalayas, Charles Maries in China and Japan, E.H. Wilson and George Forrest in China. The era came to a close in 1958 with the death of Frank Kingdon-Ward, who collected widely in China, Burma and Tibet.

Gardeners will recognize the names of these plant collectors, immortalized in many of our most popular garden plants. The gardener of today is often surprised to learn how recent many of these introductions are: some of our popular shrubs have been in our gardens for less than 100 years.

NEW PLANTS, A NEW STYLE

In the late 1800s and early 1900s William Robinson advocated permanent planting in place of bedding, combining exotics and bold-foliage plants in a native wild garden setting. Gardens began to look something like ours. Robinson's contemporary Gertrude Jekyll, regarded as the 20th century's most influential gardener, took the new palette of plant material a stage further by building on colour schemes and using plants as a material to integrate the house into the garden and the surrounding landscape.

Ann's Grove Gardens, in County Cork, Southern Ireland, exemplifies the informal style of William Robinson, with exotic and native species interplanted in the natural landscape.

A little later in the 20th century Vita Sackville-West, at Sissinghurst Castle in Kent, and the American-born Lawrence Johnston, at Hidcote Manor in the Cotswolds, combined formal and informal planting, integrating different styles of gardening with notable success.

On a more domestic scale, the growth of the suburbs saw a proliferation of small plots requiring hardy, easy-to-grow plants that tolerated the smoky atmosphere. While gardening at the grander end of the scale

Lanhydrock, near Bodmin in Cornwall, where the legacy of the Victorian plant collectors sits in a woodland setting alongside the formal bedding schemes that were so typical of the era.

still celebrated the introduction of new plants from the far corners of the world, the smaller domestic garden popularized a chosen few.

WHERE DO SHRUBS FIT IN?

The majority of ornamental shrubs have arrived in our gardens in the last 200 years, and mostly in the 20th century. Yes, of course there were woody plants in gardens – indigenous species and those introduced subsequently from Europe and beyond – but it is only in the past century that the English gardener has learned to use the various types of plant together.

The shrub provides the permanent structure in the middle layer of the landscape: it occupies the layer beneath the canopy of trees, while providing permanent height and body to the layer of herbaceous plants and smaller subjects below. Of course, sometimes tall shrubs may creep into the higher layer and many dwarf shrubs are important in the lower layer.

PLANTS OF GARDEN ORIGIN

Fifty years ago the flowering shrubs found in the average garden were few in variety: forsythia, roses, ribes, syringa, philadelphus, spiraea, cotoneaster, berberis, cytisus and a handful more. Since then, many of the introductions made by the plant hunters have become widely available, vastly increasing the range of material available to gardeners.

Even greater than the number of plants returned by the plant hunters, however, is the influx that has resulted from selection and hybridization. Variation arises in plants that grow in the wild as well as in plants that are cultivated, and over the years gardeners have selected and propagated the best forms of naturally occurring species. Fired by the quest for such improvements as larger flowers, a longer flowering season, more compact growth and higher disease resistance, they have also learned to select and modify plants through hybridization.

As far as shrubs are concerned, the hybridization process – from seed to flowering, to selection, trials and commercial propagation – is a long one. In the case of a new hybrid rose more than ten years elapse from the time the original cross is made to the launch of the new variety. Herbaceous perennials and annual bedding plants reach maturity more quickly, so the process is quicker – but many disappear as fast as they arrive.

All plant types have their phases of popularity, but shrubs remain the essential ingredient in any garden, and a good plant endures, however long it takes to reach us.

Shrubs are an essential element in the typical English garden. Today's gardener has access to a wide range of hardy shrubs that form the essential structure in the garden and link it to the natural landscape.

Speaking botanically

Latin names, as opposed to common names, may be frightening at first, but they are essential when it comes to accurate communication. A plant's common name may vary from one area to another. And when it comes to using common names in a different country, the confusion is greater still, even when the same native tongue is used.

PLANT CLASSIFICATION

FAMILY In plant classification the flowering plants are divided into a number of families. Each of these families contains a number of genera that have similar characteristics. For example, the rose family, Rosaceae, includes not only the genus *Rosa* but also a number of other genera, including *Potentilla*, *Cotoneaster*, *Malus* and *Pyracantha*. A plant's botanical name consists of the genus and the species.

GENUS The generic name is something like our surname. It always starts with a capital letter and is always a noun. It is often derived from names found in an ancient language such as Latin, Greek or Arabic. *Daphne*, for example, is named after the daughter of the ancient Greek river god. Other generic names commemorate people, in some cases the person that first discovered the plant: *Deutzia*, for example, is named after J. Deutz, *Fuchsia* after Leonard Fuchs.

SPECIES The specific name, or epithet, is more like our first name, except that it is written after the genus and always starts with a lower case letter. It cannot stand alone as a name and is not specific to that plant. As a Latin adjective, the specific name takes the gender of the generic name, so its ending agrees with the noun (although, as in any language, there are exceptions). The specific name is usually descriptive, giving us some information about the plant.

Specific names fall into four main categories:

- **Describing origin:** by continent, country, region, e.g., *sinensis, -e,* from China.

- **Describing habitat:** from mountains, woods, fields, water, e.g., *montanus, -a, -um,* of mountains.

- **Describing the plant or a feature of the plant,** such as its size, habit, leaf shape, flower colour, e.g., *fastigiatus, -a, -um,* erect growing.

- **Commemorating a botanist, plant collector, famous horticulturist, patron,** e.g., *davidii,* after Armand David, 19th-century plant collector.

SUBSPECIES, VARIETAS AND FORMA These are the botanically recognized subdivisions of a species

where distinct forms occur in the wild. These are variously known as subspecies (subsp.), varietas or variety (var.), and forma or form (f.). For example *Skimmia japonica* subsp. *reevesiana*.

CULTIVAR A cultivar is a distinct form of a species that has been selected from wild or cultivated stock and has then been maintained in cultivation by vegetative propagation. In other words, all offspring come from one original plant or clone. The cultivar name is written with an initial capital letter within single quotation marks, and follows the specific name. For example, *Acer palmatum* 'Bloodgood'.

In gardening nomenclature, 'cultivar' and 'variety' are interchangeable. Often, too, the term 'form' is used in a general way to refer to a variety, subspecies or cultivar.

CLONE To all intents and purposes a clone is the same as a cultivar: a selection of single individuals maintained in cultivation by vegetative propagation. All offspring are identical to the original.

GROUP A group lies somewhere between a cultivar and the subdivision of a species. A cultivar shows little or no variation, having originated from one individual. Members of a group can show variation, but not enough to separate them botanically. So the *Acer palmatum* Atropurpureum Group includes forms of *Acer palmatum* with purple foliage that are not named as cultivars.

HYBRID Whereas species are collected from the wild, hybrids are usually born in gardens. Over the years, gardeners have interfered with nature by hybridizing species and, in some cases, genera. Where a hybrid has originated from a cross made between two species, the new 'hybrid epithet' is preceded by a multiplication sign. For example *Elaeagnus* × *ebbingei* is a hybrid between *Elaeagnus macrophylla* and *Elaeagnus submacrophylla*.

Sometimes, when two genera are closely related, it is possible to create a hybrid between them. In this case the multiplication sign comes before the generic name. For example × *Halimiocistus sahucii* is a hybrid between *Halimium umbellatum* and *Cistus salvifolius*.

NAME CHANGES

The naming of plants using botanical nomenclature is an ongoing process. As their knowledge increases, botanists find it necessary to make changes to nomenclature. It is important to remember that the numbers of plants introduced into cultivation in the last 200 years is vast and it sometimes becomes apparent that plants that at first appeared similar are in fact sufficiently different to require separate classification. Hence changes in nomenclature. Old names, when they are well known, are often shown in parentheses after the new name. For example *Brachyglottis* 'Sunshine' (*Senecio* 'Sunshine').

SELLING NAMES

Sometimes a plant may be better known under a selling name, or trade description, than its original name. This may or may not be registered as a Trade Mark. The selling name is written without quotation marks. In this book it appears in capital letters. Normally the cultivar name is shown after it in brackets. For example, *Sophora microphylla* **SUN KING** ('Hilsop'). It is evident that the selling name in this instance is infinitely more appealing than the cultivar name and will impact on the commercial success of the plant.

PLANT BREEDERS' RIGHTS (PBR)

Certain plants may not be propagated for sale without royalties being paid to the registered breeder. Wherever such plants are offered for sale, the letters PBR must follow the plant's name. For example, *Cotinus coggygria* **GOLDEN SPIRIT** ('Ancot') PBR.

Two internationally accepted codes control all plant nomenclature. The botanical names (in other words, the generic and specific names) are covered by the International Code of Botanical Nomenclature. This is applied to wild and cultivated plants. The cultivar names and nomenclature, which are used in addition to the botanical name, are covered by the International Code of Nomenclature for Cultivated Plants. This relates only to garden plants.

PLANT NAMES ARE FUN

Whether the gardener is a natural linguist or not, botanical Latin is a satisfying language. Just as a feel for plants grows the more you work with them, so a feel for plant names develops over time. Not only are the names in a language that can be used anywhere in the world, they also provide immediately accessible information about the plant to which they refer. A few examples:

Specific epithet	Meaning	Example
alatus, -a, -um	winged	*Euonymus alatus*
fruticosus, -a, -um	shrubby	*Phlomis fruticosa*
littoralis, -e	of seashores	*Griselinia littoralis*
mollis, -e	soft	*Hamamelis mollis*
praecox	early	*Cytisus praecox*
sanguineus, -a, -um	blood-red	*Cornus sanguinea*
stellatus, -a, -um	starry	*Magnolia stellata*
sylvaticus, -a, -um	of woodland	*Fagus sylvatica*

The fascinating subject of plant names and their meanings is fully explored in Hillier's *Plant Names Explained*.

Buying shrubs

Choosing shrubs is easy: the gardener has access to an enormous range of hardy plants through mail order catalogues, nurseries and garden centres. Most shrubs are purchased after visiting a plant retailer and personally selecting the plants; because of modern production techniques, there are plenty of high-quality plants to choose from.

Today, most shrubs are 'container-grown'. That is, the plant has been grown in a pot since it was propagated. Most shrubs are propagated either by taking cuttings or by grafting. A young rooted plant is grown-on in a small pot to what is called the liner stage. Usually it is then potted into the final pot, in which it will be sold. The roots are kept intact and undisturbed at each potting, and it is important that they remain so when, finally, it is planted in the ground.

Some shrubs grow better in the open ground than they do in pots. These are lifted from the field and are potted in the autumn. If they are planted within a few months of potting, the compost may fall away from the roots because the plant has not had time to get established in the pot. These 'containerized' plants need extra care after planting, until they are established.

It used to be that all deciduous shrubs were sold 'bare-root'. Today, some hedging is still sold in this way during the winter. Plants are lifted from the field in the dormant season and are sold with little or no soil around their roots.

'Rootballed' plants are field-grown and are lifted during the dormant season, with the ball of soil around the roots preserved and the root system kept intact. This is the traditional way of supplying evergreens and large specimen shrubs, particularly those with a fibrous root system, such as rhododendrons, Japanese maples and magnolias. The rootball is often wrapped in a hessian material to keep it intact. In most cases, this should be left in position and allowed to rot away in the planting hole. If you are unsure about this, ask the nursery staff for advice: their recommendation will depend on what material has been used.

BUYING TIME

Sometimes plants are offered in more than one size. Buying bigger usually means buying time. But is that a good idea?

Today shrubs are normally measured by the size of pot in which they are grown. A plant sold in a quality nursery or garden centre should be well rooted round in its pot, so the size of pot is an indication of the plant's maturity. Sizes refer to the volume of the pot.

POT SIZE?	PLANT SIZE
9cm or 1 litre 	Starter shrubs – that is, the first stage after propagation; sometimes offered for sale during the autumn and spring. This is a good way to buy young evergreen shrubs for mixing with seasonal bedding plants in a container. It is also a good way to plant hedging economically – as long as you are patient.
2 or 3 litres 	The standard size of shrubs sold by garden centres and used for amenity planting – usually a year on from the smallest size. This is the best size to choose for general planting. There should be a healthy root system all around the outside of the rootball. However, you should still be able to see some compost. Even to the inexperienced eye, it is obvious if the plant is potbound, choked with roots, and growth has been impaired as a result.
7.5 or 10 litres 	Small specimen shrubs, popular for quick impact – often one year more advanced than the standard product. This is a way of buying time. The plants are, of course, more expensive, but it is worth the investment in the case of key plants and those that are slow to grow in the early stages. In a new planting scheme, it is worth buying some of these larger plants to achieve a degree of maturity at the outset. Remember, however, that a small plant, if given good growing conditions, often catches up with a larger one.

LARGE SPECIMEN PLANTS

Large specimens, particularly of evergreens, are becoming increasingly available. In northern Europe they are often imported from Italy, where, although the winters are cold, the rest of the year provides a long growing season and faster results. These large specimens are a good way of buying time and giving instant impact, but they come at a price. Aftercare is particularly important and the growth rate following planting may be disappointing. The plant may stand still for two or three years while the roots become established. In the long run, a smaller plant may achieve the same result.

SUBSTITUTES

When you are looking for a specific plant, perhaps one recommended by a friend or one that you have seen in a book, be prepared to consider a close substitute. New varieties are being introduced all the time, in many cases improvements on established favourites.

By insisting on the exact variety you went out to buy, you may end up turning down a better plant: *Spiraea japonica* 'Goldflame', for example, has been superseded by *Spiraea japonica* 'Firelight', a superior variety that does not revert. 'Goldflame' will still be recommended by those who are not aware of 'Firelight'.

Buying container-grown plants means that you see what you are getting. You can buy a container-grown plant in leaf and flower, in season. Illustrated labels give a very good idea of what the leaf and flower look like.

WHAT IS A GOOD PLANT?

Shrubs vary enormously in shape, size and habit. However, in most cases it is possible to spot, at an early stage, a plant that will develop into a well-shaped specimen. A properly grown young shrub branches well from the base; this is achieved by cutting back at the liner stage, while the plant is in the nursery. A well-grown shrub has strong growth and a generally healthy appearance. This is the plant to buy.

Bear in mind that some shrubs do not look good early in life – the stage at which you are most likely to see them offered for sale in the garden centre. These are highlighted in the plant descriptions in this book.

Container-grown plants (above) enable the gardener to buy and plant at any time of the year, even when shrubs are in flower.
The perfect shrub (left) has good branch framework, healthy foliage and a well-developed root system.

♀ THE AWARD OF GARDEN MERIT ♀

The Royal Horticultural Society's Award of Garden Merit (AGM) is a good indication of whether a plant is a good one to choose for your garden. Many of the shrubs in this book have been awarded the AGM (indicated by the symbol ♀).

So what does it mean? The plant has to have more than one point of interest and a unique property. It has to be easy to grow, of sound constitution and, most importantly, a good all-round garden plant. This is not to say that plants without the AGM are not worth growing. It means that, to date, the Royal Horticultural Society (RHS) has not trialled it or does not consider that the plant meets all these criteria.

Growing conditions

If you have deep, fertile, well-drained soil that does not dry out and has no perennial weeds, you cannot go wrong. However, most of us do not enjoy such conditions, and a little effort is required. The establishment and subsequent growth rate of all garden plants are affected by the quality of the environment in which they are planted. Good preparation reaps rewards.

KNOW YOUR SOIL

Soil is a complex mixture of animal, vegetable and mineral matter, living and dead, with the addition of air and water. The proportions of the constituents vary.

Normally the basic mineral content comes from the underlying rock, as a result of erosion. So if you know what the underlying rock is, you have a good idea of the type of soil.

Indigenous trees and plants are a clue to the underlying soil type. Birch trees grow on virtually any soil but bracken growing with them is a good indication that the soil is acidic.

Organic matter decomposes and mixes with the mineral content. This adds to the nutrient content and provides the sticky, glutinous substance known as humus, which keeps the mineral particles apart but also sticks to them, holding on to water and nutrients for plants to absorb.

All soils need plenty of organic matter, and they are improved by the addition of more, especially in an intensively cultivated area such as a garden.

ACID OR ALKALINE?

You can tell a lot about your soil just by looking at it and then by looking at existing plants in your garden and in neighbouring gardens, and at indigenous trees and plants in the local area.

It is important to know the pH of your soil. This is the measure of acidity or alkalinity, on a scale of 0 to 14. Soils with a low pH are acid; those with a high pH are alkaline, rich in lime. The ideal is a neutral to slightly acid soil (7.0pH), which successfully supports the widest range of plants.

If your garden is in an area surrounded by pine trees, oak trees, healthy rhododendrons and camellias, then your soil is acid. There is no need to bother with a soil test.

Lumps of chalk and flints indicate an alkaline soil, often dry and well-drained.

If the surrounding fields are flecked with white fragments of chalk, your grass is fine and short, the soil is shallow, and beech trees thrive, you are on alkaline soil. Do not bother to check. If you want to grow lime-hating, acid-loving plants, put them in containers of lime-free ericaceous compost.

A pH meter is easy to use. Water the soil thoroughly beforehand.

If soil has been imported, or if you are between soil type areas, it is worth doing a pH check. Either use a soil pH check kit or, better still, buy a pH meter, which is easier to use and is a good way of checking all parts of the garden.

COMPOSTING – THE KEY TO SUCCESS

Whatever kind of soil you have, your garden is an area of intense cultivation. To keep soil in peak condition, it is vital to add organic matter. Compost your garden and household waste and return it to the soil.

FROST WARNING

When planting in the autumn, avoid bulky organic manure unless it is very well rotted. Fresh manure contains readily available nitrogen and this can stimulate soft new growth, which is easily damaged by frost. This is particularly a problem with certain evergreens, including hebes.

INCREASING FERTILITY

Most soils carry an adequate supply of plant nutrients for growth, but for the best results, supplement this with a balanced fertilizer in slow-release form. A general, slow-release fertilizer, containing the major plant nutrients as well as trace elements, can be used for all plants except lime-haters (that is, ericaceous and acid-loving plants). Acid-loving subjects are fussy, light feeders and need a specific formulation.

IMPROVING CLAY SOIL

When preparing clay soil for planting, dig in the autumn. Leave the surface rough to allow frost to penetrate during the winter months. The freeze-thaw action of the weather does much of the cultivation. The application of lime to newly dug soil in winter works miracles. This changes the charge on the clay particles, making them stick together in groups forming larger particles; the result is a soil with more open, crumbly texture. This raises the soil pH, so is not good for lime-hating plants. Adding coarse horticultural grit and plenty of organic matter further improves heavy clay soils.

FEEDING PLANTS

Resist the temptation to overfeed, particularly at the time of planting.

Water and nutrients enter the plant through its root hairs. For this to happen, the solution of 'salts', or nutrients, in the soil water has to be weaker than the solution in the root hair cell. If it is stronger, water is drawn out of the root, the plant cannot then take in water through its roots, and it wilts. This is referred to as scorching: in dry warm weather, especially if there is a light wind, the plant goes crispy.

Fertilizer used at time of planting should be high in phosphorus, or phosphate as it is usually called. This is the nutrient used for root growth and formation, and aids establishment.

Slow-release general fertilizers supply all the nutrients that plants need during a growing season. There is rarely a need to feed with anything else.

Controlled-release fertilizers are those little spherical granules used by nurseries in container composts. They release nutrients only when the soil is moist enough and temperatures are high enough for plant growth. The granules need to be applied only once a year. They are an excellent choice for plants in containers, and are also a good option for dry situations, where other types of fertilizer could cause problems if the level of moisture in the soil drops. Liquid and soluble fertilizers are not for shrubs, unless they need a boost.

Sequestered iron is not a complete fertilizer but is an excellent tonic for yellowing ericaceous, acid-loving plants. This yellowing, known as chlorosis, is usually caused by iron deficiency. A liquid tonic, sequestered iron supplies iron in an easy-to absorb-formulation.

UNDERSTANDING FERTILIZERS

The major nutrients

N – nitrogen, for leaves and shoots   **P** – phosphorus (phosphate), for roots   **K** – potash (potassium), for flowers and fruit

Trace elements: Nutrients essential for healthy growth, but needed in small amounts, trace elements are the vitamins and minerals of the plant world. Examples include iron, magnesium and manganese.

The nutrient content of all fertilizers, and the ratio of these nutrients to one another, is indicated on the packaging.

Successful planting

Except when you are making a brand new garden, you are most likely to be planting individual subjects in existing beds, either to extend a border or to replace a plant that has been removed. Container-grown plants can be planted at any time of the year and in theory are easy to establish. In practice, getting them started in the garden can present problems, unless you follow certain guidelines.

A young container shrub has led a sheltered existence on the nursery. It has probably been under glass or polythene, being watered regularly, kept free of pests and in nice cuddly warm compost, and it will have been fed a balanced diet of controlled-release fertilizer supplemented now and then with a liquid top-up.

If the new plant is to establish quickly in your garden, its new growing environment has to be at least as appealing than that of the pot. A small hole chipped out of solid, cold, wet clay that is about to bake hard in the summer sun, is simply not inviting. The roots will stay firmly in the original compost ball, and the plant will sit still in protest.

A happy plant is an attractive plant that will grow and give pleasure without having to struggle to survive. We tend to choose what we like, but in fact the best choice of plant has to be what will grow well in the situation it is chosen for. If we choose a plant for a location that is not ideal for it, we will have to battle to get it to thrive.

LOCATION, LOCATION

Choosing the right plant for the right spot is as much about what will grow well in a particular situation as what will look right.

The plant's native habitat dictates what growing conditions it will require in the garden. For example plants with grey and aromatic foliage often hail from the Mediterranean region, so they like plenty of sunshine, relatively dry conditions and good drainage.

The more contact the gardener has with plants, the more he or she gains a feel for their requirements. We are fortunate today in that we can draw on a large pool of experience and knowledge, but this need not deter the adventurous gardener from breaking new ground or from finding out by trial and error whether or not a plant that is generally considered to be for a 'hot, dry, sunny' site will in fact tolerate shade and moist soil.

PROVIDING SHELTER

Some plants, particularly evergreens from warmer climates, suffer in the winter, but more from wind chill than from cold. In a drying wind, the plant loses water from its leaves but, if the ground is frozen, the roots are unable to draw water from the soil. This can result in damage to the plant, or even its death.

Another problem is that freezing can rupture the vessels that carry water up the plant. The damage does not show until the weather warms up, when the leaves and stems are no longer receiving a water supply.

Give a plant that is not fully hardy a greater chance of survival by planting it in the shelter of a wall, near the house, or where other shrubs or garden structures provide shelter from the wind. During severe weather, protect delicate plants with horticultural fleece, a light fabric that is placed loosely over the plant. Attach it carefully, so that it stays in position but does not cause damage. Never use polythene sheeting; this causes condensation and extreme fluctuations of temperature that will do more harm than good.

1 FIRST DIG A HOLE

The planting hole should be at least twice the size of the plant's rootball. Using a spade and a fork, break up the base of the hole to ensure good drainage and successful root penetration. Mix plenty of good garden compost, well-rotted farmyard manure, recycled green waste or proprietary planting compost both with the soil in the bottom of the hole and with the soil that has been dug out. Sprinkle a slow-release fertilizer over the soil that is to be returned to the hole and a good handful in the base of the hole. Mix in with the fork. Replace the soil mixture to leave the hole slightly deeper than the rootball of the shrub.

2 GET YOUR LEVELS RIGHT

Before you knock the new shrub out of its pot, check that the compost is wet through. It is very difficult to wet a dry rootball once it is buried.

Knock the plant out of its container and place the rootball in the centre of the hole. The surface of the compost should be just below the natural soil level.

As long as the shrub is not pot-bound, do not tease out or damage the roots. To do so would defeat the object of container planting. Any strong roots that separate themselves from the bottom of the rootball can be spread out in the planting hole, but do not interfere any more than that.

3 FIRM FOOTING

Replace the soil around the plant, mixing it well with the slow-release fertilizer and organic compost. Then gently firm the soil around the rootball with your heel. Firm from the outside of the hole in towards the rootball. Do not compress the rootball by pushing down on it with your foot.

Replace more soil to about 1cm (½in) above the compost level. Ideally you should make a dish of the soil surface so as to direct rainfall, or irrigation water, into the rootball. Water well.

WATERING

- In the early stages of a plant's life, while the root system is developing, it is really important to have a supply of water always available and to water frequently.

- The peat, or peat substitute, that is used in container composts is usually harder to wet than the soil, so when water is applied it will stay in the spaces in the soil rather than penetrating the rootball. The result: dry plant, poor growth (if any), no establishment.

- On dry soil a slow trickle is better than a torrent. Water applied quickly often runs off without penetrating the surface. Water applied slowly has time to find the spaces in the soil and so wet the particles.

- Ericaceous plants such as rhododendrons and azaleas have particularly dense fibrous root systems, which are very difficult to wet once they dry out. A very slow-dripping hose is effective or, on larger areas of planting, a seep hose.

Pruning

In today's gardens, it is pruning more than anything else that robs plants of their finest hour. Pruning is the one gardening task we never forget to do. But, sadly, both our timing and our technique are often wrong: the most destructive pest in the garden is the gardener.

A clipped peacock at Cliveden, Buckinghamshire. The desire to control plants does not mean a lack of creativity, or even humour, in the garden.

Gardening is founded on snipping, trimming, neatness and order: hedges, topiary, lawns. In the days before we had such a plethora of plants to fill our gardens, it was only by shaping plants that the gardener could create variety. Far be it from him to allow a plant to achieve its potential or to grow naturally; he must be in control.

Some great gardeners, including Vita Sackville-West and Gertrude Jekyll, combined informality with formality. Could it be that providing the gardener with structural hedges to snip was their way of ensuring that the most treasured plants were protected from the secateurs?

Spring in the garden is a time of cultivation and planting. Emerging weeds divert our attention. The grass grows quickly and needs cutting. There are tubs to fill, hanging baskets to plant, seeds to sow, vegetables to plant. Shrubs are safe: there is no time for pruning anything (except, perhaps, the roses).

Autumn, on the other hand, leaves the deciduous shrubs naked and vulnerable. It is garden clean-up time: leaves to collect, herbaceous plants to cut back, bedding plants to grub out, compost to make. And, while we are at it, how about 'tidying up' those shrubs? Before we know it, they are half their original height. Nice and tidy. And after all, they will grow again next year – a bit like a bad haircut, but with more devastating results.

Gardeners are generally nervous about pruning, until they get armed and dangerous. Then nerves turn into aggression and they set to with secateurs and loppers, chainsaws and strimmers, hell-bent on destruction. There are just a few basic rules to learn before you cut.

WHEN TO PRUNE?

The time to prune is after flowering. Very soon after flowering, not months after flowering. All shrubs are flowering plants in one way or another. If you have to prune, and want to prune, do it immediately after flowering. The new shoots that are made after pruning then have time to grow, ripen and produce flower buds for the following year. See pages 23–25.

THE GOLDEN RULES

- You do not have to prune. Pruning is a garden thing. In nature, 'pruning', if it happens at all, is a natural process. It is not an essential stage of the plant's life cycle. Many gardeners seem to think that every plant needs pruning to achieve results. This is not the case.

- The harder you prune, the more vigorous will be the growth afterwards. Plants are 'intelligent' and hormones will respond to your amputations by stimulating vigorous growth to replace what has been removed.

- Light pruning produces light lateral growth and a bushier plant. If the plant is one that flowers or fruits on this type of growth, go ahead and 'snip', but do it in a logical, controlled way.

There is a logical exception to the rule. Plants that are grown for fruit should not be pruned after flowering (or there will be no fruit). Prune selectively after the fruit has appeared. Yes, you may lose some of next year's flowers, but as long as you know what these buds look like you will know where to cut.

WHY PRUNE?

TO CONTROL SHAPE Some plants – hedges, topiary, trimmed and trained plants that provide formal structure are – are pruned regularly to control their shape. Familiar examples are box and bay. Frequent light trimming produces plenty of young fresh growth on the outside of the plant – bushy growth, with lots of lateral branching.

However, this type of pruning is disastrous when practised on other ornamental shrubs, especially the deciduous ones. The plant is robbed of its natural habit and ends up looking artificial and ugly. So often are plants subjected to this treatment, they are frequently not recognizable for what they are.

These box balls provide solid structure among informally planted shrubs and herbaceous perennials. With their size and shape controlled, they become a focal point in contrast to the irregular shapes of other plants.

Selective pruning to control the shape of the plant works if thought is given to how the plant will react when the growth is either cut back or removed. Removal of competing branches, to promote an open structure, is beneficial to both the growth habit and the health of the plant. It lets light into the leaves and allows air to circulate through the plant.

Plants growing together in a border should be pruned in relation to each other, rather than being made to stand alone as individual subjects. Shrubs that may have been planted a little too closely can often be integrated by selective removal, to ground level, of some of the branches.

TO CONTROL SIZE If a plant has got to a point where drastic pruning is required in order to control its size, ask yourself whether it is in fact too big for the location. If pruning has to be done on a regular basis, leaving the shrub more disfigured after each pruning, ask yourself whether it might be better to replace it with a less vigorous subject.

The key to success is to take action sooner rather than later. Too often a shrub is allowed to get far too big for the space it occupies.

The next question is 'How much can I cut it back by?' Each year, starting at an early stage, take a good look at the shrub, try to foresee next season's growth, and prune accordingly. Keeping a shrub under control is a manageable task if it is done in easy stages. In other words, if you are going to have to prune at some point, start at an early stage, and do it regularly. This applies particularly to the evergreen, structure shrubs and, of course, anything grown as a trimmed hedge.

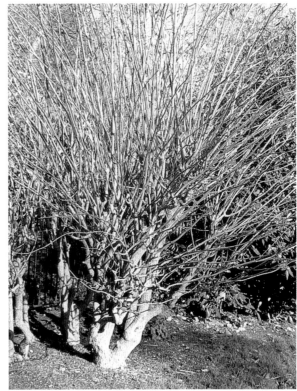

This ornamental elder is cut back or pollarded to the same point in early spring each year. Because the annual growth is always approximately the same, the height achieved is the same each year and size is restricted.

TO CONTROL PESTS AND DISEASES The first thing to remove when you prune is any diseased or damaged wood. This is essential to prevent die-back and the spread of disease to new growth.

TO PROMOTE FLOWERING AND FRUITING We prune roses and fruit trees both to promote the type of growth that will produce flower buds and to prevent the plant putting all its energies into vegetative growth.

- Many of the modern hybrid roses need hard pruning to stimulate the vigorous new growth that will produce flower buds.
- Many of the old roses respond better to lighter pruning, to stimulate twiggy growth and side branches that will bear flowers.
- Many apples and pears produce their flowers, and therefore their fruit, on small side branches called spurs. Pruning aims to build up the numbers and quality of these spurs to increase fruit production. The same is true of wisteria.

Wisteria, normally a climber, can be grown as a shrub if pruned carefully. Pruning back the long shoots creates spurs that carry the flowerbuds.

CORRECT PRUNING

- Always use a good-quality, sharp pair of secateurs and a pruning saw; clean cuts heal well and minimize the chance of infection. Never leave 'snags'.
- Cut to just above a node, with a slanting cut sloping away from the bud. This, theoretically, directs any rainwater away from the growing bud.

- Where possible, cut to an outward-facing bud, as this promotes an open structure. Use your common sense and look carefully before each cut. Once you get your eye in, it is obvious which way the bud will grow when you have removed the growth above it.
- Remember that pieces of stem left without any growth buds will die back, promoting the spread of disease.

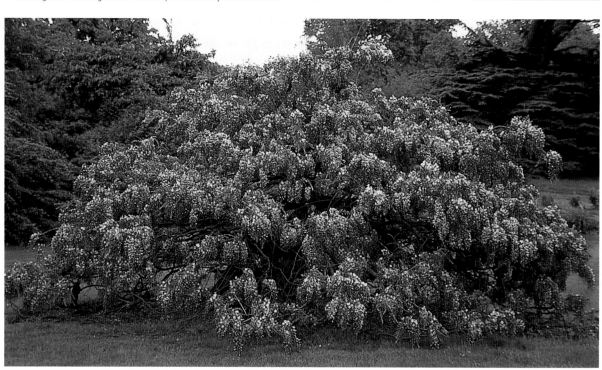

A SIMPLE GUIDE TO PRUNING THE VARIOUS TYPES OF SHRUB

This is a simple rule-of-thumb guide; there are always exceptions.

DECIDUOUS SHRUBS FLOWERING IN EARLY SPRING

e.g., forsythia, ribes

Prune after flowering. Cut out wood that has flowered, back to where vigorous new shoots are emerging. This is done selectively, paying attention to the overall shape. It is not essential every year, but should be done frequently.

DECIDUOUS SHRUBS FLOWERING IN LATE SPRING AND EARLY SUMMER

e.g., deutzia, lilac, philadelphus

Prune after flowering. Cut out wood that has flowered back to where vigorous new shoots are emerging. Take out some branches to ground level each year on mature shrubs that are overcrowded in the centre. The new growth produced will flower the following year.

DECIDUOUS SHRUBS FLOWERING IN LATE SUMMER

e.g., *Hydrangea paniculata*, buddleia, perovskia, caryopteris

Prune hard in late winter. This stimulates vigorous growth that will ripen during the summer and flower later in the year. As a rule of thumb, all these examples are cut back by two-thirds.

EVERGREEN SHRUBS

e.g., *Viburnum tinus*, *Prunus laurocerasus*, aucuba, choisya, photinia

Prune in late spring. This is a time of active growth; cutting back will stimulate a rapid flush of replacement growth.

ACID-LOVING PLANTS

e.g., camellias, rhododendrons, azaleas

Pruning is not necessary, but do it immediately after flowering if you must.

Camellias respond well to pruning, as do many rhododendrons. Deciduous azaleas must be pruned with great care to preserve the branch framework.

SILVER-FOLIAGE PLANTS

e.g., brachyglottis, santolina, helichrysum, lavender

Prune straight after flowering – or before if you prefer, in the case of undesirable yellow flowers of santolina and brachyglottis.

Pruning by the end of summer allows the plants to produce a generous flush of new silver growth before winter. Always cut back to where you can see new growth buds emerging. If you cut back into bare wood, regeneration cannot be guaranteed.

Plants that have not been pruned can also be trimmed back in mid-spring.

Shaped silver-leaved plants that are not being grown for flowering require regular trimming throughout the summer.

A SIMPLE SEASONAL GUIDE TO PRUNING

Whatever the time of year, if in doubt, leave the plant alone and consult a good pruning guide.

MIDWINTER

Prune roses. Floribundas and Hybrid Teas: cut down to three buds above ground level. New English and shrub roses: remove any dead wood and prune lightly to promote lateral growth that will produce flower buds.

LATE WINTER

Cut back caryopteris, perovskia and ceratostigma by two-thirds or more. It is easy to see the growth buds, which will produce next year's shoots and flowers, on the lower part of the stem – cut back to here.

Hard prune buddleia and *Hydrangea paniculata*. Cut mature plants back to about 1m (3ft), young plants to 60cm (2ft). This will promote vigorous arching branches.

Hard prune young plants of *Sambucus racemosa* cultivars to promote vigorous growth and good leaf colour.

EARLY SPRING

Hard prune *Cornus alba* and other subjects grown for winter stems. Cut half of the stems back to ground level each year.

Lightly prune photinia to encourage more new growth shoots of good colour.

Prune hydrangeas (except *paniculata;* see above), removing old flowerheads back to fat buds (which will flower later). On old plants, remove some older stems each year, to ground level.

MID-SPRING

Prune forsythia, ribes and any early-flowering deciduous shrubs after flowering. Cut out the older stems that have flowered, allowing new growth to come through.

Prune hebes by mid-spring. Overgrown and straggly plants can be cut back to where new shoots are emerging lower on the stems.

LATE SPRING

Prune camellias if necessary to control size.

Cut out any winter damage in evergreens such as choisya and aucuba.

Prune evergreen shrubs to control size and shape if desired.

EARLY SUMMER

Prune lilacs after flowering. They can be cut back hard; even old branches can be pruned, if done selectively. The vigorous new growth will flower next year.

Dead-head rhododendrons as the flowers fade, allowing new growth shoots to develop more freely.

Dead-head roses that repeat flower. Rather than just removing the flowerhead, cut back to an emerging, strong shoot lower down the stem.

MIDSUMMER

Prune back large-flowered abutilons by about a third. This allows enough time for new growth that will flower next year to appear.

Prune philadelphus, deutzia and weigela after flowering. Cut some of the older growth that has flowered back to the base, thinning other flowered stems to allow new shoots to grow through gracefully.

LATE SUMMER

Cut back silver-foliage shrubs such as lavander, santolina and helichrysum after flowering. Cut back to where you can see new shoots emerging deep in the plant. This leaves them time to produce a flush of new growth that will stay silver all winter.

EARLY AUTUMN

Dead-head and tidy roses as the flowers fade, except for those varieties that produce winter hips.

MID-AUTUMN

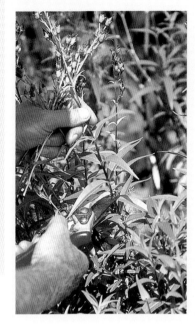

Tidy herbaceous plants as they die back, but preserve the seedheads and stems of those that remain decorative in the winter.

LATE AUTUMN

Prune vines (*vitis*) once the leaves have fallen. This must be done before midwinter or the plants will bleed.

EARLY WINTER

Winter-prune fruit trees; the same applies to ornamental crab (*Malus*), to control shape and disease.

Planting for structure

Whatever the size of the garden, the hardest thing to get right is the basic structure. It is something that frightens most of us. We worry that what we plant will get too big, cast shade or interfere with the foundations of the house. Our concerns are boundless. Often this is all due to an underlying fear of the unknown and an inability to visualize what the garden will look like in years to come, when our young plants have grown to maturity.

It may be that we find structure difficult because it is not a part of the design process that we are used to dealing with. When it comes to the house, the structure is normally already there for us. We may make alterations as time goes by, but there is usually something to start with. The same is true when we take on a mature garden.

In the house, we decorate, furnish and add finishing touches to our own taste. In garden design, this is the easy part: adding bulbs, bedding, alpines, seasonal colour and interest. We can buy on impulse and fit our acquisitions into the gaps without changing anything permanently. Nice, safe decisions.

However, gardens simply do not work without structure. Hard landscaping may provide some of this, in the form of paving, walling, pergolas, arches and garden buildings, but these elements come to life only when structural planting is added.

DESIGN GUIDELINES

The objective is to create an attractive picture to look at from the house and a comfortable space to live in outdoors.

To please the eye, gardens need the right proportion of space and planting. As a rule of thumb, this should be one-third planting and two-thirds space. The latter can be made up of grass, paving, gravel, water or even low, ground-cover plants. Most gardens tend towards a higher proportion of space, with insufficient planting.

Any garden should fit with the property to which it is attached and with the surrounding landscape. The

---

GIVE THEM SPACE

- When planning planting areas, avoid borders that run parallel to the fence line around the edge of the garden.

- Most people make their borders too narrow. The minimum depth for a border is 1m (3ft); 2m (6ft) is barely adequate, 3m (10ft) is better.

- Go out and measure the spread of an average, mature shrub, for example, choisya or ceanothus. The rule with borders is fewer, but deeper.

- To see what your garden will look like, lay a hosepipe down on the ground to mark the edge of the proposed bed. Be bold: envisage the area full of plants.

- If you start off with straight narrow borders, barely wider than the plants you put into them, in no time you will be out there with a spade making them wider so as to allow the mower to pass without damaging the growing plants. Worse still, you will be bringing the secateurs into action, trimming those new shrubs into neat, but ugly, shapes.

style, mood and design of the garden must be in keeping with the house. This is also true of the plants; these should suit the style of garden.

In a contained space, the choice can be individual. In more open situations, look at any trees, large conifers or shrubs in neighbouring gardens or in the surrounding countryside and take them into account as part of the full garden picture. Use them to expand the landscape.

Deciduous shrubs, extensions of the native hedgerow, are appropriate for rural gardens. Hollies, yew and small-leaved evergreens work well, and white- and silver-variegations seem to fit. Use yellow foliage with care. Exotics and conifers, if used at all, need careful placing.

Town gardens need solid, evergreen structure to balance the weight of masonry around them. Strong colours, yellow foliage and bold yellow variegations can work in shady situations.

VERTICAL INTEREST

Most gardens are too flat. Height is essential, to give scale to the rest of the garden and to make the space three-dimensional. The oft-requested 'tree that grows to six feet and then stops' is simply inadequate. Height need not mean heavy tree cover; light, airy trees such as birch and mountain ash will deliver. Bold upright shrubs, such as abutilon, may do the trick. For even stronger vertical accents, use climbers on pergolas and arches.

PLANT LAYERS

Successful gardens have three levels of planting:
1 Above eye level: trees, tall shrubs and climbers.
2 At eye level: shrubs and tall herbaceous plants.
3 Below eye level: dwarf shrubs, herbaceous perennials and ground cover.

A border at Le Bois des Moutiers, near Dieppe, Normandy, France, exemplifies the successful use of different levels of planting.

It is important that the structural framework provided by plants works all year round.

Trees provide the canopy above eye level. The winter silhouette of a deciduous tree provides structure just as effectively as the solid mass of any evergreen tree. Some tall shrubs contribute here too, but it is really in the eye-level landscape that they play a leading role.

Evergreens and deciduous shrubs with a strong branch framework come into their own in the middle planting layer, at eye level. Smaller-leaved, lighter-growing plants, such as pittosporums, provide structure without weight. Large-leaved evergreens, for example fatsias, contribute heavier, more solid structure and a dark background that sets off the colour of the planting in the foreground.

The lower layer is often the most scrutinized: low-growing shrubs, herbaceous perennials, bulbs and seasonal bedding plants are found here. This is where gardeners are apt to concentrate most of their effort. It is readily accessible, so it is relatively easy to rectify planting mistakes here.

CHOOSING AND POSITIONING STRUCTURAL PLANTS

Choose structure plants carefully. They are a valuable source of variety in colour and texture, as well as being architecturally useful. Give careful consideration to the positioning of plants and how they relate to their neighbours. Bear in mind colour, shape, leaf form and texture. Get it right, and the individual contribution from each plant will increase manyfold.

In newly planted areas, the planting should initially look very thin, with plenty of space for the permanent plants to grow and mature. In the early years, gaps can be filled with annuals, bulbs and temporary herbaceous planting.

TIMESCALE

We are all impatient, and plants do not give instant results. Most of the disasters that occur in the garden are the result of trying to resolve this conflict. All too often those who plant, or inherit, a hedge of × *Cupressocyparis leylandii*, for example, live to regret it.

Shrubs planted for structure take time to mature. Eventually some may get too big and perhaps after five to ten years some of the planting will need to be removed or replaced. That is part of gardening. However, it is important not to plant something that is going to present serious problems in the future.

Structure plants need not be heavy, or plain green. The light, silver-variegated form of *Pittosporum* 'Garnettii' provides height and shape without weight.

Basic evergreens

Plain evergreens and their variegated forms contribute solid structure to mixed borders of deciduous woody and herbaceous plants. Without them, planting lacks body and planting areas can become a void during during the winter months. These shrubs provide the basic framework of the garden. They are the foundations upon which the rest of the planting is built.

Arbutus unedo

Arbutus unedo ♀ (Killarney strawberry tree) is a beautiful small evergreen tree with reddish-brown, peeling bark when mature. A member of the family Ericaceae, it is unusual in tolerating lime. The white, pieris-like flowers appear at the same time as the strawberry fruits in the autumn. As a young plant, it makes a valuable bushy shrub, wind-tolerant and good by the coast. The variety **Arbutus unedo 'Atlantic'** produces flowers and fruit at an early age. **Arbutus unedo** f. **rubra** ♀ has pink-flushed flowers and is particularly prolific in its fruit production. **Arbutus 'Marina'** is similar, but is particularly suitable for pruning and maintaining as a large rounded bush.

Arbutus makes a good alternative to photinia where a slower-growing, denser plant, and one with smaller foliage, is needed.

Buxus sempervirens ♀, or common box, grows to make a large shrub or small tree with masses of small, round, dark green leaves. It is found all over southern Europe, northern Africa and western Asia. It is naturalized through southern England, but it is not clear whether it is a British native or was introduced by the Romans.

Box has been a quintessential element of garden structure throughout Europe for centuries. Its positive response to clipping and shaping has resulted in its use for hedging and topiary of all kinds. Its hardy nature and its longevity make it indispensable for the construction of parterres. Indeed, there are some formal gardens where it is the only plant used.

There are many cultivars, all with different rates of growth and growth habits. Some of the variegated forms are particularly fine (see page 57).

Buxus sempervirens 'Suffruticosa' ♀, or edging box, is the very dwarf form commonly used for formal edging to paths and beds. Leaves are medium, ovate and a bright shiny green. This plant is slow-growing, and therefore easily controlled, and is ideal for making the lowest of hedges. It can be grown in modern, gravel parterres and clipped to make interesting raised shapes – true

Box at Bourton House Garden, Gloucestershire.

vegetable masonry! **Buxus microphylla 'Faulkner'** is an alternative to *Buxus sempervirens* 'Suffruticosa', and also widely grown. It is compact, with a more spreading habit.

Contemporary minimalist garden design makes extensive, and creative, use of box both for topiary in containers and for 'cloud' beds and hedges – a reflection of the endurance and adaptability of this plant in our gardens.

Box is easy to grow and generally needs little attention. Although it is a hardy plant, the new growth can be hit by frost in spring, but the plant soon grows through any damage. Box is

Buxus sempervirens 'Suffruticosa'

BOX BLIGHT

In recent years, box blight has become a problem. Initially this can be mistaken for nutrient deficiency, but the disease quickly progresses to patchy die-back, with the foliage becoming yellow, dry and parchment-like.

Treatment: cut out the affected growth and burn it. Keep the plant watered and fed with a balanced soluble feed. The less stress the plant suffers, the greater its chance of recovery. Spray with Bordeaux mixture or a traditional copper fungicide.

very susceptible to nutrient deficiency, especially when grown in containers or on light, well-drained soils. Potassium deficiency shows itself as bronzing of the foliage, particularly in winter. Potassium is very soluble and quickly washed away by winter rainfall but the problem can be rectified by applying a general, slow-release fertilizer.

Elaeagnus × ebbingei is a hybrid between *Elaeagnus pungens* from Japan and *Elaeagnus macrophylla* from Korea and Japan. This is a big, fast-growing, vigorous shrub that will deliver screening and shelter while contributing an attractive feature to the garden. The mature leaves are fairly large, dark green and silver beneath. The new shoots are grey-olive with russet down. Its most surprising attribute is the fragrance of its flowers, produced under the foliage in early winter. Visually, the appearance of the tiny, creamy-white flowers does not transform the bush but the fragrance is unmissable, often sending the gardener in search of some exotic bloom hidden beneath the undergrowth.

It was only in 1929 that *Elaeagnus × ebbingei* was introduced into our gardens, so perhaps it is no surprise that it is not more extensively used. It is used in amenity planting schemes where quick results and wind-resistance are required. It is excellent by the sea.

The silvery underside of the foliage and a tolerance of dry conditions make this an plant ideal for providing structure in mixed planting that has a high proportion of silver and grey foliage. Its subtle colour makes it a good mixer; it is easy to accommodate and provides a sympathetic backdrop to any foreground scheme.

Elaeagnus responds well to pruning, though this should be done carefully if the bony frame of the plant is not to become more of a feature than the foliage. Selective hard pruning of stems is more desirable than cutting back moderately.

Elaeagnus × ebbingei

It also responds well to clipping if this is done from an early stage, so it makes an excellent hedge. It is easier to cut than laurel because the leaves are smaller.

The waxy dust that covers the leaves can be irritating to the nose when handling the plant, so take precautions.

Ilex aquifolium ♀, our native holly, has been revered for its shiny, dark, evergreen leaves since ancient times. Early man marvelled at its powers. While other trees shed their leaves and creatures hibernated in the frozen days of winter, holly shone green and, what is more, produced fruit and reproduced, defying the elements and celebrating the birth of life itself with its shiny red berries. Holly was recognized as a plant with magical powers. Branches were used to surround livestock pens – not only did its spiny leaves make a physical barrier to predators, its magical powers warded off evil spirits. Holly planted by the cottage door kept witches away. No man dared fell a holly tree. As our only broad-leaved native evergreen, the holly reigned supreme.

Holly has medicinal uses. Writing in the 17th century, Culpeper claimed that red holly berries brought relief from

Ilex aquifolium 'J.C. van Tol'

colds and clammy phlegm, while yellow berries relieved phlegm brought on by excess alcohol. A medicinal tea was made from the leaves.

In the garden, the cultivars of *Ilex aquifolium* are superb, stately structure plants. They take time to reach maturity but are worth the wait.

The variegated forms of ilex (see Plant Profile, page 62) are more widely planted than the plain green. Of the green cultivars, *Ilex aquifolium* 'J.C. van Tol' ♀ is the most sought-after. Shiny, dark green, almost spineless leaves contrast with the prolific crops of red berries. This cultivar is self-pollinating, so can be planted on its own.

Ilex aquifolium 'Ferox' (hedgehog holly) is male, so produces no berries. It is interesting for its small, very spiny leaves: the spines grow not only from the leaf edges but also from the upper surface. It is lower and slower-growing than others and, having resided in our gardens since the 17th century, is thought to be the oldest holly variety still in cultivation.

Ilex crenata 'Convexa' ♀ is a superb form of the Japanese holly. The leaves are like those of box but larger, much darker and glossier. It has a dense, bushy habit and, although it makes only a small shrub, is an imposing structure plant. Ideal to trim and shape, it is a wonderful alternative to box for a low hedge. It freely produces shiny, black fruits in the late autumn.

Ilex × meserveae 'Blue Girl'

Ilex × meserveae 'Blue Prince'

Ilex × meserveae, the blue hollies, were raised in New York to cope with the severe winters of eastern North America. They are bushy shrubs, up to 2m (6ft) high, with black-purple shoots and softly spined leaves that are smaller than other varieties. The glossy foliage is dark blue-green, providing a welcome change from the emerald greens of other hollies. Female varieties have scarlet fruits. **'Blue Angel'** and **'Blue Girl'** are female, **'Blue Boy'** and **'Blue Prince'** male. Their hardiness has made them popular in continental Europe as well as America. The blue hollies are an excellent choice for structural plants in contemporary schemes, combining well with metal and slate.

Laurus nobilis ♀, the bay laurel, is the true laurel. The first recorded date of cultivation in Britain is 1562, but it is probable that this plant was introduced long before then. It played a significant part in the culture of ancient Rome – it was the leaves of the bay laurel that were used to adorn dignitaries and heroes – and it is likely that the Romans brought it to Britain with them. The aromatic leaves are widely used for their culinary qualities and feature extensively in dishes across the Mediterranean region, where the plant is widespread.

Left unpruned, *Laurus nobilis* makes a dense pyramid. The foliage is dark and matt, the perfect background for other plants. It can be susceptible to frost damage in extreme conditions, but tolerates the salt air of coastal areas. It is good on shallow chalk soils, enjoying the good drainage and low nutrient content. The small, yellowish-green flowers appear in April, clustering the branches of plants that have not been repeatedly clipped.

KEEPING A BAY IN TRIM

Trained bay is easily maintained by pinching, as long as this is done when the new, soft shoots first flush. Pinch each shoot back to two leaves and buds, paying attention to maintaining the shape of the plant.

A high percentage of bays used in gardens are trained, often as 'lollipops' or pyramids. *Laurus nobilis* responds well to clipping and training, so was embraced by continental European and, later, British gardeners for this purpose. Belgium is the centre for high-quality trained bay, with large nurseries dedicated to this purpose.

Left untrained, *Laurus nobilis* makes an excellent informal structure plant; its vertical growth habit makes it very useful for screening. There is a good golden form: *Laurus nobilis* 'Aurea' (see page 42).

The large-leaved Japanese and Chinese **privets** are not often used as big structure plants, although they have excellent qualities. *Ligustrum japonicum* is a very dense, medium-sized shrub with olive-green leaves, similar to those of a camellia. It has white flowers in late summer and is excellent as a hedge or screen. The best variety is **Ligustrum japonicum 'Macrophyllum'**, with dark foliage and broader leaves. **Ligustrum japonicum 'Rotundifolium'** is an interestingly architectural shrub with rounded, thick, dark leaves. It is very slow and compact, and usually grows into an interesting shape.

Ligustrum lucidum ♀, the Chinese privet, is much larger-growing, often making a small tree. With long, pointed leaves, it resembles a large version of

PLANTING PARTNERS

Both the yellow-fruiting holly *Ilex aquifolium* 'Bacciflava' and the bronze-yellow cultivar *Ilex aquifolium* 'Amber' ♀ (left) are attractive plants to combine with yellow-variegated evergreens such as *Elaeagnus pungens* 'Maculata'.

Viburnum tinus 'French White' ♀, with its large heads of white flowers, is a strong-growing form that combines well with white-variegated shrubs such as *Pittosporum* 'Garnettii'.

Viburnum tinus 'Purpureum', with its purplish new growth, combines well with golden-foliage deciduous shrubs, particularly *Sambucus racemosa* 'Sutherland Gold' ♀.

Ligustrum lucidum

Myrtus communis

Osmanthus × burkwoodii

Phillyrea angustifolia

the hedging privet. Its habit is very symmetrical and in autumn it has conspicuous panicles of white flowers. It makes a good choice where a large background shrub is needed quickly.

Myrtus communis♥, the common myrtle, is a Mediterranean shrub grown in England since the 16th century. It is hardy in milder areas, particularly by the coast, and grows well in the shelter of a sunny wall. In ideal conditions it will reach 4m (13ft), growing successfully on any well-drained soil, including chalk. The pretty foliage is shiny and rich dark green. The white flowers are produced in summer and may be followed by purple-black berries. Because of its traditional and medicinal connections, it associates well with herbs and aromatics. It is an appropriate choice to have by the house as a symbol of health and wellbeing.

A compact form *Myrtus communis* subsp. *tarentina*♥, has small narrow, dark green leaves, pink-tinged flowers in autumn and white berries.

Osmanthus are holly-like evergreens, good structure plants that grow on virtually any soil. The variegated forms are perhaps the best-known but there are some excellent plain green forms, well worth remembering when it comes to choosing easy-to-grow evergreens.

Osmanthus decorus, previously known as *Phillyrea decora*, deserves to be planted more often than it is. Forming a large, broad dome, it is an excellent, tough and easy-to-grow plant with large, leathery shiny leaves and small fragrant white flowers in spring.

Osmanthus × burkwoodii♥ is the best known osmanthus. Previously offered as × *Osmarea burkwoodii*, it has been in our gardens since 1930. It is hardy and compact, with upright growth, light tan stems and neat oval, dark green, leathery leaves. It produces profuse white, very fragrant flowers in late spring. This is a really useful shrub that can be grown in sun or shade, and it can be trimmed to shape in more formal schemes.

A very useful alternative to a green holly for smaller gardens, *Osmanthus heterophyllus* 'Gulftide'♥ looks like a small, dark green holly, with leaves often twisted, very spiny and glossy. Growth is compact; the plant rarely gets large.

Phillyrea is a genus that offers some excellent evergreen structure plants. It is a pity it is not more widely known. *Phillyrea* are handsome creatures of the olive family, closely related to osmanthus.

Phillyrea angustifolia is the most attractive species, with neat narrow, shiny dark green leaves. Although a compact, rounded shrub, it has a wonderfully loose quality, with elegant sprays of foliage that are useful for cutting. The flowers are like those of box: creamy-yellow and carried on the fine stems, in the leaf axils, in May and June. It is a good coastal plant. Its finest quality is its gentle movement in the breeze; it lacks the stiffness of so many structural evergreens.

Phillyrea latifolia has broader leaves and is larger-growing than *Phillyrea angustifolia*. Often confused with the holm oak, *Quercus ilex*, it offers a useful alternative where *Quercus ilex* would grow too large. The leaves are small, neat and dark green; white flowers are produced in spring. It becomes looser in habit as the plant matures and the branches become weighed down by the masses of fine foliage.

Viburnum tinus must be mentioned here (see pages 186–87 for a fuller account). Probably our most popular and widely planted evergreen shrub, *Viburnum tinus* provides solid structure on any site, in virtually any conditions except very waterlogged. It responds well to trimming, but the main problem is deciding when to trim, as the plant has such a long flowering season. Pruning is best done in March and April as the flowers are fading, though this will sacrifice the blue-black berries on those plants that produce them.

Lighter and brighter evergreens

Not all evergreen shrubs need to be solid and heavy. The evergreen shrubs described here provide structure in the garden while remaining light and bright in character. They can also be particularly useful for enlivening a dark, shady corner. Small leaves, shiny foliage and different shades of green provide lighter, brighter highlights than heavier evergreens.

Choisya ternata ♀, the Mexican orange blossom, is perhaps second only to *Viburnum tinus* as a widely planted evergreen flowering shrub. It is a very useful, medium-sized shrub, making a neat rounded bush and needing no attention. The trifoliate leaves are shiny, dark green and strongly aromatic when crushed, characteristic of the family Rutaceae, to which it belongs. The family includes citrus and the herb rue.

Choisyas flower best in an open position but will grow in sun or in shade, on any soil. The white, scented flowers are carried in clusters in the leaf axils through late spring and early summer and again in autumn. In fact, some plants are rarely out of flower.

Choisyas need no pruning, but you can trim them after flowering if you need to control size. Ideally, do this from an early age, as plants that have been cut back hard into the old wood, after they have been allowed to grow too large for their situation, rarely recover.

Choisya ternata is everyone's ideal shrub: easy to grow, with a long season of flowering, evergreen, scented and trouble-free. If it has one drawback, it is that it can be slow to get started, so patience is required for the first few years.

One of the few evergreen shrubs reviled by deer and rabbits, choisya is invaluable for those living in areas where these animals are a problem.

The yellow-leaved cultivar, *Choisya ternata* SUNDANCE ('Lich') ♀ does not flower as freely as *Choisya ternata*, but compensates with the brilliance of its young yellow foliage. The tips can be subject to frost damage, but this is easily rectified by trimming in early spring. See also page 40.

Griselinia littoralis ♀ is a native of New Zealand, notable for its rounded, glossy, apple-green leaves. The upright, yellowish stems and ochre tint in the foliage are reminiscent of seaweed and are an acquired taste. Care is needed when siting this plant; the variegated forms may be easier to accommodate than the plain, but can look out of place in the traditional English garden.

However, griselinias offer lighter alternatives to heavy evergreens such as

Griselinia littoralis

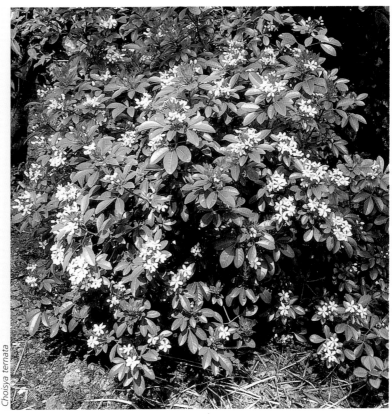

Choisya ternata

laurel, and mix well with golden-variegated plants. They grow quickly, make a good screen, and respond well to trimming, so they make excellent hedging plants. They are very useful in coastal locations (*littoralis* means 'of sea shores'). These shrubs are not for cold areas and do not thrive on chalk. See also page 61.

Pittosporum tenuifolium

Pittosporum tenuifolium ♀ is a native of New Zealand. At one time considered tender for any but the mildest localities, it is now widely grown. The species is a columnar shrub of neat habit. Small, pale green undulate leaves are carried on dark twigs; although there are masses of leaves, the shrub has the effect of being solid without being dense and is well clothed to the ground. Tiny, chocolate, honey-scented flowers are produced in spring; although they are not showy, they are a pleasing contrast to the foliage and the fragrance is noticeable in the garden. *Pittosporum tenuifolium* is good in seaside gardens. Although it prefers good drainage, it seems happy on heavy clay. The foliage is widely used in floristry, so it is a shrub that flower arrangers appreciate. The plant responds well to clipping, so its shape and size are easily controlled and it makes an excellent hedge.

There are many cultivars, with white- and gold-variegated and purple foliage. (See pages 49, 64).

Photinia × fraseri is best known as a chalk-tolerant substitute for pieris. (For pieris, see pages 63, 109.) The popular photinia is a large, vigorous, evergreen shrub. The glossy, leathery dark green leaves are similar to those of the Portugal laurel but have a serrated edge and are more upright along the branches. They resemble individual, large rose leaflets – a clue to the family this plant belongs to: Rosaceae.

The new growth is an attractive coppery red and is the feature for which the plant is best known. The clusters of white flowers, very similar to those of hawthorn but larger, are pretty in the spring. The popular forms of the plant are very hardy, and even the soft new growth is fairly frost-resistant – certainly much more so than that of pieris.

Photinia is a large, easy-to-grow shrub that thrives on any soil, unless conditions are very wet. Colour is better when there is a reasonable amount of sunshine, but the plant is shade-tolerant.

Photinia × fraseri 'Red Robin' ♀ is the best-known and most popular clone, and probably the most spectacular. It was raised in New Zealand but is tough and hardy in the UK. The new growth is brilliant red and is considered equal to pieris in the brilliance of its display.

Photinia × fraseri 'Robusta' is equally useful. It is even more hardy and vigorous but its new growth is more coppery red.

Young container-grown photinia plants often look weak and lax in habit, but their appearance belies their later performance. Hard pruning after planting helps to promote vigorous growth and good branch structure from the base.

Photinias make excellent screening plants and mix well with other large evergreen and deciduous shrubs to provide an effective visual or sound barrier. They respond well to pruning and trimming, so they are ideal as a hedge or for training as a standard. In this form, they make a useful and showy evergreen tree. Trimming results in a flush of new growth.

DOUBLE FLUSH

To get the maximum red foliage effect from your photinia, trim it twice a year, in March and again in July. The second of the two flushes of new growth that result from trimming normally lasts all winter.

Photinia × fraseri 'Red Robin'

Bold-foliage evergreens

Evergreen shrubs with large glossy leaves make a bold statement in the garden and provide a welcome contrast to small, fine green and variegated leaves. Too many small-leaved plants can look fussy and lack impact. Large-leaved plants have great presence against them, providing contrast in the structure planting.

Aucuba japonica (spotted laurel) are the unsung heroes of the garden. These evergreen, shade-loving shrubs grow in just about any soil or situation, however sunless. They have the ability to compete with the roots of trees such as beech and horse chestnut. Even in such adverse conditions, they perform well, their bold, glossy foliage making them a very attractive feature of the garden. The variegated forms bring a little sunshine to the darkest corners.

As the name suggests, *Aucuba japonica* originate from Japan. Being remarkably hardy plants, they are often grown in continental Europe as container plants for winter decoration. They survive unscathed on the pavements of Amsterdam and Brussels in the freezing, windy conditions of mid-winter. They are also very resistant to atmospheric pollution, so suit urban areas. At the other end of the scale, they make sturdy indoor plants and are ideal for draughty hallways and lobbies where more tender subjects would die.

The flowers are insignificant, small and reddish-purple, produced in April. On female plants attractive red berries follow. To fruit well, female plants need a reasonable amount of sunshine and a male pollinator.

The first form to be introduced from Japan, in 1783, was *Aucuba japonica* **'Variegata' ('Maculata').** It has yellow-speckled leaves and is female. See pages 57 for the variegated aucubas.

Of the plain green aucubas, *Aucuba japonica* **f. *longifolia*** ♀ is well worth looking out for. *Aucuba japonica* **f. *longifolia* 'Salicifolia'** ('leaves like a willow') has very narrow leaves on sea-green stems and is particularly prolific in its fruit production.

Aucuba japonica **'Rozannie'** ♀ is a true bold-foliage evergreen with broad, toothed, dark leaves. It is a compact female form that berries well when pollinated.

The aucubas make rounded bushes 2–3m (6–10ft) high and are good solid structure plants. They require no pruning, but if you do want to cut the plants back, to reduce size, do it carefully, with secateurs. Clipping with shears results in unsightly remnants of disfigured leaves.

Sometimes aucubas show blackening of the new shoots in winter. This is not due to frost damage but is the effect of drought during the previous summer. Cut out the damaged growth and the plant quickly recovers.

Fatsia japonica ♀ (castor oil plant) is the ultimate big, green, glossy evergreen. It is exotic in character, yet, perhaps because of its affinity with the ivy, it is in touch with the landscape of Britain.

A native of Japan, it is quite hardy once established. It grows well in any well-drained soil and tolerates any aspect. It is at its best in shade or semi-shade, when the foliage is rich dark green; in full sun the foliage is harder

Fatsia japonica

Aucuba japonica f. *longifolia* 'Salicifolia'

and more olive in colour. The leaves are palmate and on a happy plant are remarkably large. Fatsia flowers in late autumn and early winter, producing a creamy-white inflorescence, like a giant ivy flower, arising from the apical bud. It looks particularly striking against the backdrop of deep green foliage.

Fatsia is an excellent choice for a pot and also for coastal gardens. Left to thrive, it will make a large shrub of spreading habit.

The variegated form *Fatsia japonica* 'Variegata' ♀ is now widely available and, being less vigorous than the plain form, is an excellent plant for the small garden. It tends to be a little more tender, so a sheltered spot is ideal. It looks superb underplanted with a small-leaved, white-variegated ivy.

PRUNING FATSIA

After several years in a container, fatsia can sometimes get leggy and bare at the base. In this situation, hard pruning, down to 30cm (1ft), will result in vigorous growth and healthy new foliage.

Magnolia grandiflora is a magnificent evergreen traditionally grown as a wall shrub in colder climates. Known as the southern magnolia, it is a native of the south-eastern USA but is widely grown as a specimen tree in Mediterranean countries. In the UK it makes an excellent, open-ground, large shrub if given shelter and full sun. The huge creamy, deliciously fragrant flowers are produced in summer and early autumn on mature plants. Some cultivars flower early in life; choose one of these if you are growing the plant for flowers as well as foliage. See also pages 134–35.

Magnolia grandiflora 'Exmouth' ♀ is the most popular variety. Its large leaves are soft green above, reddish brown and felty on the underside. The very large flowers are produced from

Magnolia grandiflora

an early age. *Magnolia grandiflora* 'Galissonnière' is a particularly hardy variety and, with an upright columnar habit, makes an excellent formal structure plant. The dark leaves are reddish-brown on the underside, looking superb with the huge fragrant flowers. *Magnolia grandiflora* 'Victoria' ♀ is another very hardy variety selected in Victoria, British Columbia. The leaves are an exceptionally rich brown beneath.

Magnolia grandiflora 'Little Gem' appeals to those who have a small garden and a strong desire for this beautiful evergreen. However, it is a tender plant and very slow-growing in the early stages of its life.

Magnolia grandiflora needs sun and good drainage. It resents being planted too deep and reacts by standing still, even on the finest soil. It will grow on chalk as long as there is good soil depth and plenty of organic matter is added.

The New Zealand flax, which is not a shrub in the true sense but is generally treated as if it were, is an invaluable structure plant and belongs with this group of shrubs. *Phormium tenax* ♀ is often overlooked in favour of its more colourful relations (see pages 55, 66, 125); the plain green species, however, is a hardy character, with magnificent sword-shaped leaves that can reach a

Phormium tenax

height of 2m (6ft). It suits contemporary schemes, and is a valuable architectural plant to balance heavy masonry. In summer, established plants produce statuesque, antler-like flower spikes, bronze-red in colour, reaching at least 4m (13ft). *Phormium tenax* stands up to exposed conditions and is excellent by the sea. It grows on any fertile soil and in any situation, looking as good beside water as it does in the desert.

Prunus laurocerasus ♀, the cherry laurel, is so widespread in Britain it could be mistaken for a native. In fact it reached Britain in the 17th century from eastern Europe and south-west Asia. It

Prunus laurocerasus 'Rotundifolia'

PRUNING LAUREL HEDGES

Because of its large leathery leaves, any cherry laurel used as a hedge or a shaped subject should be clipped early in the year. New growth will then quickly hide the damaged leaves. If you cut it any later, you will be left with unsightly chopped leaves spoiling the appearance for the rest of the season. Cut smaller specimens with secateurs for best effect.

is true that this is probably the most tolerant shrub when it comes to colonizing shade and areas overhung by trees, but in the garden it should be regarded as a screening plant.

Cherry laurels grow quickly, attaining a height of 6m (20ft) if left unchecked. They make excellent broad hedges and were loved by the Victorians, including Gertrude Jekyll, for this purpose.

The variety *Prunus laurocerasus* 'Rotundifolia' has shorter rounder leaves and is highly suited to clipping, so is perfect for hedging or for making into solid shapes in the border. A seedling of 'Rotundifolia', *Prunus laurocerasus* ETNA ('Anbri') is dense and upright, making a broad shrub. The attractive bronze young foliage becomes dark green with age.

Its ease of cultivation means that many cultivars are often selected as low-maintenance landscape plants. The shiny, dark green foliage of the low, compact *Prunus laurocerasus* 'Otto Luyken' ♀, once widely grown as a garden shrub, is the perfect foil for its showy, upright spikes of white flowers. Unfortunately, however, shot-hole virus, which affects the new growth at the end of the branches, often spoils the foliage. This virus can affect all prunus, deciduous and evergreen, but especially the less vigorous types.

Prunus lusitanica ♀, the Portugal laurel, makes a beautiful specimen tree if it is allowed to grow to maturity. It is normally seen as a rounded bush, and suits clipping and training. The dark green leaves are thinner and finer than

Prunus lusitanica

those of the common cherry laurel, carried on attractive red stems and leaf stalks. It is surprisingly hardy and it tolerates chalk. This plant deserves wider consideration as a structure plant.

Viburnum davidii ♀ was introduced by plant collector Ernest Wilson from western China as recently as 1904. Its extensive use as a garden and landscape plant shows the versatility and appeal of this wonderful evergreen. It grows on any soil, in sun or shade, and is excellent as a permanent subject for a pot.

Viburnum davidii

Often referred to as a good ground-cover shrub, it is far more than this. Left to reach its potential, it spreads to form a mound up to 1m (3ft) high and 1.5m (5ft) wide. Growth is neat and compact.

The large, perfect, leathery oval leaves are conspicuously veined along their length. They are glossy, a deep green above and lighter beneath. The leaf and flower cluster stalks are often red; the dull white flowers are usually produced in late spring and early summer. On female plants, these are followed by small, egg-shaped, blue-black fruits that persist through winter. A male pollinator is required if a female plant is to fruit; planting in groups is desirable. The way to be sure of getting a female plant is to buy it in fruit.

Viburnum davidii's bold form suits contemporary and oriental schemes and works well with gravel, pebbles and rock. It contributes bold structure to a shade planting of pulmonarias and vincas.

FOLIAGE EFFECTS

Flowers will come and go but the contribution made to the garden picture by leaves is long-lasting. It is the colour and texture of foliage that should form the basis of any planting scheme. While structure shrubs create a solid green framework, coloured foliage sets the tone: cheerful yellow, dramatic wine, uplifting gold or silver variegations, and ethereal silver. A dull garden is a garden that lacks variety. Shrubs that are well chosen for their foliage effects are the foundation of good planting.

RIGHT: *Cotinus coggygria* 'Velvet Cloak' in combination with an orange hemerocallis

Yellow and gold

The last two decades of the 20th century saw the introduction of many golden-leaved variations of familar shrubs; other yellow plants were also much loved. Since then, however, yellow has become less popular in the garden, while purple- and silver-variegated foliage and pastels have come to the fore. Daffodil sales have fallen as hyacinth and crocus sales have soared. Marigolds are neglected, while impatiens and petunias are snapped up for pots, baskets and borders.

Golden-yellow foliage is a sure way to brighten up the garden. Since yellow attracts the eye, its positioning needs careful consideration. Use it where you want to draw attention – such as a gateway, an entrance or a focal point – and avoid planting it where it will distract from the focus of the design.

Some yellow-leaved plants scorch in sunlight, so try not to plant them in open situations. Most yellow foliage loses some colour in shade and reverts to a light lime green, which is less striking. Golden-leaved plants tend to be at their best in late summer, and they always complement the oranges and reds of early autumn.

GOLDEN EVERGREENS

The heavy spotting and variegation of some of the **aucubas** give an overall effect of a yellow-leaved shrub. The yellow-splashed foliage of *Aucuba japonica* 'Marmorata' is particularly strong, making this plant a natural choice where a golden-leaved evergreen is needed, especially for a shady site. Aucubas also make superb structure plants (see also pages 35, 57, 96, 122).

Many consider *Choisya ternata* SUNDANCE ('Lich') ♀ to be one of the finest yellow-leaved evergreens, and for a patch of sunshine in the shrub border all year round, it is hard to beat. Although not as free-flowering as

Golden foliage and yellow flowers blend to create a sunny picture.

MIXING AND MATCHING

For best effect, aim to include sufficient plain green and yellow-variegated foliage in the scheme to dilute the yellow and allow the individual plants to shine.

Lime green, as seen in *Alchemilla mollis* ♀, softens yellow and links it with plain greens. The bronze-purple of *Foeniculum vulgare* 'Purpureum' (bronze fennel) provides a good foil for the yellow and adds depth and interest.

Choisya ternata (see page 33), this plant makes up for the lack of flowers with a spectacular display of glossy golden leaves throughout the year. Sometimes the growing tips can be clipped by frost, but if you nip these back in early spring, the plant will quickly recover. Its solid structure is ideal with lighter deciduous shrubs, for example *Philadelphus microphyllus* or *Spiraea* 'Arguta' ♥. Avoid planting with pink shrubs – the combination of colours is not pleasing.

The newer, golden-leaved **Choisya GOLDFINGERS** ('Limo') has finer foliage and the colour is softer yellow. The golden-leaved form of *Choisya* 'Aztec Pearl' ♥, it can be slow to get going, with a very horizontal growth habit when young. It improves with age, but for faster and more robust effect choose SUNDANCE.

Diosma ericoides 'Sunset Gold' is widely available in garden centres in spring, when it is covered with small white, starry flowers. It is very much like a heather but with more arching, horizontal growth, and rather tarnished golden foliage. It is tender and needs neutral or lime-free soil, and is also very susceptible to drying out. For a similar foliage effect from a plant that succeeds

At Denmans, Sussex, *Escallonia laevis* 'Gold Brian' (right) draws the eye to a focal point, the blue seat.

more easily, choose one of the infinitely superior golden forms of *Erica arborea*.

Erica arborea, the tree heath (see page 132), is native to southern Europe, south-west Asia, and north and east Africa. Although it will form a medium to large shrub, once established it can be pruned hard after flowering to promote long sprays of flowers the following season. The fragrant, tiny round flowers with brown stamens are profuse in early spring; they produce clouds of pollen when shaken. *Erica arborea* 'Albert's Gold' ♥ is vigorous and hardy, with bright yellow young foliage; 'Estrella Gold' ♥ is smaller, very hardy, and has similar new growth.

> ### WHERE TO GROW TREE HEATHS
>
> Although recommended for acid soils, these shrubs are more lime-tolerant than many of the callunas. They will grow successfully on clay soils if the pH is not too high. Tree heaths are excellent subjects for bridging the gap between conifers and broad-leaved shrubs in mixed plantings.

Escallonia laevis, which originates from Brazil, boasts two cultivars that are regarded as golden-foliage evergreens: *Escallonia laevis* 'Gold Brian', with yellow foliage, becoming dark green with age; and *Escallonia laevis* 'Gold Ellen', with green leaves that are broadly margined with yellow, giving the overall effect of a golden shrub. Both cultivars have the characteristic sticky, aromatic, lustrous foliage and straight horizontal branches of escallonia. Both produce deep pink flowers; to some the combination with the golden leaves is pleasing, to others it is unattractive. Although these plants are reasonably hardy, they are not suitable for cold, exposed situations. The Mediterranean character of these shrubs sits well with plants such as phormiums and grasses.

Although there are no broad-leaved hebes bearing golden-yellow foliage, *Hebe ochracea*, one of the so-called

Choisya ternata SUNDANCE ('Lich')

Erica arborea 'Albert's Gold'

Choisya GOLDFINGERS ('Limo')

Escallonia laevis 'Gold Ellen'

Ilex crenata 'Golden Gem'

Laurus nobilis 'Aurea'

Lonicera nitida 'Baggesen's Gold'

whipcord hebes, has foliage with a distinct ochre-gold tarnish. This colour is otherwise confined to conifers, which it resembles. Its habit, too, is like that of a prostrate juniper – a low, irregularly layered star shape. Small white flowers appear in summer but are of secondary importance to the foliage, which makes more of an impact in other seasons, particularly winter. *Hebe ochracea* 'James Stirling' ♀ is the excellent cultivar normally grown. Often combined with conifers and heathers, this is good at the front of a yellow-themed planting scheme. (See Good Companions, below.)

A golden-leaved form of the Japanese holly, *Ilex crenata* 'Golden Gem' is a small, compact shrub with a flattened top and yellow leaves. The colour is at its best during the winter and spring, so it could be used to bring colour to the rock garden or to winter containers. It is slow-growing and needs little attention. As a female holly, it is able to produce berries but in fact it rarely flowers.

The golden-leaved bay laurel, *Laurus nobilis* 'Aurea' ♀, is thought by many gardeners to be an ugly duckling of a plant. As a young container-grown shrub, it can be straggly, and appears

chlorotic with its uneven yellow foliage. As a large, mature shrub, however, it has the same statuesque, dense pyramidal habit as the green-leaved bay laurel, but with a lighter character. In low winter sunshine the leaves are particularly golden and glorious. It is an excellent alternative to a large yellow conifer, and suits either a rural or an urban setting. It can be clipped and pruned to shape. Do this in spring, as the foliage starts to green, and just before new shoots appear. If there is space, allow it to reach its potential.

Privet, or *Ligustrum ovalifolium*, is one of our most widely planted shrubs, used mainly for hedging (see page 122). It is easy to grow on any soil and is a tolerant plant, shedding its leaves only in cold conditions. Its wide use as a suburban hedge in the latter part of the 20th century has meant that privet has been overlooked as a shrub suitable for general garden use. The golden privet, *Ligustrum ovalifolium* 'Aureum', will grow to make a large, graceful shrub of up to 3m (10ft). Upright and arching, the thin branches produce bright, rich yellow leaves, sometimes with a green centre. The habit is more open and sparse in shade, making it a useful shrub to lighten a dark corner. Its white flowers are strongly fragrant.

Lonicera nitida 'Baggesen's Gold' ♀ is an amazingly versatile plant, used variously as a winter container plant, an evergreen shrub and a hedging plant. *Lonicera nitida* (see page 122) is a dense,

GOOD COMPANIONS

Plant *Fuchsia* 'Genii' ♀ (1) with other yellow-leaved plants, such as *Hosta* 'Golden Tiara' ♀ and the grass *Carex elata* 'Aurea' ♀ (2) or, for a striking contrast, with a purple heuchera such as *Heuchera* 'Plum Pudding' (3).

Hebe ochracea 'James Stirling' ♀ (4) is a good partner for *Spiraea japonica* 'Firelight' (5) and a pleasing textural contrast with *Euonymus fortunei* 'Emerald 'n' Gold' ♀ (6).

Osmanthus heterophyllus 'Goshiki'

Pittosporum tenuifolium 'Warnham Gold'

small-leaved, dark evergreen shrub with straight twigs. It ultimately reaches 2m (6ft), and has been widely used for hedging because of its quick growth and positive response to clipping. It was introduced to our gardens in 1908 and was quickly employed in suburban gardens as a substitute for box.

If it is left unclipped, *Lonicera nitida* 'Baggesen's Gold' grows into a graceful plant, with leaves that are yellow during summer, turning a yellow-green hue in autumn. The tiny leaves makes this a particularly attractive shrub. When the plant is in shade, the foliage colour is a yellow-green throughout the year; on poor soil the colour is a paler, almost primrose yellow on occasions.

Osmanthus heterophyllus 'Goshiki' is normally regarded as variegated, but the overall effect is certainly more of a soft yellow shrub than one with conspicuous variegation. The small, holly-like leaves are mottled with yellow and are bronze-tinted when young. The colour tends to be lighter and more yellow in full sun. This is a superb evergreen shrub of compact habit and a uniform, mounded shape. It is a very good choice for a container as an alternative to box, and is an excellent structure shrub in mixed plantings. The soft colour sits easily with a wide range of plants and is gentler on the eye than many gold or variegated plants.

For stronger foliage effect, consider *Osmanthus heterophyllus* 'Aureus' (all gold), which has dark green foliage and bright, deep gold young growth. This is a bold shrub, and a good choice for the foreground when planted with gold-variegated evergreen shrubs.

A superb yellow-leaved shrub for effective, light structure is *Pittosporum tenuifolium* 'Warnham Gold' ♀, with greenish-yellow young foliage that matures to golden-yellow. The leaves are softly wavy and loose in habit, but they achieve dense cover. In winter the colour intensifies to soft old gold, which looks delightful against dark evergreens or clear blue winter skies. As the plant matures, it makes a tall narrow cone.

YELLOW AND GOLD PLANT COMBINATIONS

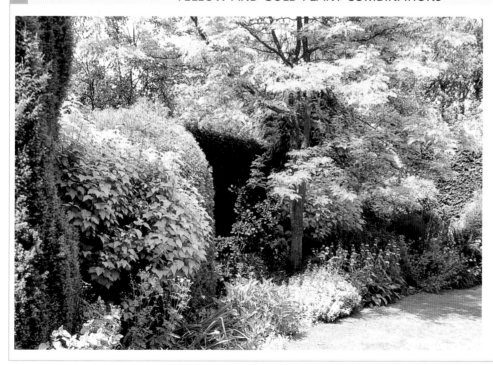

The Yellow Border at Le Clos du Coudray, Normandy, in France. This perfectly illustrates how stunning combinations are created when golden-leaved trees, such as *Robinia pseudoacacia* 'Frisia' ♀, *Gleditsia triacanthos* 'Sunburst' ♀ or *Ptelea trifoliata* 'Aurea' ♀, are mixed with attractive golden-leaved shrubs and yellow-flowering herbaceous plants.

DECIDUOUS SHRUBS WITH GOLDEN FOLIAGE

All maples are highly valued for their most attractive foliage (see also pages 50–51). If you decide you would like an *Acer shirasawanum* 'Aureum' ♀ (*Acer japonicum* 'Aureum') in your garden, do not procrastinate – plant it now. Growth is slow, and it takes some time to reach its potential. However, even when the plant is not much more than a small twig, the stunning acid-yellow colour of the foliage is an eye-catcher. The shrub's elegant, spreading habit is distinctly oriental. The leaves are rounded and sharply toothed, transforming from yellow to orange-red in autumn. A shrub for dappled shade and shelter, this acer does not like drought and the foliage will scorch in full sun. It associates well with hostas, grasses, ground-cover plants and pebbles in an uncluttered scheme. This is not a shrub to mix with flowering subjects.

A recent lack of interest in **berberis** has led to a decline in the popularity of *Berberis thunbergii* 'Aurea'. However, it is very striking when the wonderful bright yellow new growth appears – a shade that suits the small round leaves, carried on wand-like branches; this colour changes to pale green as the season progresses. The foliage can scorch in strong sun. This is a problem not suffered by the more recent cultivar *Berberis thunbergii* BONANZA GOLD

Acer shirasawanum 'Aureum'

('Bogozam'), with orange-red shoots that turn yellow-green as they mature.

Caryopteris are delightful plants for sunny positions on well-drained soil, and thrive on chalk. The aromatic leaves are usually a soft grey-green, which blends beautifully with the fluffy blue of the late-summer flowers. *Caryopteris* × *clandonensis* 'Worcester Gold' ♀ has golden-yellow, flushed foliage. While the combination of yellow leaves and blue flowers is not unappealing, it does not mix well with some autumn herbaceous plants. It is unattractive with sedum and echinacea, for example, but works well with rudbeckia.

The virtues of the red stems of *Cornus alba* 'Aurea' ♀ are extolled in

Cornus alba 'Aurea'

the section on shrubs for winter (see pages 177–78). It is a plant that works hard year-round, however, for there are few yellow-leaved plants with such soft grace as this one. The large, well-spaced leaves are an almost translucent shade of yellow, and they complement variegated or green shrubs, without shouting. As a further bonus, the leaves

Berberis thunbergii 'Aurea'

Caryopteris × *clandonensis* 'Worcester Gold'

LATE-SUMMER BLUES

All golden-leaved subjects look stunning in association with blue flowers. Remember that there are some excellent late-summer blues: caryopteris, ceratostigma, perovskia and the autumn-flowering ceanothus. These shrubs bloom when many gold-foliage plants are at their best.

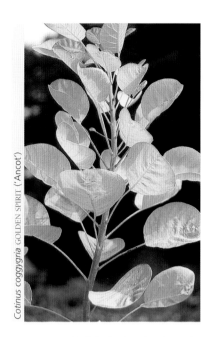

Cotinus coggygria GOLDEN SPIRIT ('Ancot')

shoots and leaves that are lime-yellow in sun, lime-green in semi-shade. The flowers are small for a hybrid fuchsia, with a violet corolla and cerise calyx – a pleasing contrast to the yellow of the foliage. *Fuchsia* 'Genii' works well with other yellow-leaved plants, such as hostas and grasses, and is striking with purple heucheras, which combine beautifully with the flowers (see Good Companions, page 42).

Philadelphus coronarius 'Aureus' ♀ is probably the most widely planted of the deciduous yellow-leaved shrubs. The leaves are bright acid yellow when young, maturing to greenish yellow. In semi-shade the leaves are more lime yellow and contrast superbly with purple-leaved shrubs such as the elder *Sambucus nigra* f. *porphyrophylla* 'Eva' ♀ (formerly known as 'Black Lace', see page 54). The new foliage is at its best when the late tulips are in flower (see Good Companions, page 47).

Philadelphus coronarius 'Aureus' is generally a tough, tolerant plant that will withstand poor, dry soil, although occasionally its leaves scorch in hot sunshine. It is a medium-sized shrub and, although not as free-flowering as most philadelphus, it produces plenty of very fragrant, single, creamy-white flowers with yellow stamens. Prune immediately after flowering, cutting out some of the old wood that has flowered and leaving the vigorous new shoots.

turn a wonderful shade of salmon in autumn, before falling to reveal the winter stems. Selective pruning of half of the stems to ground level each year ensures well-coloured new wood, and keeps the shrub light and open in character. It is very useful for sun or shade, on any soil, and is particularly tolerant of wet conditions.

Cotinus coggygria GOLDEN SPIRIT ('Ancot') is a relatively new introduction that is proving to be an excellent plant. It grows well and, like all the more familiar purple-leaved smoke bushes (see page 54), has excellent leaf form. This is a large shrub, reaching about 2m (6ft) in height and spread. It responds well to pruning, and the long, straight sprays of foliage produced after it has been cut back are among its attractions. This plant is useful in a large pot as long as it is pruned hard each spring. After a hot summer, it has sensational orange-salmon autumn colour, even in shade.

Fuchsia 'Genii' ♀ is a dwarf shrub that develops its best colour in full sun and does not scorch. It is surprisingly hardy, and in mild localities it can be regarded as a permanent garden subject. The habit is upright with red

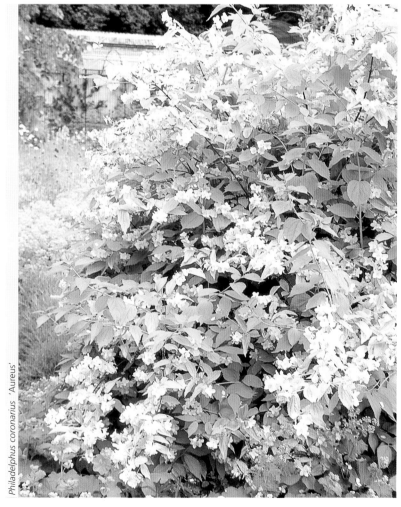

Philadelphus coronarius 'Aureus'

Physocarpus opulifolius 'Dart's Gold' ♥ is a compact shrub that thrives anywhere. Its flowers are white, tinged pink, and appear all along the branches in early summer. The leaves are similar in shape to those of *Ribes*, (flowering currant) but are bright yellow, staying this colour for a long period, and are much more scorch-resistant. (See Good Companions page 93.) This is less often seen than the dark-leaved *Physocarpus opulifolius* 'Diabolo' (see page 54).

Ribes sanguineum 'Brocklebankii' is a smaller, slower-growing shrub than most flowering currants. The leaves are attractive in form and colour (a rich golden-yellow), but they tend to scorch in sun and jar with the pink flowers, produced at a time when most people find the contrast of yellow forsythia and pink cherries more than enough.

Ribes sanguineum 'Brocklebankii'

Rubus cockburnianus 'Golden Vale'

Rubus cockburnianus is a strong-growing bramble, with arching purple stems overlaid with a white bloom. *Rubus cockburnianus* 'Goldenvale' ♥ has the same white stems, exposed in winter, but this cultivar is blessed with brilliant golden-yellow, fern-like leaves in summer. This variety is not nearly as invasive as the species, and can be pruned hard at the end of winter to

keep it in control. This is truly a plant for all seasons, happy in sun or shade, and deserves wider planting.

A golden form of our native, purple-berried elder, *Sambucus racemosa* 'Plumosa Aurea' is one of the most graceful yellow-leaved shrubs. It is a medium to large shrub with deeply cut golden foliage, conical rather than flat flowerheads, which crowd the branches

PLANT PROFILE

Spiraea

Spiraeas are hardy shrubs, easy to grow on any soil and requiring little care. Prune these foliage types in early spring, before the new growth really gets going, as light or as hard as you wish. Because they stay looking good for a long period, spiraeas are excellent garden-centre plants. Unfortunately, this has led to over-planting, but with their pleasing habit and attractive foliage they are useful low-growing shrubs for many planting schemes. Some plants, such as *Spiraea japonica* 'Goldflame', will produce reverted green shoots; cut the green shoots out as soon as they appear to retain the golden colour of these shrubs.

Spiraea japonica 'Candlelight' ♥ is a compact shrub with foliage a clear yellow that gradually deepens. It does not revert, and has good autumn leaf colour. The pink flowers contrast with the foliage, but this is not a subtle combination.

Spiraea japonica 'Firelight' has orange-red young foliage and a graceful, arching habit. The autumn colour is fiery red. (See Good Companions, page 42.)

Spiraea japonica 'Goldflame' is one of our most popular dwarf shrubs. It has upright growth and deep rose-red

flowers. The young leaves are bright, reddish-orange on tan-barked stems. They eventually become rich yellow, then green. (See Good Companions, right.)

Spiraea japonica GOLDEN PRINCESS ('Lisp') ♥, of dwarf habit, has bronze-red foliage that gradually turns a brilliant yellow and, in autumn, red. Its flowers are deep pink.

Spiraea japonica MAGIC CARPET ('Walbuma') ♥ has a spreading habit and bright red new foliage, turning yellow. The compact flowerheads are deep pink. It is a good plant for ground cover and containers.

MORE YELLOW AND GOLD SHRUBS *Acer negundo* 'Kelly's Gold' • *Calluna vulgaris* 'Beoley Gold' • *Ceratostigma willmottianum* DESERT SKIES • *Cornus mas* 'Aurea' • *Corylus avellana* 'Aurea' • *Erica carnea* 'Aurea' •

Sambucus racemosa 'Plumosa Aurea'

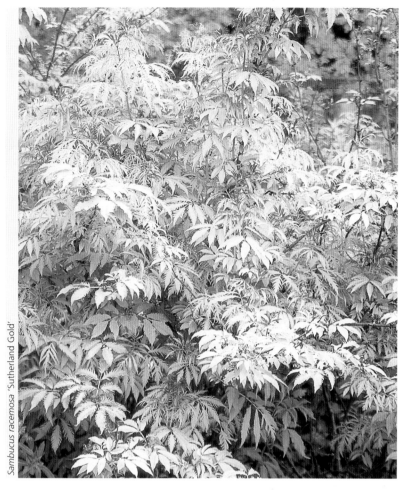

Sambucus racemosa 'Sutherland Gold'

in mid-spring, and clusters of scarlet fruits, which in this golden form are insignificant. It is best in light shade, as it is prone to scorch in full sun. Another golden cultivar, *Sambucus racemosa* **'Sutherland Gold'** ♀ is perhaps not as fine and graceful, but is scorch-resistant and therefore more useful. Prune in late winter, selectively cutting back some of the older branches to healthy buds near the base of the plant. Cutting half-way tends to produce clumsy growth.

There are several varieties of weigela with golden-yellow foliage. *Weigela* **'Looymansii Aurea'** is an old variety, found as a seedling in 1873. The foliage is light gold and is best grown in partial shade: in full sun, the colour is harsher

Weigela BRIANT RUBIDOR ('Olympiade')

and the leaves scorch. A disadvantage of this plant is that the gold foliage looks unpleasant with the pink flowers. Today, we tend to grow the cultivar **Weigela** BRIANT RUBIDOR **('Olympiade')** more frequently. The leaves are yellow or green, with a broad yellow margin, and the flowers are a dark carmine-red, which looks better with the foliage.

GOOD COMPANIONS

Philadelphus coronarius 'Aureus' ♀ makes a wonderful backdrop to *Tulipa* 'Black Parrot' ♀, 'Queen of Night' or 'Black Hero' (1).

Underplant a spiraea that has orange-red new growth, such as *Spiraea japonica* 'Goldflame' (2) with early-flowering dwarf bulbs *Scilla siberica* or a blue *Anemone blanda* (3).

Ilex aquifolium 'Flavescens' • *Kolkwitzia amabilis* 'Maradco' • *Leycesteria formosa* GOLDEN LANTERNS '(Notbruce) •
Ligustrum lucidum 'Golden Wax' • *Ptelea trifoliata* 'Aurea' • *Ribes alpinum* 'Aureum' • *Viburnum opulus* 'Aureum' •

Purple and plum

The Red Border at Hidcote Manor Garden, Gloucestershire.

Wild, hot colours become stronger and richer when blended with deep plum, wine and bronze – tones that exist in plants at all levels, from the leafy canopy of trees such as acer to the ground-cover carpeting of ajuga or heuchera. Purple is often planted as a contrast to yellow. It stands bold and beautiful against orange and gold while, with its ingredient colours of red, blue, brown and pink, it has a softening and melting effect on bright shades of yellow.

MIXING AND MATCHING

Shrubs with purplish-red foliage mix well with many other colours of leaf and flower, but each combination produces a very different effect.

Purplish-red foliage provides a strong contrast to yellow, which works where dramatic effect is required, and to draw the eye, but can be overpowering. Usually a yellow-leaved shrub against a purple-leaved shrub is too much: two solid masses competing against each other. For example, imagine *Cotinus coggygria* 'Royal Purple' alongside *Choisya ternata* 'Sundance'.

However, if the partners are at different levels in the planting scheme, they are different in form or one is much lighter in structure than the other, the effect can be stunning: purple cotinus beneath golden gleditsia, 'Black Parrot' tulips against golden philadelphus, or perhaps purple heucheras under golden spiraeas.

The addition of purple foliage adds weight, and depth, to any planting of silver, blue and pink. It contributes a richness that makes a scheme more interesting and eye-catching. Purple-leaved deciduous shrubs, such as *Sambucus* (elder) and *Corylus* (hazel), combine particularly well with cottage garden favourites such as herbaceous geraniums, artemisias, delphiniums and lavenders. They also make dramatic supports for climbers such as *Clematis texensis* and *Clematis viticella*, the midnight velvet background of the purple foliage being the perfect canvas for the embroidery of the clematis flowers.

Wine-red foliage is a dramatic complement to hot colours. Try adding the chocolate-leaved varieties of those exotic summer visitors – cannas, dahlias and begonias. Structural, red-leaved plants such as berberis, cotinus and pittosporums look stunning with *Dahlia* 'Bishop of Llandaff'. In late summer, any of these will provide the perfect backdrop for crocosmias or heleniums.

EVERGREEN PURPLES

There are very few purple evergreens. The purple *Pittosporum tenuifolium* 'Purpureum' has shiny, crinkle-edged leaves of deep bronze-purple in autumn and winter, carried on wiry, upright stems. The new spring growth is fresh, bright apple-green, and the transition to darkness intensifies gradually through the year. This is a shrub with a spindly habit, and is rarely offered for sale because it has such an unappealing gait while in a container. However, once the plant is established, its light bony form is an attractive addition to any scheme, and it is useful for cutting.

A shorter, smaller, more compact cultivar is *Pittosporum tenuifolium* 'Tom Thumb' ♀ – an excellent small shrub. The density and intensity of its foliage in winter is stunning, making it the ideal partner for the glowing winter stems of cornus (see pages 177–78), or the pretty, nodding blooms of *Helleborus orientalis*. It is also an excellent long-term subject for a container: a glazed oriental pot is the perfect foil for the colour and texture of the leaves. This shrub was originally raised in New Zealand but proves to be very hardy in the northern hemisphere.

On a lighter note, *Pseudowintera colorata*, also from New Zealand, likes a little shelter and dislikes shallow chalk. It is excellent in semi-shade, in a pot containing ericaceous compost. The leaves are grey-olive in the centre but flushed pink and edged and blotched with Merlot-purple. A pleasing low mound of a shrub, this is a good choice to plant with azaleas and low-growing rhododendrons for interest year-round.

Salvia officinalis 'Purpurascens' ♀, the purple-leaf sage, is the perfect mixer (see Good Companions, right). It has made the move from the herb garden to the flower border and in the process has become one of our best-loved dwarf

Pittosporum tenuifolium 'Tom Thumb'

Pittosporum tenuifolium 'Purpureum'

Pseudowintera colorata

shrubs. The dusky purple foliage, which becomes richer in summer and greyer in winter, is perfect for softening paving, as a container plant, for the front of the border or to combine with grey foliage. Delightfully aromatic, the leaves of sage can be used in cooking. It is therefore a suitable partner for rosemary and thyme in hot, dry planting schemes. As is the case with most Mediterranean plants, this sage prefers good drainage and relatively dry soil, but it is surprisingly accommodating and will even survive heavy clay provided it is not waterlogged. Excellent on chalk, sages are short-lived on heavier soils, and you should replace plants approximately every three years. *(Continued on page 52.)*

(Continued on page 52.)

GOOD COMPANIONS

Make a purple and silver cameo with *Hebe* 'Mrs Winder' ♀ ('Waikiki') (1), *Salvia officinalis* 'Purpurascens' ♀ (2), *Lavandula stoechas* subsp. *pedunculata* ♀ ('Papillon') (3) and *Santolina chamaecyparissus* ♀ (4).

Acer

The Japanese maples are the aristocrats of the deciduous red-foliage shrubs or small trees. In spring the feathery scarlet leaves unfurl, like tiny fishing flies resting on the branches. The soft foliage then shimmers gracefully through the summer months, until the display of fiery autumn tints sets the plant ablaze, putting its more introvert companions firmly in the shade.

Japanese maples make excellent subjects for containers for sheltered positions. Their architectural form and mature character suits minimalist schemes, where the individual beauty of the plant can be appreciated.

Global interest in Japanese maples has resulted in a myriad of named cultivars. As a rule of thumb, the *palmatum* types are fairly upright and normally carry their branches in attractive layers. The cut-leaf types (the Dissectum group) are generally lower-growing, forming a mound. Most of the upright, red-leaved varieties are derivatives of the *Acer palmatum* Atropurpureum group. These make large shrubs of graceful habit.

Sometimes considered delicate, these maples are susceptible to wind damage; in exposed surroundings, shelter them with hardier neighbours. They enjoy the dappled shade from taller trees, but if deprived of too much sunlight they lose colour and the rich burgundy foliage becomes a muddy green. Grow them in lime-free, loam-based compost, and water well throughout the growing season.

Acer palmatum types prefer moist, well-drained, loamy soil, and grow best in neutral-to-acid conditions. The stronger-growing varieties succeed on chalk, and often are surprisingly tolerant of inhospitable conditions.

In all cases, pruning of Japanese maples should be necessary only to rectify damage or to remove dead and diseased wood. Trimming can ruin the plant's natural shape and beauty. Do not prune in winter as branches cut during the dormant season tend to let disease into the plant. For more on acers, see pages 66–67, 168–69.

Acer palmatum 'Fireglow' with *Tulipa* 'Queen of Night'.

Acer palmatum 'Bloodgood' ♀ (right) is an excellent form, widely grown for its deep reddish-purple foliage, which turns red in autumn. The winged fruits, conspicuous on mature plants, are also attractive. *Acer palmatum* 'Fireglow' is similar but more vigorous and generally considered to be an improvement on 'Bloodgood'.

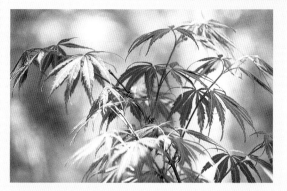

Acer palmatum 'Burgundy Lace' ♀ is broad-spreading, forming a mound of feathered foliage, wider than it is high.

Acer palmatum 'Trompenburg' ♀ has deep purplish-red young leaves that turn greener later in the season, before putting on a good display of bright red autumn colour. The leaves are deeply divided, with narrow lobes and rolled margins. This is a very tough acer.

Acer palmatum 'Beni-maiko' has delicate leaves on fine branches, giving wonderful movement. The young leaves are fiery red, later pink, then greenish red. All shades appear on the plant at the same time, creating the effect of an Impressionist painting.

Acer palmatum var. *dissectum* 'Crimson Queen' ♀ is a cut-leaf type, with rich reddish-purple foliage that holds its colour well. The downward-swept branches and deeply cut foliage resemble the plumage of an exotic bird.

Acer palmatum 'Corallinum', a slow-growing cultivar with small, deep-cut leaves that open bright salmon pink.

Acer palmatum var. *dissectum* 'Inaba-shidare' has large purple leaves with red stems. This is a strong-growing cultivar that retains its colour throughout the season before turning red in the autumn.

Hebe 'Amy'

Hebe 'Caledonia'

Cut back the flower spikes of the purple-leaved sage in summer, after the flowers fade, to encourage new growth. Plants can also be trimmed in late spring to promote bushiness. Ideally, plant as small, young plants in groups of three. If one fails, others will fill the space. (See Good Companions, pages 49, 83.)

The **hebes**, mostly originating from New Zealand, include some of our best-loved purple-leaved evergreens. (For cultivation of hebes, see page 76). *Hebe* 'Mrs Winder' ♀ ('Waikiki') is one of the most widely planted hebes. A shrub of rounded habit, it grows to about 1m (3ft). The small shiny, purple leaves are lovely with the bright blue flowers in summer and autumn. A reasonably hardy hybrid, this hebe nearly always makes a good recovery if

---

LOOKING AFTER HEBES

If you need to prune your hebes, to control their size or to promote bushiness, do so after the danger of severe frost has passed. Cut the branches back to a point where new green shoots are emerging. Cutting back hard into bare wood is risky, and there is no certainty that the plant will recover.

Larger-leaved hebes may suffer from leafspot diseases, particularly after mild, damp winters. Treat this by cutting back and treating the new growth, as it emerges, with a systemic fungicide.

---

damaged by bad weather. Combine it with lavenders and grey-leaved subjects (see Good Companions, page 49).

Hebe 'Amy' has long, oval, pointed leaves, which are larger than those of many other hebe cultivars. Purple when young, they become dark green as they mature, but the whole plant always has a purple hue. On a sheltered site, winter colour is good. The small, violet-purple bottlebrush flowers appear through summer into autumn on upright stems, making a small rounded bush. Another reliable purple-leaved evergreen is *Hebe* 'Caledonia', a dwarf, compact, rounded shrub with plum-tinted foliage and violet flowers from late spring into autumn.

Hebe 'Pascal' ♀ is a comparatively new variety. Compact and upright in habit, it has stunning, deep burgundy foliage in winter and throughout spring, becoming bronze-green in summer; it has mauve flowers in summer and early autumn. *Hebe* 'Twisty' has interesting, upright branches and pointed purple leaves that spiral from the stem without stalks. The effect is reminiscent of the foliage of a purple monkey puzzle tree. (See also *Hebe* 'Red Edge' ♀, page 76.)

Several *Hebe speciosa* cultivars have reddish-purple new growth that turns dark green as it ages. The lovely *Hebe speciosa* 'La Séduisante' is a small shrub with large, narrow bottlebrush sprays of crimson flowers accentuating the red colour of the new leaves. It needs a sheltered wall or a position near the house; it is good for seaside gardens.

DECIDUOUS PURPLES

Acers – see Plant Profile, pages 50–51.

With their tough, thorny and resilient stems, **berberis** are very efficient at deterring intruders. However, their contibution is far greater than this. *Berberis thunbergii* f. *atropurpurea* 'Rose Glow' ♀ makes a small bush with perfectly rounded, reddish-purple, pink-splashed leaves; where there is some shade, they become a rich copper. The colour intensifies as winter approaches. Plant it where the early sun shines through the leaves, transforming the erect stems into flaming wands. It thrives in any site. (See Good Companions, page 100.) The cultivar 'Harlequin' is very similar but has slightly smaller leaves and more pink mottling.

A very compact, dwarf cultivar good for small gardens is 'Atropurpurea Nana' ♀. It is also useful in a rock garden and is excellent, although rarely used, as a dwarf hedge. (See Good Companions, opposite.) 'Bagatelle' ♀ is an even more compact shrub.

The upright forms of purple berberis deserve to be more popular than they are. They are striking statement plants, excellent when planted to rise out of a mass of softer, lighter foliage. *Berberis thunbergii* f. *atropurpurea* 'Helmond Pillar' grows to 2m (6ft) and has rich purple foliage that turns a sensational shade of red-orange in autumn. 'Red

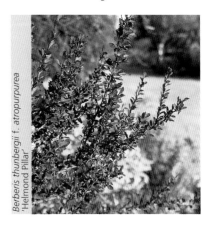

Berberis thunbergii f. atropurpurea 'Helmond Pillar'

Berberis thunbergii f. atropurpurea 'Rose Glow'

other plants is recognized (see Good Companions, below). It prefers a sunny position and requires good drainage.

The purple-leaf filbert, also known as hazel, *Corylus maxima* 'Purpurea' ♀ has large, rounded, heart-shaped leaves of a similarly intense colour to that of the purple beech. If allowed to grow, it will make a large spreading shrub with reddish-brown catkins borne in early spring, and later carrying red-purple nuts with prominent calyces. Hard, selective pruning produces strong upright growth.

The leaves are carried at an attractive horizontal angle to the branches and, like beech, are particularly attractive when young with sunlight shining through them. It is an easy plant to grow

Chief' is a smaller upright shrub, with bright red stems and narrow, red-purple leaves. It is not as column-like, and its branches become more arching as the plant matures.

If space allows and you need a big, dramatic, purple-leaved shrub, *Berberis × ottawensis* f. *purpurea* 'Superba' ♀ ('Purpurea') is unbeatable, especially as a boundary plant. It produces vigorous, upright arching stems and superb wine-purple foliage. Small yellow flowers are produced in spring, but are insignificant compared with the foliage. This is an excellent screening plant, and a good contrast to the solid form of the larger yellow conifers.

Cercis are normally regarded as small trees, usually growing on a single stem.

However, their stature is often more shrub-like. Certainly, *Cercis canadensis* 'Forest Pansy' ♀ could not be regarded as vigorous. The pink flowers, which are produced on the dark, woody branches, are inconspicuous and secondary, while the leaves are truly glorious: heart-shaped and a rich reddish-purple colour, turning purple-gold in autumn. The growth habit is very attractive, with spreading branches forming a broad, funnel-shaped head. This plant has become more popular in recent years as its ability to combine successfully with

Corylus maxima 'Purpurea'

BERBERIS – NO HALF MEASURES

The larger berberis are not a pleasure to prune; good armour is required. They are, however, spoilt by half-hearted snipping, and cutting 60cm (2ft) off the end of the branches just produces whippy shoots, way up in the air. Selective pruning of older branches, right to the base, is the only approach. If a stately specimen is too tall, it has been planted in the wrong position.

GOOD COMPANIONS

Consider *Berberis thunbergii* f. *atropurpurea* 'Atropurpurea Nana' ♀ (1) as an effective contrast to *Lavandula angustifolia* 'Hidcote' ♀ (2) in a formal scheme.

Cercis canadensis 'Forest Pansy' ♀ (3) is very striking when planted with *Cerinthe major* 'Purpurascens' (4), the broad bean flower.

and suits informal planting schemes with other shrubs such as buddleia, philadelphus, deutzia and shrub roses.

The purple-leaved smoke bushes, **cotinus** are the deepest, darkest and arguably most handsome of all shrubs. *Cotinus coggygria* 'Velvet Cloak' is perhaps the finest. Its deep red-purple leaves hold their colour well into autumn before they turn red. *Cotinus coggygria* 'Royal Purple' ♀ is the best known, with deep wine-purple leaves that redden towards autumn (see Good Companions, page 142).

Smoke bushes are always late to break into leaf but, when they do, they steal the show. The rich mantle of leaves demands showy jewels to enhance its beauty. Burnt orange daylilies are the perfect adornment to the purple leaves (illus. pages 38–39).

Physocarpus opulifolius 'Diabolo' ♀ is a gregarious shrub that associates well with herbaceous plants, evergreens and roses. It is an ideal plant for an open, sunny position. In full sun, the foliage can be so dark that it is almost black. It is excellent as a background to shrub roses, and combines well with herbaceous perennials to provide good structure in mixed plantings. (See Good Companions, opposite and page 113.) Hard pruning increases vigour and improves foliage. Prune early in the season, while the plant

Cotinus coggygria 'Royal Purple'

Sambucus nigra f. porphyrophylla 'Gerda'

is dormant, or after the flowers have faded, as with any of the deciduous flowering shrubs. Simply prune out the wood that has flowered, leaving the new, vigorous shoots to grow through.

Sambucus, or elder, responds to the same treatment. Purple-leaved elders have deservedly become very popular. *Sambucus nigra* f. *porphyrophylla* 'Eva' ♀ (formerly known as 'Black Lace'), a cultivar introduced in 2003, is less vigorous but has superb, finely cut foliage. This is an excellent plant for giving depth to herbaceous plantings: try it mixed with silver-leaved plants, herbaceous geraniums and sweet peas. (See Good Companions, opposite.) *Sambucus nigra* f. *porphyrophylla* 'Gerda' ♀ (formerly known as 'Black Beauty') makes a dramatic impact in any border and is fast-growing as long as it is pruned hard in its first season. In subsequent years, it can be cut back hard towards the end of winter.

Viburnum sargentii 'Onondaga' ♀ is a large, vigorous shrub similar to the guelder rose, *Viburnum opulus*. New foliage is deep wine-red, and the whole plant displays wonderful reddish-purple autumn colour when it is grown in full sun. The flattened flowerheads resemble small lacecap hydrangeas; the individual fertile flowers are red in bud and when open reveal purple stamens.

The sterile florets surrounding them stay white. Offset by the purple foliage at the end of the branches, this is a most striking combination (illus. page 147).

Viburnum sargentii 'Onondaga' is a tall, very upright shrub; poor pruning easily spoils this habit, and it is not a plant that responds well to control. If pruning is necessary, remove whole stems selectively to ground level, after flowering. It grows well on any soil, including chalk, but needs an open, sunny position if it is to display good foliage colour. This is a useful shrub for country gardens, where it mixes happily with native plants.

Weigela florida 'Foliis Purpureis' ♀ is not the most intense of the red-leaved shrubs, the foliage being more brown-purple in hue. However, this colour is no less useful in the garden, and there is the bonus of a mass of mauve-pink, funnel-shaped flowers in late spring and early summer. This combination of flower and foliage is most pleasing – unlike the pink and red blooms displayed by many of the golden-leaved shrubs. It is also more compact and slower-growing than most weigelas. To get the best from the foliage and flowers, provide a sunny aspect.

Weigela florida WINE AND ROSES ('Alexandra') is a recent cultivar with deep red-purple foliage that becomes bronze-green edged with purple as the

COTINUS PRUNING TIPS

Smoke bush, the common name for cotinus, comes from the purplish-grey inflorescences that, seen from a distance, resemble puffs of pink smoke. These are produced on two- to three-year-old wood, so if you want flowers, keep pruning to a minimum. Cotinus can be slow to get going, but hard pruning in the first year or two helps. Hard pruning also improves the size of the foliage. Do this in late winter, cutting stems back to two or three buds.

MORE PURPLE AND PLUM SHRUBS *Acer palmatum* 'Red Pygmy' • *Acer palmatum* 'Hessei' • *Berberis thunbergii* f. *atropurpurea* 'Dart's Red Lady' • *Berberis thunbergii* f. *atropurpurea* 'Red Pillar' •

season progresses, turning deep purple in autumn. The growth is dense and spreading; the flowers, borne in late spring and early summer, are reddish pink. Another new cultivar is *Weigela* NAOMI CAMPBELL ('Bokrashine'), with deep chocolate foliage and bright red flowers, also borne in late spring and early summer – a striking combination that sits well with dark blue ceanothus.

Weigela florida 'Foliis Purpureis'

Weigelas are easy shrubs to grow, and they thrive on chalk and clay soils. Ideally, remove flowered shoots immediately after flowering to allow new, vigorous growth to come through.

SPIKY MIXERS

Phormiums with plum-coloured foliage and rich red **cordylines** are dramatic creatures that make a strong statement in pots on the patio or in a courtyard, or rising from the border.

The red-leaved cordylines are less vigorous than the plain green *Cordyline australis* (see page 87) but they still make small trees in very mild locations. Often seen as specimens gracing a terrace, they also suit both traditional and contemporary planting schemes. *Cordyline australis* 'Torbay Red' is the best form, with deep burgundy-red foliage and broad leaves. *Cordyline australis* 'Red Star' has bronze-red foliage. The red cordylines are not quite as hardy as the green ones, so winter protection is frequently needed.

The purple-leaved phormiums are surprisingly versatile plants, in spite of

Cordyline australis 'Red Star'

Phormium 'Platt's Black'

their exotic appearance. The broad, sword-shaped foliage of the larger varieties suit specimen planting in patio containers, gravel and as exclamation marks in the border, rising out of lower, softer planting.

Phormiums like good light and good drainage. The coloured forms can suffer in winter, so some form of protection is advisable in areas with cold winters. They are excellent plants for coastal gardens. Plant phormiums near the front of the border, where they can rise above surrounding planting, their spiky forms bringing mixed plantings to life.

Phormium 'Platt's Black' is one of the darkest hardy foliage plants: it has narrow, arching, inky purple leaves of less than 1m (3ft) long. *Phormium* 'Dark Delight' is slightly larger, with broad, dark bronze-purple leaves, that point downwards at the tip.

Phormium tenax Purpureum Group ♀ is a large plant, reaching 2m (6ft). The bold leaves are bronze-purple and contrast superbly with both grey foliage and soft yellow grasses. This is one of the hardiest forms and reliably produces striking architectural spikes of bronze-red flowers once established.

GOOD COMPANIONS

The ebony foliage of *Physocarpus opulifolius* 'Diabolo' ♀ (1) is stunning underplanted with *Helichrysum italicum* 'Korma', against the silver of *Elaeagnus* 'Quicksilver' ♀ (2), or with the russet shades of the reflexed turk's caps of *Lilium henryi* ♀ (3).

For stunning summer effect, let a shocking-pink everlasting pea, *Lathyrus latifolius* (5), clamber through. *Sambucus nigra* f. *porphyrophylla* 'Eva' ♀ (5).

Coprosma depressa 'Karo Red' • *Cordyline australis* 'Red Sensation' • *Corylopsis sinensis* var. *sinensis* 'Spring Purple' • *Phormium tenax* 'All Black' • *Prunus cerasifera* 'Nigra' • *Sambucus nigra* f. *porphyrophylla* 'Thundercloud' •

Gold and silver variegated

Variegated plants occur only rarely in the wild; they are mostly a phenomenon of gardens. Whenever a variegated clone has arisen, its worth has been recognized by gardeners and nurserymen, who have propagated it and preserved it for ornamental use.

In the garden, shrubs with variegated leaves perform a function similar to that of flowering shrubs: they provide variety and they break up the solid green of most foliage. Whereas flowering shrubs provide limited, seasonal interest, the majority of important variegated shrubs are evergreen and therefore make a contribution all year round. They are useful to lighten shady areas, and many succeed in positions where flowering shrubs simply will not perform.

Light variegated shrubs such as *Cornus alternifolia* 'Argentea' brighten the planting.

HOW VARIEGATION OCCURS

Variegation occurs when certain areas of a leaf lack the green pigment chlorophyll. White patches are caused by a total absence of pigments; yellow variegation arises when pigments other than chlorophyll are present. Variegation is produced when there is a cell mutation; this usually happens when something goes wrong with the genetic information in the growing point of a shoot. All cells from the mutant cells then lack the green pigment chlorophyll in certain areas of the leaf. Chlorophyll is responsible for photosynthesis (food manufacture); without chlorophyll, there is a reduction in the plant's capacity to produce food and, consequently, a reduction in growth rate.

Some variegations are stable, and all resulting growth has the same variegation. In other cases, reversion occurs and the original green growth takes over (see box, page 63).

MIXING AND MATCHING

In the garden, remember that strong variegation introduces colour and therefore attracts attention. Yellow variegations draw the eye; they are valuable for softening the effect of adjacent golden-leaved plants, as well as for providing a transition into green-leaved plants. Always consider what effect the colour yellow has on flowering plants.

White variegations are softer and cooler than yellow variegations. They do not generally combine well with yellow variegations or with golden foliage, but are good with plain greens, which they soften and lighten. Some silver variegations work in association with grey-leaved plants.

Both yellow and white variegations provide a striking combination with purple foliage. All variegated evergreens extend the season of interest.

EVERGREEN VARIEGATED SHRUBS

The versatile qualities of the aucubas are extolled elsewhere in this book (see pages 35, 88). Excellent plants for shady areas and tolerant of any soil, they are some of our most popular variegated evergreens. The variegation in some cases is so strong that they fulfil the role of gold-leaved evergreens.

Aucuba japonica 'Crotonifolia' ♀ has large leaves boldly spotted and blotched with gold and has been regarded as the best golden-variegated aucuba. A female variety, it produces berries, but they are of secondary importance to the striking foliage. *Aucuba japonica* Marmorata' is an improvement on 'Crotonifolia', resistant to scorch in an open sunny position. *Aucuba japonica* 'Golden King' ♀, a male form, is similar, but has an even more striking variegation. Plant this one in semi-shade as it can scorch in full sun.

Variegated forms of common box, *Buxus sempervirens,* are delightful structure plants. The tiny, variegated leaves lighten their solid shape and compact habit. *Buxus sempervirens* 'Elegantissima' ♀ is a slow-growing form that makes a dense, compact dome. Leaves are small and often misshapen, green with an

Buxus sempervirens 'Latifolia Maculata'

Aucuba japonica 'Marmorata'

Buxus sempervirens 'Elegantissima'

Aucuba japonica 'Crotonifolia'

PLANTING PARTNERS

The unusual yellow marking of the variegated aucubas makes them good companions to other more uniformly golden variegated shrubs, such as *Elaeagnus pungens* 'Maculata' and *Euonymus japonicus* 'Aureus'. They are also an excellent backdrop to golden-foliage shrubs such as *Philadelphus coronarius* 'Aureus' ♀ and *Cornus alba* 'Aurea' ♀, plants that also enjoy semi-shade rather than full sun. See also page 96.

---

irregular, creamy-white margin. This is considered the best 'silver box', a brilliant specimen plant for making a statement, perhaps at the corner of a bed or to mark an entrance. The larger leaves of *Buxus sempervirens* 'Latifolia Maculata' ♀ are irregularly blotched dull yellow. The young growth in spring is particularly bright and attractive. Dense and compact, this shrub forms a large mound and can make an excellent hedge, clipped either formally or perhaps as an irregularly shaped 'cloud hedge'.

Coronilla valentina subsp. *glauca* 'Variegata' ♀ is a charming, small, variegated shrub for a sheltered spot. It is also an excellent plant for the conservatory. *(Continued on page 60.)*

57

Euonymus

Euonymus has become a household name because of the popularity of *Euonymus fortunei* 'Emerald 'n' Gold' and 'Emerald Gaiety', those dwarf, sprawling ever-greens so widely used to bring foliage interest into seasonal planting, containers and amenity planting schemes. The evergreen euonymus have produced numerous variegated clones; in fact, in gardens it is rare to find a plain green variety. All euonymus are easy to grow and thrive on any soil, including chalk.

Euonymus fortunei is a hardy trailing evergreen that grows as ground cover in sun or shade, with a habit similar to that of the English ivy. It has the ability to produce roots at intervals and has juvenile and adult stages. The various cultivars, nearly all variegated, show the characteristics of the species to varying degrees. Some have the ability to climb, if given encouragement; some are self-clinging. Most are grown as low shrubs and evergreen ground cover.

The favourites *Euonymus fortunei* 'Emerald Gaiety' ♥ and *Euonymus fortunei* 'Emerald 'n' Gold' ♥ are small, compact and bushy. 'Emerald Gaiety' is a hardy, versatile plant that mixes happily in just about any planting. It associates particularly well with hostas to provide winter structure and interest. 'Emerald 'n' Gold' is perhaps more vigorous than 'Emerald Gaiety' and climbs if supported. Its colour is stronger, so it needs careful positioning but, being old-gold, it does not shout as loudly as many yellow-variegated plants.

Euonymus japonicus, the Japanese spindle, from China and Japan, has given rise to many tough ever-green, variegated shrubs ranging in size from small to large. Young plants are often grown in containers, for both indoor and outdoor use. These shrubs grow in any situation and tolerate pollution, shade and coastal exposure. (See Planting Partners, page 57.)

Varieties of *Euonymus japonicus* 'Microphyllus' are small, dense and compact shrubs with much smaller

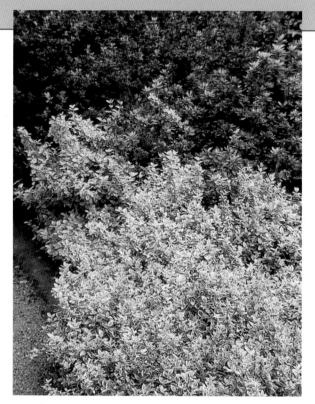

Euonymus fortunei 'Emerald 'n' Gold' adds year-round colour to a border.

leaves than other *Euonymus japonicus*. They provide an alternative to box or hebe.

Some variegated euonymus have a tendency to revert (see box, page 63), including *Euonymus fortunei* BLONDY ('Interbolwi'), whose leaves, carried on slightly yellow stems, have a broad yellow blotch in the centre. *Euonymus japonicus* 'Aureus' ('Aureopictus'), whose glossy leathery leaves have bright golden centres, tends on occasions to produce green and plain yellow shoots. 'Bravo' is a new cultivar, with more subtle, creamy variegation, and is less liable to revert. Cut out any reverted, plain shoots as they appear.

Euonymus fortunei 'Harlequin' is a best-seller – the name is attractive, the variegation is unusual (small, narrow, dark green leaves are heavily mottled white), and it looks good in a pot, but in the garden it is a weak plant and scorches in full sun, so is not worth growing in a border.

See pages 170–71 for the deciduous euonymus, grown for the glorious colour of their autumn foliage.

Euonymus fortunei 'Emerald Gaiety' ♀ has small, dark green leaves irregularly edged with white and often variegated with paler green. They tinge pink in winter, especially on poor soil and in full sun. Try it with hostas, including a blue-leaved variety such as 'Blue Wedgwood'.

Euonymus fortunei 'Silver Queen' is a small, compact shrub, yet has the potential to grow to 2m (6ft) or more against a wall. It has a glorious variegation: the new leaves open creamy-yellow and become dark green with a broad, cream margin. A light, bright, sophisticated plant, it is slow to grow at first, but it is well worth persevering with. In a shady spot it associates well with *Viburnum tinus*.

Euonymus fortunei 'Emerald 'n' Gold' ♀ has all the attributes of 'Emerald Gaiety' except that it has gold-margined leaves that turn creamy gold, flushed pink, in winter.

Euonymus japonicus 'Ovatus Aureus' ♀, the most popular of the large-leaved euonymus, has slower, more compact growth than many. The growth is upright, the leaves are edged and patterned with creamy yellow. It needs a sunny, open position to retain its colour and variegation; in shade it can become predominantly green.

Euonymus japonicus 'Chollipo' ♀ is an excellent large, dense shrub, with upright growth. The leaves are dark green and leathery, broadly edged with yellow. *Euonymus japonicus* 'Latifolius Albomarginatus' ('Macrophyllus Albus') has large dark green leaves with a broad white edge.

Euonymus fortunei 'Tustin' ♀ is a brilliant ground-cover plant, particularly good on shady banks. Its long, narrow leaves are veined with pale yellow-green, making it an excellent choice to underplant mahonia – for example, *Mahonia* × *media* 'Winter Sun'.

Elaeagnus × ebbingei 'Limelight'

Elaeagnus × ebbingei 'Gilt Edge'

The coronilla's long, arching stems are smothered in very small blue-green compound leaves, somewhat like those of *Ruta* (rue). These are so broadly margined with rich cream that the plant appears to be cream, flecked with green. The bright yellow, fragrant, vetch-like flowers appear in profusion in late winter and then intermittently throughout the year. The harsh colour of the flowers is softened by the cream of the foliage.

Unlike most of the variegated plants, *Elaeagnus × ebbingei* 'Limelight' is fast-growing. It is a large shrub, with all the attributes of *Elaeagnus × ebbingei*. The new shoots are silvery brown and the leaves are always green at first, with silvery scales. As they mature, they develop a broad central brushstroke of deep yellow and pale green. The leaves, like those of *Elaeagnus × ebbingei*, remain silver on the underside. This is one of the softer yellow-variegated evergreens, both in growth habit and colour. It makes a big bold shrub, good for screening. It is able to keep pace with *Prunus laurocerasus* ♥, *Photinia × fraseri* and other vigorous shrubs that are valuable for screening.

Elaeagnus × ebbingei 'Coastal Gold' has broad, wavy-edged leaves, silvery at first then pale yellow, edged and blotched with green. *Elaeagnus ×*

ebbingei 'Gilt Edge' ♥ is less vigorous and slower-growing than 'Coastal Gold'. It is notable for its conspicuous leaves, which are attractively margined with golden yellow. It is less tolerant of exposure than other varieties, and grows best in semi-shade. In strong sunshine and on cold exposed sites, the leaf edges can scorch.

Elaeagnus pungens 'Maculata' is one of the most popular variegated shrubs. It has a more spreading growth habit than *Elaeagnus × ebbingei*, with stiff horizontal branches that become spiny on mature plants. The dark green leaves have large, irregular splashes of bright gold – very striking. (See Good Companions, page 63.)

A large plant that is not often seen, despite its pleasing, subtle variegation, is *Elaeagnus pungens* 'Goldrim' ♥. This is a sport of 'Maculata' and has glossy, deep green leaves that are narrowly margined with bright yellow. For smaller gardens, the more compact *Elaeagnus pungens* 'Frederici' is a very good choice. Its narrow leaves of creamy yellow have an irregular green border; this is a pretty variegation, in soft colours.

VARIEGATED ELAEAGNUS: A FEW TIPS

Cut out any reverted, plain green shoots as they appear; they are more vigorous than the variegated shoots, and in time will take over. Variegated elaeagnus are useful for lightening neighbouring dark evergreen shrubs. All produce fragrant, small creamy flowers appear in autumn. Beware: the strong variegation screams with pink- or red-flowering shrubs.

Fatsia japonica 'Variegata'

Griselinia littoralis 'Dixon's Cream'

Fatsia japonica 'Variegata' is one of only a few large-leaved variegated evergreens. The variegation is subtle: greyish-green, hand-like leaves are tipped with creamy white. It is not as large, or as vigorous, as the plain green *Fatsia japonica* (see page 36), and not quite as hardy. A good courtyard plant and a superb architectural plant for a pot, it suits sheltered shade. It is worth protecting with horticultural fleece in severe winter weather; this prevents the growth tips being damaged by frost.

Griselinias offer an unusual foliage form; the rounded leaves stand out well against other green or variegated shrubs. They are a useful choice where a tall, loosely upright variegated shrub is needed. They are excellent coastal plants. *Griselinia littoralis* **'Variegata'** ♥ has rounded, apple-green leaves boldly marked with creamy white. It combines well with the cherry laurel and is a good screening plant. *Griselinia littoralis* **'Dixon's Cream'** has even more striking leaves, splashed and marked creamy white over a larger area. It is a sport of 'Variegata'; similar in habit, it is much slower growing because of the amount of variegation. (See also page 33.)

Variegated **hebes** may not be the hardiest of small evergreen shrubs but they are certainly widely planted. **Hebe**

× *franciscana* **'Variegata'** ♥ is now more frequently used as a bedding plant than as an evergreen garden shrub. Millions are produced in Holland each year, specifically to bring foliage interest to seasonal containers. The deep mauve flowers contrast well with the elliptical leaves edged with creamy white. A good plant for seaside gardens, elsewhere it is perhaps most useful for window boxes and containers in sheltered situations.

Hebe × franciscana 'Variegata'

Variegated sports of the small-leaved hebes make popular impulse-buys in garden centres. Their colourful foliage and neat habit look good in a container, and strikingly different from anything else on offer. However, their long-term performance in the garden is yet to be proved. They dislike high temperatures and very dry conditions, so they are often casualties in hot summers.

One of the best is **Hebe** **'Pink Elephant'**, a compact and hardy sport of 'Red Edge'. The leaves are edged with creamy yellow and tipped pink; the colour darkens to burgundy in winter. The white flowers in summer are of little interest. **'Sweet Kim'** is similar, but perhaps not as robust. **Hebe** **'Dazzler'** has slender, purple-flushed shoots and narrow leaves edged cream and pink. The newer **Hebe** **'Heartbreaker'** is a more upright and robust selection of Hebe 'Dazzler'.

The novelty variegated hebes are good plants for patio containers and can suit contemporary schemes, but they usually look out of place in a more traditional planting scheme.

Ilex

The hollies boast more good variegated forms than any other type of plant. Whether you require silver or gold variegation, holly is an obvious port of call. The disadvantage of the hollies, if there is one, is their slow growth at an early age and their ungainly habit as young plants. On the other hand, they are permanent, long-lived garden residents that do not decline with age.

The foliage of variegated hollies contributes so much to the garden throughout the year that fruiting is of secondary importance. When choosing your holly, remember: if the name sounds masculine, the holly is probably female, that is, it fruits. One exception to this rule is the old, creamy-white variegated variety, *Ilex aquifolium* 'Silver Milkmaid', which is female.

Hollies are easy to grow and succeed on just about any soil. Well-prepared soil and watering during establishment will pay dividends in getting them through the slower early stages of growth.

All variegated hollies have a tendency to revert, (see box, page 63) especially when young. Cut out any plain green shoots; they are more vigorous than the variegated shoots and, if left, take over.

Hollies suit both town and country gardens and can be used in formal and informal planting. It is worth planting them alongside a faster-growing partner, one that will fill the role in the early years and can be removed as the holly matures – perhaps an evergreen ceanothus or rhamnus.

Ilex × *altaclerensis* 'Golden King' ♀ (left) is a large, vigorous holly that matures to a broad, formal cone. It has broad, almost spineless leaves, with a wide gold margin. A female, it berries well in the presence of a male pollinator; the fruit is red-brown. This is regarded as the best gold-variegated holly. 'Lawsoniana' ♀ is 'Golden King' in reverse: the broad green leaves are splashed golden yellow in the centre. It berries well, with red-brown fruits.

The silver hedgehog holly, *Ilex aquifolium* 'Ferox Argentea' ♀, boasts sweeping purple twigs and dark green leaves variegated creamy white. Spines edge the leaves and cover the leaf surface. More lax than many hollies, it is useful in mixed planting where its light colour and habit bring evergreen interest.

Ilex aquifolium 'Handsworth New Silver' ♀ is an upright, stately shrub, with purple stems and delightful silver-variegated foliage. The leaves are narrow, dark green, mottled grey and edged creamy white. A female clone, in a good year it produces masses of bright red berries. 'Silver Queen' ♀ has similar variegation but broader leaves. The young shoots are black-purple, the new leaves shrimp-pink; it does not fruit.

Ilex aquifolium 'Madame Briot' ♀ is an excellent variety, with purple stems and well-spaced spiny leaves, dark green mottled yellow. A female clone, it produces plenty of scarlet fruit.

REVERSION

Most variegated plants have a tendency to produce plain green shoots. These naturally have more chlorophyll and a greater capacity to produce food, therefore they grow more vigorously. Left on the plant, they will eventually take over and smother the variegated plant. Cut out any plain green shoots as they appear, right back to the point where they emerge from the main stem. The earlier this is done in their development the better. In the case of some variegated plants, such as *Elaeagnus pungens* 'Maculata' (right), this will probably have to be done regularly throughout the life of the plant.

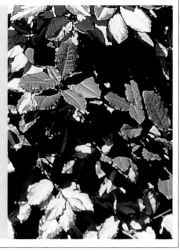

The variegated form of **Chinese privet** is very different from the familiar privet used for hedging. *Ligustrum lucidum* **'Excelsum Superbum'** ♀ is a very large shrub or small tree with big, bright green leaves marked with paler green and edged with greenish-yellow. Unrestricted, it has a superb, broadly conical habit. Large sprays of fragrant flowers appear in autumn. This is an elegant shrub, superb as a specimen, and ideal to lighten heavy laurels and conifers planted for screening.

Luma apiculata ♀, previously known as *Myrtus luma*, is a beautiful evergreen shrub, or small tree, from Chile. The bark is a feature of mature specimens: the cinnamon-coloured outer layers peel away to reveal cream bark beneath. The leaves are dark green and pointed, flowers are white, in late summer and autumn. The variegated cultivar *Luma apiculata* **'Glanleam Gold'** ♀ is more compact. The leaves are smaller and the habit denser. The individual leaves have a creamy white margin and are tinged red when young, especially at the end of the shoots. This lovely variegated evergreen mixes well with low herbaceous planting. (See Good Companions, right.) It is also good in a pot on a sunny patio.

The variegated **osmanthus** are good alternatives to holly for small gardens,

quite apart from being fine variegated evergreens in themselves. *Osmanthus heterophyllus* **'Variegatus'** ♀ is the best. Small, dark green, holly-like leaves are edged bright creamy white. A neat, compact plant, it easy to grow in sun or shade, on almost any soil. (See Good Companions, page 65.) *Osmanthus heterophyllus* **'Aureomarginatus'** is similar, but has leaf margins of deep yellow. The growth is never as good; there are better gold-variegated evergreens. Because it has the overall appearance of a soft golden shrub, the

best-known osmanthus, *Osmanthus heterophyllus* **'Goshiki'**, is included in the golden-foliage shrubs (see page 43).

Photinia davidiana **'Palette'**, also called *Stranvaesia davidiana* 'Palette', is a slow-growing, bony shrub with thin foliage. It is intensely variegated, the leaves being blotched and streaked with cream and pink when young. A novelty, it attracts attention in the garden centre when presented in a pot. In the garden, however, it is a poor plant and never earns its keep. Its appeal lies in the unreal colouring of its foliage.

The variegated **pieris** are some of our most delightful variegated shrubs but are confined to gardens on acid soil if they are to be grown in the open ground. They are, however, wonderful subjects for pots, as long as they are grown in a lime-free, loam-based, compost. They enjoy a position out of full sun, so are good for a shady terrace. The pieris are described more fully in the section on acid-loving plants, page 109, but the two best cultivars for variegated foliage are *Pieris japonica* **'White Rim'**, also grown as 'Variegata', and *Pieris japonica* **'Little Heath'** ♀. Both are excellent silver-variegated plants but

GOOD COMPANIONS

Underplant *Elaeagnus pungens* 'Maculata' (1) with a carpet of golden creeping Jenny, *Lysimachia nummularia* 'Aurea' ♀ (2).

Luma apiculata 'Glanleam Gold' ♀ (3) associates well with woody herbs such as *Rosmarinus officinalis* 'Severn Sea' ♀ (4) and *Thymus* 'Doone Valley' (5).

Pieris japonica 'Little Heath'

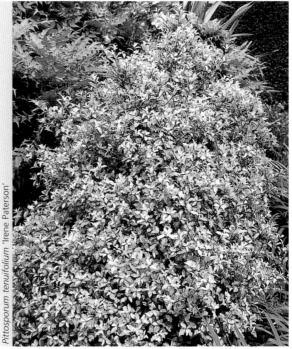

Pittosporum tenuifolium 'Irene Paterson'

Pieris japonica 'Little Heath' is the more unusual, having smaller, neater foliage and pinkish leaf and flower buds.

Pittosporums provide us with some lovely light-variegated shrubs. Good structure plants, pittosporums grow quickly, soon giving height without robbing space. The most popular of the species is *Pittosporum* 'Garnettii' ♀ (*Pittosporum tenuifolium* 'Garnettii'). It is also the easiest to grow. It quickly makes a large, broad, conical shrub, but responds to light clipping if needed (illus. page 28). Its grey-green leaves are margined creamy-white, often spotted pink in winter; they look especially pretty when the tiny chocolate flowers appear on the branches in spring. This is a must for the flower arranger's garden, and sits well in either town or country.

Pittosporum tenuifolium has such small, neat foliage that the variegated forms give the overall impression of having silver or lime foliage rather than being distinctly variegated. They are some of the prettiest variegated shrubs; hence their popularity.

Pittosporum tenuifolium 'Gold Star' has yellow-green leaves edged with dark green, and there is a prominent white midrib on the older leaves. The shrub is compact and upright and is an excellent structure plant. It is a good choice when a softer variegation is required. *Pittosporum tenuifolium* 'Eila Keightley' and 'Abbotsbury Gold' share the same blotched greenish-yellow foliage. The former shows the variegation more distinctly on the older foliage. The overall effect is yellow-green, so it is a useful neighbour for lightening up dark evergreens and for softening the bright variegation of plants such as *Elaeagnus pungens* 'Maculata'. *Pittosporum tenuifolium* 'Irene Paterson' ♀ is slow-growing because of the amount of variegation in its foliage. The young leaves are creamy white, becoming marbled in green and white as they mature. This is a lovely shrub, and it always stands out in any planting scheme.

Pittosporum tenuifolium 'Silver Queen' ♀ has small, neat foliage of silver grey-green, edged with white. The leaves are less crinkled than those of many varieties; the habit is neat and compact. More solid is *Pittosporum tobira* 'Variegatum', with whorls of round-ended leaves that are shiny grey-green, irregularly edged with creamy white. It is not the hardiest of plants, but is happy in a sheltered position in the south of England and near the coast. The flowers, in clusters at the end of the branches, are more conspicuous than on many pittosporums. They open white, turn yellow with age, and are deliciously fragrant. A rounded, slow-growing shrub, this pittosporum is good at the base of a warm wall.

Prunus laurocerasus 'Castlewellan', originally grown as 'Variegata' and often called 'Marbled White', is an interesting evergreen with grey-green leaves heavily marbled white. It is slow-growing but eventually makes a large, dense bush. The habit is more open when the plant is grown in shade. It combines well with, and is an interesting alternative to, defined white-variegated shrubs such as

Pittosporum tenuifolium 'Silver Queen'

Rhamnus alaternus 'Argenteovariegata'

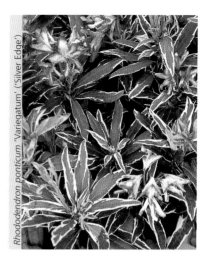

Rhododendron ponticum 'Variegatum' ('Silver Edge')

Pittosporum 'Garnettii' and *Cornus alba* 'Elegantissima'. It makes the perfect partner for the latter's red winter stems.

The variegated form of Portuguese laurel, *Prunus lusitanica* 'Variegata' is not a vigorous plant, but it can be a most attractive addition to evergreen planting under the dappled shade of lighter trees. It has the attractive red leaf stalks of the species, and has horizontal branching, from which the white-margined leaves hang elegantly. It is good on all soils, including chalk. (See Good Companions, below right.)

Also easy to grow on any soil and succeeding in sun or shade, *Rhamnus alaternus* 'Argenteovariegata' ♀ is fast-growing and an excellent choice where a tall but light subject is needed urgently. It is more susceptible to cold than some evergreens and traditionally has been grown against a wall. With winters becoming milder, it has ventured out into the open garden, but it is not good on exposed sites. Frost and cold winds may cause it to shed its leaves, but it usually recovers. To be on the safe side, a rhamnus should be firmly staked throughout its life. It can become top-heavy in maturity and is then a likely casualty in winter gales.

The growth habit is upright and sweeping. The individual leaves are margined cream and marbled with shades of grey and green, giving a pale silver-green effect overall. If a plain green shoot appears occasionally, cut it out. Mature specimens become bare at the base so it is wise to underplant with a contrasting companion, perhaps *Choisya ternata* or *Fatsia japonica*.

Rhododendrons are subjects for the section that features plants for acid soils, pages 101–105. However, some of the variegated forms of hybrid rhododendron are such excellent foliage plants they deserve a mention here. Yes, they need ericaceous soil but, as long as they are grown in lime-free, loam-based, compost, they are also excellent subjects for pots.

Rhododendron 'Goldflimmer' is one of the best. A variegated form of the vigorous *Rhododendron ponticum*, it is a surprisingly compact, slow-growing shrub. The leaves are dark green, with irregular streaks of yellow around the edge. The flowers are lilac, marked with brown spots, and appear later in the rhododendron season.

Sometimes seen for sale under the name 'Silver Edge', *Rhododendron ponticum* 'Variegatum' has leaves margined with creamy white.

GOOD COMPANIONS

A good pairing for a container is *Osmanthus heterophyllus* 'Variegatus' ♀ (1) and the silver grey- and cream-variegated ivy *Hedera helix* 'Glacier' ♀ (2).

The pink tinge in winter on the leaves of *Prunus lusitanica* 'Variegata' (3) makes it a wonderful partner for the dark foliage and pink buds of *Viburnum tinus* (4).

Viburnum tinus 'Variegatum'

Viburnum tinus 'Variegatum' is considerably less vigorous and weather-resistant than the plain green forms. The leaves are strongly variegated in creamy yellow, and are particularly attractive in combination with the pinkish buds and white flowers. It prefers a reasonably sheltered site and semi-shade. In strong sun, the leaf edges may brown, and it struggles on a cold, exposed site.

SPIKY VARIEGATIONS

The leaves of **cordyline** and **phormium** introduce a different and dramatic form to the garden, an exciting contrast to the rounded shapes of most plants. Both species like sunshine and good drainage. They are excellent subjects for planting in gravel and growing in pots, but can look out of place in a traditional scheme. (See also pages 55, 87, 124–25.)

With its creamy-white striped leaves, *Cordyline australis* 'Torbay Dazzler' ♀ is a striking plant for a warm patio. It is not as vigorous as the green form.

The **phormiums** have some of the most exotic foliage of any garden plant. They also introduce pink, red and orange variegations – rarely seen elsewhere. As a rule, the flamboyantly coloured forms are less hardy than the more subtle ones.

Phormium 'Yellow Wave' ♀ is the most reliable yellow variety. With yellow-green striped leaves of drooping character, it reaches 1m (3ft) in height.

Phormium 'Duet' ♀ has more upright foliage, margined with creamy white, while *Phormium tenax* 'Variegatum' ♀ has similar leaves but is a much larger-growing variety of phormium. The leaves of *Phormium* 'Sundowner' ♀ are up to 1.5m (5ft) long, bronze-green with deep pink margins. *Phormium* 'Maori Chief' is slightly less hardy, but has upright leaves of scarlet, crimson and bronze. *Phormium* 'Pink Panther' has ruby-red leaves with pink margins.

Cordyline australis 'Torbay Dazzler'

Phormium 'Yellow Wave'

VARIEGATED SEMI-EVERGREEN AND DECIDUOUS SHRUBS

The forms of *Abelia* × *grandiflora* are semi-evergreen shrubs popular for their late-summer and autumn flowers; some are variegated. *Abelia* × *grandiflora* 'Francis Mason' has small shiny, dark green leaves with a yellow margin. However, the variegation is not distinct unless the plant is grown in full sun on dry soil. The newer variety, *Abelia* × *grandiflora* 'Hopleys', has a more prominent variegation; and in the autumn its leaves flush pink, picking up the pink of the flowers. The best-known of the variegated abelias, however, is *Abelia* × *grandiflora* CONFETTI ('Conti'). This is a much smaller shrub than the others, with light, arching growth and leaves margined white. It is a pretty plant, but not robust.

Even at the best of times, the young foliage of the Japanese maples is at risk from scorch by strong winds and bright sunlight; and the variegated forms are especially vulnerable. The variegated forms of *Acer palmatum* are some of the most delicate of variegated plants. A few are worthy garden plants; others are only for the enthusiast. *Acer palmatum* 'Kagiri-nishiki' ('Roseomarginatum') is one of the easiest. Reasonable vigour and a light, arching habit are in its favour. The lobed leaves are often somewhat distorted, pale green and irregularly variegated with white and coral pink – very pretty. It tends to revert, and any plain green shoots should be cut out.

Acer palmatum 'Asahi-zuru' is also vigorous by palmatum standards. It is a spreading shrub, with white-blotched leaves, sometimes all white or pink when young. It is regarded as one of the most stable variegated Japanese maples.

The variegated forms of the box elder, *Acer negundo* 'Flamingo', have long been grown as shrubs, as well as small trees. The light, variegated foliage of *Acer negundo* 'Variegatum' was prized as a pot plant, and often grown by municipal parks departments for indoor decoration. *Acer negundo* 'Flamingo' has pretty, pale green foliage edged with soft pink, changing to white. It is a very appealing plant at the stage when it is offered for sale, but disappoints when it is grown in the garden as it stretches upwards to form a leggy shrub with poor leaf colour. The secret of success is hard pruning in early spring, back to one or more short stems. This annual pollarding results in vigorous growth and good leaf colour.

The variegated *Buddleja davidii* 'Harlequin' is striking, even as a young shrub in a pot. The long green leaves are boldly variegated with creamy white, in strong contrast to the reddish-purple flowers. The habit is low and arching. The plant is not nearly as vigorous as most buddleias. *Buddleja davidii* 'Santana' ('Thia') is similar, with yellow-variegated foliage and wine-red flowers. Both are sports of 'Royal Red' and tend to revert. There are other variegated buddleias, but these are the best. All buddleias are valuable for their summer flowers, attractive to butterflies (see also pages 74, 148–49, 163).

Buddleias are best hard pruned in February, to promote vigorous growth and prolific flowering. The variegated forms need lighter pruning: cut back by half rather than two-thirds.

An excellent foliage plant with large heart-shaped leaves, *Clerodendrum trichotomum* 'Carnival' is at its best in late summer and autumn. The leaves are blue-green, mottled grey-green, with a broad and striking cream margin. From August on, clusters of fragrant white flowers emerge from pretty pink calyces and are carried in graceful clusters. It makes a horizontally branched shrub up to 1m (3ft) in height. The leaves are very slow to open in late spring; the plant

Acer palmatum 'Kagiri-nishiki'

Acer negundo 'Flamingo'

Clerodendrum trichotomum 'Carnival'

Cornus alba 'Elegantissima'

needs a warm, sunny position to thrive. When touched, the foliage smells of rubber. It is resistant to rabbits and deer.

The variegated forms of *Cornus alba* are all-year-round shrubs, with colourful winter stems and interesting foliage in summer (see pages 177–78).

Cornus alba 'Elegantissima' ♀ is one of the brightest and whitest of evergreen shrubs. It is a vigorous plant and, if left unpruned, forms a large flowing mound up to 3m (10ft) high. The foliage is soft and pretty. The leaves are green in the centre, mottled and broadly margined with white. One of the best variegated plants for damp sites, it succeeds in sun or shade. For small gardens, choose *Cornus alba* 'Sibirica Variegata', smaller-growing and less vigorous than 'Elegantissima'. It is similar in foliage but often has pinkish leaf tints, particularly in the autumn. (See Good Companions, pages 69, 184.) *Cornus alba* 'Spaethii' ♀ offers a golden yellow variegation. 'Gouchaultii'

is similar, but often has orange-red tints. *Cornus sericea* 'White Gold' ♀ is similar in foliage colouring to *Cornus alba* 'Elegantissima', but has yellow stems. This gives a pleasingly fresh effect.

Cornus mas, the cornelian cherry, is a large, densely branched shrub, often seen in British hedgerows. It is a delight in early spring when small yellow, pom-pom flowers appear all over the bare branches. Although long cultivated, this shrub is too large, and has too short a season of interest, for most gardens. However, the variegated form, *Cornus*

TRIED AND TESTED

The variegated forms of shrubs described here have all proved themselves as reliable plants. Many more are available, and gardeners may be tempted by new arrivals. Beware of novelties, however. The tried and tested variegated shrub is likely to be the more reliable choice.

mas 'Variegata' ♀, is a superb plant, and one of the best variegated shrubs. It is much less vigorous than the species, with an open, light branch structure and broad, pointed white-margined leaves. In the autumn, as well as good leaf colour, it has scarlet cherry-like fruits.

Cornus controversa 'Variegata' ♀ is really a small tree, and is certainly a plant for specimen planting. It is one of the most magnificent of variegated hardy plants with its horizontal tiered branching and hanging silver-white variegated leaves. A mature specimen, well grown, is a splendid sight. In the early stages of growth it is worth staking and training the leader, to encourage the plant to gain height. It should never be pruned to change its shape; allow it to develop naturally.

Cornus alternifolia 'Argentea' ♀, the pagoda dogwood, is one of the most beautiful silver-variegated shrubs. Fine, light horizontal branches of dark wood carry a froth of small, creamy-white margined leaves. Seen from a distance, a mature shrub seems to sit like a white cloud in the border. If grown with a single stem, it makes a superb subject for the oriental garden; as a multi-stemmed shrub, it is outstanding as a specimen or for mixed planting. Growing to 3m (10ft) tall, *Cornus alternifolia* is a hardy plant from North America and is tougher and easier to grow than its appearance suggests.

A low, spreading shrub, *Cotoneaster atropurpureus* 'Variegatus' ♀ (also known as *Cotoneaster horizontalis* 'Variegatus') does not have such a bold herringbone branch structure as *Cotoneaster horizontalis*. It is also less vigorous. The tiny dark green leaves are margined with cream and become tinged with red in autumn, making a delightful display with the red berries. (See Good Companions, right.)

Fuchsia is associated with seasonal planting, being one of our most popular bedding plants. In milder locations, fuchsias are favourite garden shrubs, thriving in sun or shade, flowering from early summer through autumn. Their graceful habit, light foliage and pendent flowers make them versatile plants that combine well with other shrubs and herbaceous plants (see page 153).

The best-known fuchsia is *Fuchsia magellanica*. It has slender, arching growth and delicate, red-and-purple hanging flowers. *Fuchsia magellanica* var. *gracilis* 'Variegata' ♀ is the best of the variegated fuchsias. Its green leaves edged with creamy yellow and flushed pink make a pleasing combination with the flowers. Although it is less hardy than the green form, it is still a good shrub for a sheltered location. *Fuchsia magellanica* var. *gracilis* 'Tricolor' ('Tricolor') is more spreading and smaller. The little leaves are grey-green tinged pink when young and becoming white-edged as they mature. The ends of the shoots retain a pink flush throughout the season. The flowers are red-and-purple, perhaps smaller than those of the species. More tender than all these cultivars, *Fuchsia magellanica* var. *molinae* 'Sharpitor' has white flowers and grey-green leaves margined white. It is a pretty plant, and a good choice for mild areas.

Fuchsia 'Tom West' Meillez is a superb foliage plant. More tender than *Fuchsia magellanica*, it is usually grown as a patio subject. The young leaves are bronze, edged dark pink, becoming blue-green with pink edges. The shoots are reddish purple, and the flowers are red and purple. This is a colourful plant.

Cornus controversa 'Variegata'

MORE GOLD AND SILVER VARIEGATED SHRUBS *Acer palmatum* 'Butterfly' • *Acer campestre* 'Carnival' • *Aralia elata* 'Variegata' • *Azara microphylla* 'Variegata' • *Ceanothus* 'Zanzibar' • *Elaeagnus pungens* 'Dicksonii' •

Fuchsia 'Tom West' Meillez

Fuchsia 'Sunray' is a small bushy shrub, with pale green and cream leaves, edged and flushed with red. It has red-and-mauve flowers. This is a good choice for a small garden or patio.

Hydrangea has variegated forms, of which **Hydrangea macrophylla** 'Tricolor' is probably the best. A lacecap hydrangea, it has pale-pink flowers, turning to white. The leaves are green, variegated with grey and pale yellow – an attractive combination.

Hypericum × *moserianum* 'Tricolor' has great appeal as a garden-centre plant and looks good in a pot. In the garden, it often disappoints. It is a dwarf shrub with arching stems and classic, golden-yellow hypericum flowers of good size. The leaves are prettily mottled with pink, white and pale green. It needs a sheltered site and can be prone to rust in a damp season. Prune back hard in early spring to promote vigorous new growth.

The variegated form of the mock orange, **Philadelphus coronarius** 'Variegatus' ♀ has leaves variegated creamy white, and the same creamy-white, deliciously scented flowers as the species: single, simple and beautiful. Although *Philadelphus coronarius* is excellent on very dry soil, the variegated form can develop browning of the leaf tips and margins when grown on dry soil in full sun. It is better planted in light shade, where the foliage will stand out against a dark background and the delicious scent can permeate the

garden. **Philadelphus** 'Innocence' is another single, very free-flowering variety, with delightful arching growth and creamy-white variegated leaves. This is a lovely, light and pretty shrub.

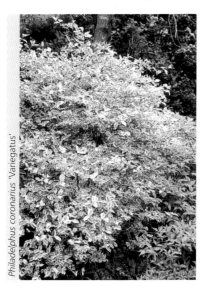

Philadelphus coronarius 'Variegatus'

Weigela 'Florida Variegata' ♀ is one of the best and most popular variegated shrubs. The growth habit is compact, leaves soft green edged creamy white, flowers pink – lovely in combination with the leaves. This is a very easy shrub to combine with roses and perennials, particularly herbaceous geraniums. (See Good Companions, below.) **Weigela** 'Kosteriana Variegata' is very similar but a little more upright. The leaves turn to shades of pink and red in autumn, adding a further season of interest. Both varieties should be pruned lightly after flowering to remove some of the stems that have flowered. This encourages vigorous new growth from the base. Do not trim to shape, as this will take away the lightness and grace of this plant.

GOOD COMPANIONS

The pink tints in the foliage of *Cornus alba* 'Sibirica Variegata' (1) complement the purple foliage of *Berberis thunbergii* f. *atropurpurea* 'Rose Glow' ♀ (2).

The salmon-red flowers of *Schizostylis coccinea* ♀ (3) work well with the autumn berries of *Cotoneaster atropurpureus* 'Variegatus' ♀ (4) grown against a wall.

Extend the flowering season of *Weigela* 'Florida Variegata' ♀ (5) by letting *Clematis* 'Purpurea Plena Elegans' ♀ (6) scramble through it.

Silver and grey

Those who garden on sand or thin, chalky soil truly appreciate grey- and silver-leaved plants such as santolina and lavender. Hailing from Mediterranean regions, they are naturally drought-resistant and remarkably tolerant of sunny sites, where many plants just shrivel up and die. Gardeners on heavier, clay soils find that these plants do not like soggy winter weather.

Silver-leaved plants are good mixers with any colour scheme.

The value of the silver- or grey-leaved shrubs is indisputable: their foliage is the perfect foil for almost any other colour in the garden. They naturally associate well with plants from similar hot, dry, sunny climates, such as cistus, helianthemum, rosemary, salvia, thyme and many others (see pages 82–87). They are usually tough and thrive on poor, well-drained soil in full sun.

CARING FOR SILVER-LEAVED PLANTS

On heavy soils, add plenty of sharp grit at the time of planting to improve drainage. Mulch with a generous layer of gravel or sharp grit to prevent rain from splashing soil onto the foliage.

Before winter, make sure you remove any leaves that have fallen from surrounding deciduous plants. These can easily lodge on the felty foliage of silver subjects, holding the wet and causing damage during the damp months.

Most silver-leaved plants are short-lived. Once they become old and fail to perform, replace them with new stock. Fortunately, they are quick to establish and grow to maturity.

Silver foliage is an adaptation to environment, a means of conserving water and reducing its loss. The woolly covering of pale fibres over the foliage creates a microclimate around the leaf surface, reducing air movement and slowing evaporation of water. In some cases, this woolly coating disappears from the upper surface as the leaf matures and the leaf then reveals more of its underlying green colour. This allows more light to reach the surface for photosynthesis, the means by which the plant makes its food. However, the underside stays protected, keeping its silver appearance. As an added means of reducing water loss, many silver-foliage plants have reduced the size of their leaves: a leaf that is narrow or finely cut loses less water than one with a large surface. Edges that curl under protect the underside of the leaf from water loss.

Silver-leaved plants are frequently aromatic; the presence of oil in the foliage helps to prevent desiccation by strong sun and drying winds. The oil also protects the plant by repelling animals and insect pests, and its smell, combined with the felty nature of the leaves, appears to be unattractive to deer and rabbits.

Acacia baileyana 'Purpurea' ♀ is a lovely form of the Cootamundra wattle. Usually considered a conservatory plant, it is now often grown outside in sheltered situations. The finely cut, fern-like foliage is blue-grey and the new shoots a deep purple – a wonderful contrast. The bright yellow flowers in spring are of secondary importance and lack the subtlety of the soft, delicate foliage. This is a good shrub to grow against a wall. Being light and leggy in habit, it is also useful for providing height among mounds of other grey-leaved plants, for example santolinas and lavenders.

Acacia baileyana 'Purpurea'

Artemisia abrotanum ♔ (lad's love, southernwood) has been in cultivation in Britain since the 16th century, the original attraction being its aromatic leaves. One of the many herbaceous and woody artemisias, it is very easy to grow and quickly makes a small upright shrub with grey-green downy leaves. Greyish flower buds appear at the end of the stems in summer; these are best trimmed off to preserve the foliage and to prevent the shrub from opening up under the weight of the foliage when wet. In garden centres, it is often found with the herbs rather than other shrubs.

Artemisia 'Powis Castle' ♔ is the best-known and most widely grown artemisia. The foliage is deeply cut and feathery, the habit compact when young, becoming sprawling. It makes good ground cover, and when planted on top of a wall it cascades over the

Artemisia 'Powis Castle'

edge. This artemisia likes full sun and well-drained soil, and dislikes wet, cold sites and heavy soil; on clay add plenty of grit when planting.

Artemisia 'Powis Castle' does not respond well to hard pruning; cut back the stems only to where new growth buds are clearly visible. Sometimes it will sprout from the base, but it rarely breaks from bare wood. Watch out for blackfly, which are particularly attracted to the new growth. Be careful which insecticide you use, as some grey-leaved plants are sensitive to certain chemicals.

MIXING AND MATCHING

Silver plant material has a wonderfully fragile quality when used en masse. It suggests sunny days and hot countries, but is also perfect in the light of cooler climes. It is ideal for softening paving, walling and hard landscape materials, and works well in pots, tubs and other containers.

Silver-grey foliage adds colour and texture to the garden. It can be used as an addition to foliage of other colours, or as the predominant foliage. Silver reflects the light of open spaces, and its soft hue complements solid structure. Grey-foliage shrubs work well in plantings of sun-loving herbaceous perennials.

Most grey-leaved plants suit seaside situations and cope with salt winds. In the high light levels, the blueness of the grey works wonderfully with bright orange eschscholzia and the neon shades of mesembryanthemum.

Silver-leaved planting in Derek Jarman's coastal garden, Dungeness, Kent.

Silver-grey is the perfect partner for blue, looks soft and pretty with pink, sparkles with lavender and is positively regal with purple. It also has an affinity with dark red, especially the large, bold blooms of peonies and poppies. Silver foliage provides the perfect setting for gems such as amethyst alliums and sapphire brodiaea.

Be careful when juxtaposing silver with other foliage. Silver-grey shrubs with large leaves can look fine with heavy evergreens, but those with more delicate foliage can be overpowered by them and need to be combined with less solid plants.

Silver is happier in association with white variegation than it is with yellow. While grey is not a natural partner for golden foliage, it contrasts stunningly with plum-purple shades. Silver *Elaeagnus* 'Quicksilver' ♔ planted with *Physocarpus opulifolius* 'Diabolo' ♔, for example, is a striking combination that works on its own or can be built into mixed plantings (see Good Companions, page 55).

Lavenders

The lavenders are among our most popular garden plants. They are evergreen, versatile and associate well with roses and herbaceous plants, as well as paving and stonework. The aromatic foliage is as important a feature as the flowers, which include pink-, white- and blue-flowered cultivars, and a mass of shades in between. There are tall and short lavenders, some compact growers, others of larger, looser habit. Most varieties make an excellent low hedge, and are suitable for coastal planting.

While lavenders thrive in open, sunny positions on well-drained soil, they are tolerant of some shade and will survive on heavier soils. Lavenders are short-lived, and those growing on heavy soils have a shorter life span than those on sand or chalk.

Lavandula angustifolia is the common, silver-leaved species, with strongly aromatic foliage and tall grey stems bearing pale grey-blue flower spikes. It is one of the best for hedging and is sold in vast numbers for this purpose. This lavender invariably gets larger than anticipated: if you plan to allow it to flower, ensure that you give it sufficient space. Alternatively, pinch it regularly during the season, to maintain silver new growth and a compact habit. Numerous *Lavandula angustifolia* cultivars are widely available, of which *Lavandula angustifolia* 'Hidcote'♥ is probably the best-known. Introduced in 1920 and still a favourite, this is a superb cultivar for edging rose beds or simply to plant informally in front of shrub roses.

Lavandula × *intermedia* is a hybrid of *Lavandula angustifolia* with *Lavandula latifolia*. Again, there are many varieties in cultivation, generally larger, more vigorous and later-flowering than the cultivars of *Lavandula angustifolia*. *Lavandula latifolia* has large, branched flowerheads, a characteristic that is often shown in the offspring.

Lavandula stoechas♥, the French lavender, is a more dwarf, compact, aromatic, shrubby little plant with

Lavandula angustifolia at Barrington Court, Somerset.

upright growth and dense, stubby flowerheads of dark purple flowers. The flowers are produced over a longer period than other lavenders, appearing in succession throughout the summer. Less tolerant than other species, it needs good drainage and a warm, sunny position. Many cultivars have appeared in recent years, including some that look very attractive; however, most are not very hardy and are best grown in pots near the house, where the eaves protect the plants from damage caused by winter rain.

If you allow lavender to flower, trim the plant back immediately after flowering, to enable the new silver growth to emerge. This will keep the plant looking reasonable through the winter months. French lavenders tend to be more upright than others and need trimming to retain their bushiness. They are best lightly pruned in mid-spring, just before the flower buds appear. Do not cut back hard into bare wood, only to where growth shoots are clearly visible. Periodic trimming and dead-heading during the flowering season will keep them looking good.

Lavandula angustifolia 'Loddon Blue' ♀ is compact and small-growing, with purple-blue flowers. It is excellent for pots and low borders.

Lavandula angustifolia 'Loddon Pink' ♀ is about the same size as 'Hidcote', but with greener foliage and pink flower spikes.

Lavandula angustifolia 'Munstead' is similar to 'Hidcote' but has paler, lavender-blue flowers.

Lavandula × intermedia 'Arabian Night' ♀ produces long spikes of purple-blue flowers.

Lavandula × intermedia Dutch Group ('Dutch') is a vigorous plant, with broad grey leaves and lavender-blue flowers; easily reaches 1m (3ft).

Lavandula × intermedia 'Grosso', a shorter plant than 'Dutch', has mid-blue flowers in midsummer and very aromatic foliage.

Lavandula 'Sawyers' ♀ is a superb, compact bushy plant with silver-grey foliage and large pointed flower spikes of deep purple.

Lavandula angustifolia 'Hidcote' ♀, with its compact growth, fine grey-green foliage and dense spikes of violet-blue flowers, is a good plant for hedging. The blooms are at their best in midsummer, and should be trimmed off the plants by late summer to allow for another flush of growth. The flowering time coincides with the peak of the rose season.

Lavandula angustifolia 'Imperial Gem' ♀ is very similar to 'Hidcote' but has purple flowers and more silver foliage. It is excellent for low, compact hedges and stays silver all winter if cut back after flowering.

Lavandula angustifolia 'Miss Katherine' ♀ is a very fragrant, compact form with masses of deep pink flowers and grey-green foliage.

Lavandula angustifolia 'Wendy Carlisle', a delightful plant, has neat, upright growth, aromatic grey foliage and silver and white flowers.

Lavandula stoechas subsp. *pedunculata* ♀ is an excellent plant, with short flower spikes on long, wispy stems. The flowers have long, butterfly-like bracts at the top, hence the name 'Papillon', under which it is sometimes sold. The flowering season often extends from late spring to mid-autumn.

Lavandula stoechas 'Willow Vale' ♀, a superb plant, has vigorous, grey-green foliage and long, purple, crinkly bracts.

Ballota pseudodictamnus ♀ is a beautiful dwarf shrub from the Mediterranean region, perfect for any dry, sunny garden. A greyish-white, furry covering gives a woolly look to the stems and rounded leaves, and pinkish-white flowers are borne in whorls in midsummer. This shrub forms a mound as a young plant; cut back hard each spring to preserve the shape. This is a good plant to combine with purple sage and the prostrate forms of rosemary.

Brachyglottis – see *Senecio*, page 79.

Buddleias may not seem an obvious choice when considering silver-leaved shrubs, but there are some that are well worth including. *Buddleja fallowiana* is a medium to large deciduous shrub, with white-woolly stems and leaves, and fragrant, pale lavender flowers in

Buddleja 'Lochinch'

Buddleja alternifolia 'Argentea'

WHERE CONTRAST IS NEEDED

Since many grey-leaved plants are light, with narrow, fine foliage, a silver scheme often needs the contrast of bolder forms. To find something that is both bold and silver, you may need to turn to herbaceous plants.

Few plants rival the dramatic architectural foliage of *Cynara cardunculus* ♀, the cardoon (left). This is a truly statuesque border plant, with magnificent blue-green silver leaves that erupt from the ground in early spring and stay the course throughout much of the year. The thistle-like flower spikes are a bonus, as are the blooms of the silver, felty rosettes of verbascum (Aaron's rod or mullein). These appear reliably from random seedlings on poor sandy soil or chalk. If you do not want seedlings all over the garden, remove most of the flower spikes as the blooms fade.

Remember, too, that most silver shrubs form round mounds of fluffy, soft texture – and they need contrast. Spiky phormiums, grasses, lilies and irises all help to relieve these soft shapes.

large panicles. Unfortunately, it is not the hardiest of buddleias and needs a warm, sheltered wall to thrive.

Buddleja 'Lochinch' ♀, the hybrid between *Buddleja fallowiana* and *Buddleja davidii*, is hardier, and one of the best buddleias. It is a medium-sized shrub of bushy, compact growth. The young stems are downy grey, as are the leaves. Later, while the underside of the leaves stays white and felty, the upper surface becomes sage-green in colour. The flowers are pale violet-blue with an orange eye, sweetly scented and, like all buddleia flowers, attractive to butterflies. This is a lovely shrub, easy to grow and combine with herbaceous perennials, roses and cottage garden flowers. Prune in late winter, cutting all stems down to about 1m (3ft) in height.

Buddleja alternifolia 'Argentea' is the silver-leaved form of the graceful *Buddleja alternifolia*. It is a large shrub with fine, arching, spreading branches. It looks beautiful on a bank or falling over a wall. The narrow, willow-like leaves flank the wispy branches, which in early summer are garlanded with

Convolvulus cneorum

Corokia cotoneaster

scented lilac flowers. There is no need to prune this buddleia; just give it a sunny space in which to grow.

Convolvulus cneorum ♀, a very popular shrub in garden centres today, was introduced to Britain from south-eastern Europe around 1640. Its silver, silky leaves, compact dwarf habit and white trumpet flowers are an appealing combination. If planted in a well-drained site in full sun, it is surprisingly hardy and needs little maintenance. The flowering period is long – from early summer into autumn – making this convolvulus an excellent choice for patio containers. The flower buds can be trimmed off regularly if a mound of silver foliage is required; the new shoots have a striking, almost metallic quality. *Convolvulus cneorum* 'Snow Angel' is a more compact form, with bold silver foliage and funnel-shaped, white to pale pink flowers.

Corokia cotoneaster, the wire-netting bush, is a curious evergreen plant from New Zealand. The fine, twiggy branches and small silver leaves create an attractive wiry mass of a bush, studded with tiny yellow flowers in late spring. It is quite unlike any other shrub and will, if given ideal conditions, eventually make a large plant. It is not a shrub for cold, exposed sites.

Elaeagnus angustifolia, the oleaster, is widely naturalized in southern Europe

and, like santolina, has been cultivated in Britain since the 16th century. It is a large spiny, deciduous shrub with silvery grey willow-like leaves – similar to those of *Pyrus salicifolia* (the weeping pear). Tiny fragrant flowers in early summer are followed by oval amber fruits.

The best form to grow is *Elaeagnus* 'Quicksilver' ♀ (once sold as *Elaeagnus angustifolia* Caspica Group), a superb large shrub that grows quickly with vigorous, but graceful, upright then arching branches. The foliage is silver and reflective. Unlike many elaeagnus, this plant is deciduous, and the leaves

wilt and fall in autumn. The new foliage, when it appears in spring, is a delight when associated with blue ceanothus. (See also Good Companions, below.)

It is rare to find a silver-leaved plant that offers height, so this plant is very valuable. Do not underestimate its potential size: it can easily reach 3m (10ft) in five years. It does not grow well in a pot, so container-grown plants often look weak until established in the garden. *Elaeagnus* 'Quicksilver' sways beautifully in the breeze, and in many gardens sits more happily than eucalyptus. *(Continued on page 77.)*

GOOD COMPANIONS

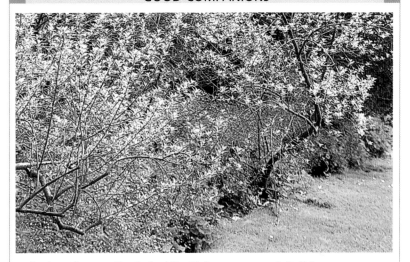

Underplant *Elaeagnus* 'Quicksilver' ♀ with *Brunnera macrophylla* ♀ for a pretty springtime combination.

Hebe

Hebes are perennially popular with gardeners for their evergreen foliage and attractive summer flowers. They are excellent plants for sheltered locations on well-drained soil, and tolerate relatively exposed coastal situations. However, they dislike heavy soil and poor drainage, and many seem happier on chalk than on acid soils. As a general rule, the larger-leaved hebes are more tender and susceptible to frost damage than those with small leaves.

The hebes provide some of our most useful silver-foliage shrubs (for purple-leaved hebes, see page 52). All silver hebes have small leaves and are much hardier than their larger-leaved cousins. Although most hebes are native to New Zealand, the small- and grey-leaved species tend to originate from cooler, higher altitudes. They are low-growing, compact plants, excellent for containers or the front of borders, to provide solid, evergreen structure among low-growing purple and soft grey subjects. The silver hebes successfully fit into seaside gardens, associate particularly well with gravel, stone and paving and, while they like good light, will tolerate semi-shade – although this may be at the expense of colour. They may suffer in very hot, dry conditions in summer.

Generally, silver hebes do not require any pruning. If plants become straggly, they can be cut back to wherever new shoots are visible on the branches low down in the shrub.

Hebe albicans ♀ forms a dense, rounded mound of blue-grey foliage. The closely packed tips of the new shoots form the outside of the shrub, so it is always the best part of the plant that meets the eye. Short spikes of white flowers, pretty against the tough grey foliage, are produced in summer. This is a very hardy plant, tolerant of poor soil, pollution and difficult situations.

Hebe 'Red Edge' ♀ (below) is the best-known hybrid of *Hebe albicans;* it is a dual-purpose plant, as its foliage turns burgundy in winter.

Hebe 'Pewter Dome' ♀ is a particularly fine hybrid, with dense foliage. It is lower-growing and more compact than *Hebe albicans*.

Hebe pimeleoides 'Quicksilver' ♀ is a dwarf shrub, prostrate in habit, with purplish-black stems. It has pale lilac flowers in summer and tiny silver-blue, well-spaced leaves, creating a lighter, prettier plant than more compact varieties. It is good in gravel, and with purple sage and rosemary. (See also Good Companions, page 79.)

Hebe pinguifoilia 'Pagei' ♀, one of the most familiar dwarf evergreen shrubs, is hardy and easy to grow. It spreads to make a broad mat of silver foliage that looks good all year. The small white flowers appear in late spring and early summer. It is a good ground-cover plant, excellent in paving.

Hebe recurva 'Boughton Silver' ♀ has a different habit from the other silver hebes – more open, with slender branches and longer, narrower leaves. The foliage is silvery blue.

Elaeagnus 'Quicksilver'

Elaeagnus 'Quicksilver' may produce suckers; these are worth cultivating, as the plant is not long-lived and often needs to be replaced after eight or ten years. It grows on any soil, but is not at its best on shallow chalk.

Helichrysum italicum ❀ (*Helichrysum angustifolium*), the curry plant, is the most intensely aromatic and brightest of the silver stars in the garden. The growth is more open than lavender, so the plant gets less sodden in winter. Look out for

---

EUCALYPTUS AS A SHRUB

For an evergreen silver plant with height, consider growing eucalyptus as a shrub. Eucalyptus has the ability to regenerate from the base, and readily produces growth buds at the bottom of woody stems. If you regularly cut it back hard from an early age, it produces vigorous, fast-growing, straight stems of juvenile foliage; this is normally of a more intense colour than the adult foliage of trees. This technique is called stooling. *Eucalyptus gunnii* ❀ is frequently grown in this way; its round, silver-blue, juvenile leaves are particularly attractive.

Helichrysum italicum 'Korma' ❀, a more compact form, with broader leaves of bright burnished silver. The flowers, are cream in bud, opening to a softer yellow than seen on other helichrysums.

Cut flower stems back to the base as the flowers fade, and trim plants lightly to encourage new silver growth that will persist through the winter months. It is an excellent container plant for gardeners who forget to water; it prefers full sun, but tolerates some shade.

Helichrysum italicum 'Korma'

Hippophae rhamnoides ❀, the sea buckthorn, is a tall, slender, angular shrub with thorny silver-grey branches and narrow, silvery leaves. It grows almost anywhere, is wind- and salt-tolerant, and is excellent for providing height where space is limited and conditions are hostile. It is an excellent choice for banks of poor sandy soil. In winter female plants, if they have a male partner, produce orange-yellow berries that are bird-resistant; they look most attractive on the bare stems in the winter sunshine against a blue sky.

For **lavenders**, see the Plant Profile on pages 72–73.

HOW TO BUY BUCKTHORN

Hippophae rhamnoides is a plant to buy during the winter, as a bare-root hedging plant. It is inexpensive and establishes easily. Plant the stems in a group of three or five, 1m (3ft) apart, to produce a more substantial shrub. Prune hard at an early stage if a more branched plant is required.

The grey-foliage forms of *Ozothamnus rosmarinifolius* offer a welcome upright alternative to the fluffy mounds produced by most silver-leaved subjects. Native to Tasmania and south-eastern Australia, *Ozothamnus rosmarinifolius* are surprisingly hardy, evergreen plants if given good, well-drained soil and the sunniest spot in the garden. They are excellent plants for a dry, sheltered site, perhaps against a wall. In summer red buds appear on mature plants, later opening to white-scented flowers. Unlike the flowers of many silver-leaved shrubs, these are an attractive feature.

Ozothamnus rosmarinifolius 'Silver Jubilee' ❀ is the most widely grown cultivar, although not the hardiest. It has silvery grey foliage. *Ozothamnus* 'Threave Seedling' is becoming a more popular alternative, with slightly broader leaves of an attractive silver-grey. (See Good Companions, page 79.)

Ozothamnus require no pruning, and resent it later in life. Young plants can be encouraged to branch if the tops are nipped out at an early stage. The shrubs are best planted in late spring as a

---

FOR A SILVER EFFECT

Some white-variegated shrubs have the effect of silver foliage, in particular *Pittosporum* 'Garnettii' ❀ and *Pittosporum tenuifolium* 'Irene Patterson' ❀. In the case of *Pittosporum* 'Garnettii', the white edge to the leaf becomes one with the pale peridot-green of the rest of the leaf, resulting in the shrub having a silver-grey effect when seen from a distance. The foliage of *Pittosporum tenuifolium* 'Irene Patterson' is a more creamy white colour; it can be used in combination with grey-leaved subjects as long as there are white flowers present.

Ozothamnus rosmarinifolius 'Silver Jubilee'

Phlomis italica

Salix elaeagnos subsp. *angustifolia*

young plant rather than as a large specimen. Plants that have established naturally and have rooted well into the garden soil seem to overwinter successfully. If drainage is poor, add sharp grit when planting.

Phlomis are excellent plants for a dry, sunny position and poor soil. *Phlomis fruticosa* ♀, the Jerusalem sage, is an evergreen, grey-green felty shrub with whorls of yellow flowers throughout the summer. On a well-drained site, it is remarkably hardy. *Phlomis italica* is not as hardy, but is the most desirable variety. The leaves and stems are very hairy, with a wonderful tarnished-silver quality. The flowers are lilac, carried at the top of the stems in summer. If stems do get knocked back by the frost, the plant usually shoots from the base and often suckers.

Ruta graveolens **'Jackman's Blue'**, or rue, is a herb long cultivated in Britain for its medicinal properties. It has pretty, divided leaves with tiny, rounded leaflets and makes a small semi-evergreen, aromatic shrub. The foliage of the variety 'Jackman's Blue' is a brilliant blue-grey. The flowers in summer are small and mustard yellow but, while they are not unattractive, the plant is better off without them – both habit and foliage colour are

superior if the flowers are removed. Easy to grow on well-drained soil, the plant has only one drawback: the foliage can cause severe skin irritation and blistering if handled in sunlight.

Salix exigua, the coyote willow, is a very upright, large shrub, with reed-like stems of greyish brown and long silky, silver leaves. Fine catkins appear at the same time as the leaves. Of more delicate constitution than most willows, this shrub can be difficult to establish on some soils.

For wet sites and alongside water, *Salix elaeagnos* **subsp.** *angustifolia* ♀ (sometimes called *Salix rosmarinifolia*) is a better choice. This is an altogether more vigorous shrub and denser in habit. The leaves are grey and woolly, becoming green above and silver beneath as they mature; the foliage moving in the wind is a delightful sight.

RUE PLANTING TIPS

Plant rue (*Ruta*) in sun for best foliage colour. The colour is superb with lighter, fluffier grey-leaved plants. It is also good with purple: heucheras and *Festuca glauca* are natural partners. It is an excellent choice for containers on a sunny patio, especially terracotta or ceramic pots with blue-green glazes.

The stems are reddish brown and very useful for winter colour.

Santolinas, the cotton lavenders, are evergreen and remarkably frost hardy – the most weather-resistant of the silver-foliage plants and more tolerant of heavy soil than most. Santolinas are mostly sold as young plants suitable for containers, for both summer and winter planting. In a well-drained soil they stay looking good throughout the winter months and make a useful contribution of lighter foliage to winter plantings. Santolinas are also tolerant of semi-shade and can be used effectively under trees to provide evergreen ground cover. If trimmed regularly, santolinas can be shaped into a dome or ball, and make a superb dwarf evergreen hedge. They are easier to manage and more consistent than lavender, but their aromatic quality is perhaps not so universally appealing.

Santolina chamaecyparissus ♀ (*Santolina incana*) is the most widely grown kind, with woolly, silver, thread-like foliage and bright lemon-yellow flowers in midsummer. It originated in the Pyrenees but has been cultivated in Britain since the 16th century, when it was a useful ingredient in the knot garden. *Santolina chamaecyparissus* **'Lambrook Silver'** has fine foliage and

MORE SILVER AND GREY SHRUBS *Atriplex halimus* • *Berberis temolaica* • *Buddleja* 'Silver Anniversary' • *Calluna vulgaris* 'Silver Queen' • *Cistus* × *argenteus* 'Silver Pink' • *Cytisus battandieri* • *Euryops pectinatus* •

lemon-yellow flowers, of a milder hue than those of the species. *Santolina chamaecyparissus* 'Lemon Queen' also produces lemon-yellow flowers. *Santolina chamaecyparissus* var. *nana*♔ is more compact, ideal for sunny areas of stonework and paving as well as pots and containers. *Santolina chamaecyparissus* 'Pretty Carol' bears soft grey foliage and pale yellow flowers. (See Good Companions, pages 49 and right.)

Cut santolinas back hard in early spring, to where the new growth is emerging near the base of the woody stems. You should also cut them back

Santolina chamaecyparissus

after flowering – or just before, if you dislike the yellow flowers – to prevent heavy growth developing. This can weigh down the branches when the plant gets wet in the winter months.

Senecios, among the best shrubs of garden and landscape planting, have now been reclassified as *Brachyglottis* – a name reluctantly used by gardeners who already know the plants well. They come from New Zealand and Tasmania.

Senecio 'Sunshine'♔, often known as *Senecio greyi*, is an easy plant, a safe choice where evergreen silver foliage is required on heavier soil; it is also excellent in coastal gardens. If left to grow without cutting back, it will form a broad mound up to 1m (3ft) high and 2m (6ft) across. The leaves are silver when young, becoming dark green on top and silver below with age. The flower buds are silver gems, opening to

brash yellow daisies, which some gardeners may prefer to remove.

This shrub does tend to open up in the centre, so is best pruned just before or just after flowering, cutting back to where new growth is emerging half way down the branches. This encourages the new shoots, with their bright silver foliage, to develop. *Senecio* 'Sunshine' is an accommodating plant, so if you should leave it unpruned for a season or two, you can rejuvenate at a later date. Although this shrub prefers an open, sunny, even windswept site, it tolerates semi-shade. It is also probably the hardiest of the grey-leaved evergreens.

Senecio monroi♔, from South Island, New Zealand, is a smaller shrub of denser habit. It forms a broad dome and

Brachyglottis (Senecio) 'Sunshine'

has oval leaves that undulate along the edges. The underside is covered with dense white felt, the upper surface is grey-green. This cultivar is not often seen and is much less widely available than *Senecio* 'Sunshine'. It is less tolerant of heavy soil and damp sites.

GOOD COMPANIONS

For contrast of shape and a good combination of colours, mix *Hebe pimeleoides* 'Quicksilver'♔ (1) with the spiky blue grass *Festuca glauca* (2).

Position *Ozothamnus* 'Threave Seedling' (3) alongside *Salvia officinalis* 'Purpurascens'♔, the purple sage, or a white-flowered cistus, such as *Cistus* × *obtusifolius* 'Thrive' (4).

Grow a santolina, such as *Santolina chamaecyparissus* 'Lambrook Silver', under the weeping pear, *Pyrus salicifolia* 'Pendula'♔ (5), to create a beautiful silvery scene (as seen here at Apple Court, Lymington, Hampshire).

Hebe albicans 'Blue Star' • *Helianthemum* 'Rhodanthe Carneum' ('Wisley Pink') • *Perovskia* 'Blue Spire'• *Potentilla fruticosa* 'Manchu' • *Rosa glauca* • *Salix repens* var. *argentea* • *Teucrium fruticans*•

SITUATIONS

Getting the right plant in the right place is the secret of successful planting. Plants chosen only for their appearance, with no regard to the growing conditions, may disappoint the gardener. Thriving plants look good and reward with their performance; plants that are struggling for life contribute little. Shrubs are part of the permanent fabric of any garden, so deciding what to plant where is crucially important. Choosing successful planting partners – good companions that complement each other – increases the value of any individual plant.

RIGHT: Lake Mount, Glanmire, County Cork, Ireland

Hot, dry, sunny sites

A hot, dry, sunny position can be a curse or a blessing depending on what you plant. Many plants suffer severely from drought in summer, while others thrive on a good baking. Provided you choose plants that hail from very hot climates, you will not go far wrong: natives of southern Europe, north Africa, the south-western USA, parts of South Africa and Australia generally thrive in these conditions.

The Dry Garden, Savill Garden, Windsor Great Park.

Many plants of Mediterranean origin are surprisingly hardy and can withstand cold as well as drought. However, they resent wet conditions. The damp English winter is far from ideal, but give them a dry spot, poor soil and sunshine to look forward to and they are perfectly happy. Most grey-foliage plants in this book (see pages 70–79) delight in these conditions – helichrysums, santolinas, lavenders and ballotas, to name but a few. Without damp around their roots and leaves, they retain foliage colour even through winter. Evergreen plants such as sedums and sempervivums are also useful additions to dry, sunny plantings, especially to fill gaps in paving and to edge dry borders.

Callistemons, or bottlebrushes, with their spectacular red flowers in summer, have established themselves as popular garden shrubs in milder areas, thriving if given a sunny, well-drained position. *Callistemon citrinus* 'Splendens' ♀ is remarkably hardy and stands up to frost and drying winter winds better than many evergreens; it suits coastal gardens and it associates well with decking

and terracotta paving. *Callistemon salignus* ♀ is less often seen but is one of the hardiest bottlebrushes, with willow-like growth and pale yellow flowers. Callistemons do not mix well with traditional English planting. They are at their best with exotics and silver foliage (see Good Companions, opposite).

After flowering, callistemons must be cut back to immediately behind the seedhead. None of the old seedheads should be visible. This ensures vigorous new growth and a compact habit.

Ceanothus are the best of the blue-flowering shrubs for late spring and

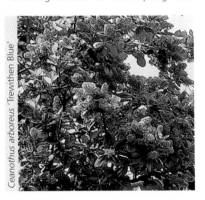

Ceanothus arboreus 'Trewithen Blue'

summer (see Plant Profile, page 140). All like full sun and good drainage, as the common name, Californian lilac, suggests. They grow on most soils but will tolerate very shallow chalk only if the soil is improved with organic matter. Ceanothus are fast-growing and can be grown as freestanding or wall shrubs.

Evergreen varieties of ceanothus are more tender than deciduous ones, so

GETTING PLANTS GOING

Beds against sunny walls can often be problematic, particularly where overhanging eaves keep rainfall off the ground. In such areas, all new plants need special attention – even the most drought-resistant subjects. In particular, container-grown plants that have been potted in peat-based compost need watering until their roots are established. Without regular watering in the initial stages, roots do not venture into the surrounding soil and the plants quickly dry out.

are ideal for a warm position. Those with small leaves are more susceptible to frost than larger-leaved varieties, such as *Ceanothus arboreus* 'Trewithen Blue' ♀. In a favoured spot, this gets very large and is glorious in spring, with a haze of huge panicles of deep blue flowers. For a sunny bank, choose the hardy *Ceanothus thyrsiflorus* var. *repens* ♀. It grows to an extensive low, evergreen mound of glossy, bright green foliage with masses of fluffy, mid-blue flowers in late spring (see Good Companions, page 85). *Ceanothus* 'Centennial' is also prostrate, but more compact, with neat, dark green foliage on fine stems and violet-blue flowers in late spring and early summer. Particularly tolerant of drought, it is excellent in pots and alongside paved areas, and is a good choice for the smaller garden.

Cistus × obtusifolius 'Thrive'

Cistus, also known as sun roses, are popular for their reliability, ease of cultivation and attractive flowers, which are short-lived but freely produced, usually in midsummer. True Mediterranean plants, they are found in the wild from the Canary Islands to the Caucasus, and revel in hot sunshine, poor soil and dry conditions. Hybrids have arisen in the wild and in gardens, creating a range of sizes and growth habits; most have white or pink flowers. (See Plant Profile, page 150.)

One of the hardiest and most widely planted of the sun roses, **Cistus × hybridus** (*Cistus × corbariensis*) grows larger than many, producing a rounded

GOOD COMPANIONS

For an exotic touch of colour, try planting *Callistemon citrinus* 'Splendens' (1) with a *Phormium* 'Yellow Wave' (2).

Coronilla valentina subsp. *glauca* ♀ (3) is beautiful planted with the purple sage, *Salvia officinalis* 'Purpurascens' (4), and magenta helianthemums, such as 'Ben Ledi'.

Plant *Erysimum* 'Bowles' Mauve' ♀ (5) with sages and thymes. The fluffy, shrubby thymes such as *Thymus vulgaris* 'Silver Posie' (6) enjoy exactly the same conditions as erysimum.

mound about 1m (3ft) high. The white flowers, with bright yellow stamens, emerge from green or shrimp-pink buds. **Cistus × obtusifolius** 'Thrive', a neat, compact plant, is a better choice for a smaller garden. It has dark green foliage, which can be bronze-tinged in winter, and freely produces white flowers with yellow stamens from late spring on; these appear over a long period, sometimes even in late summer. (See Good Companions, pages 79, 85.)

The hardiest of the sun roses is **Cistus laurifolius** ♀, which can reach 2m (6ft) high. The leaves are dark green and leathery, and the flowers white with yellow centres. The less hardy **Cistus ladanifer** ♀, the gum cistus, has sticky, lance-shaped leaves; the strikingly large flowers are white with dark red basal blotches. The hybrid between *Cistus ladanifer* and *Cistus laurifolius*, **Cistus × cyprius** ♀, has the attributes of both

Cistus laurifolius

CISTUS AFTERCARE

When planting cistus, always give them plenty of space to spread sideways; drawn and leggy growth is hard to correct. Pinch back the growth of young plants in their first season to encourage a bushy habit. Many of the sun roses do not respond kindly to pruning, although *Cistus × hybridus* and *Cistus × obtusifolius* 'Thrive' may be pruned after flowering. If you do prune, never cut back into old wood, and only prune back to where you can see vigorous young shoots emerging from the branches.

Genista aetnensis

Genista lydia

Grevillea 'Robyn Gordon'

Grevillea 'Fireworks'

parents: vigorous growth, good-looking foliage, hardiness. Look out for *Cistus* × *cyprius* var. *ellipticus* f. *bicolor* 'Elma' ♀, whose glorious flowers, silky and pure white with yellow stamens, look superb against the polished green leaves.

With its lax arching growth and beautiful blue-green, rue-like foliage, *Coronilla valentina* subsp. *glauca* ♀ is a very attractive small shrub for the base of a sunny wall. It bears clouds of bright yellow flowers in mid-spring, and others intermittently through the year – even, on a very sheltered site, in winter. (See Good Companions, page 83; also 119.)

A superb, woody-based form of the perennial wallflower, *Erysimum* 'Bowles' Mauve' ♀ makes a rounded evergreen shrub with dark greyish-green leaves and spikes of soft purple, wallflower-scented flowers. It is not long-lived, so take cuttings every couple of years and have replacements ready to replant. A well-drained, sunny site prolongs its life. (See Good Companions, page 83.)

Genistas are related to *Cytisus*, the brooms, and need similar treatment (see page 139), though many are tougher and very suitable for hot, dry, sunny conditions. *Genista hispanica* (Spanish gorse) is one of the most reliable shrubs for a hot, dry but inhospitable site such as a dry bank. It will grow on virtually any soil and is lime-tolerant. Forming a dense, prickly mound (which deters rabbits and deer), it produces masses of yellow flowers in late spring. It may not be the most beautiful plant, but it is effective on a dry bank when planted with santolina, rosemary, cistus and other maquis-type plant material. *Genista lydia* ♀ is a well-known shrub, useful for tumbling over steps, low walls and onto paving. The fine stems curve gracefully to form a low mound of soft green, and the chrome yellow flowers are bright and smother the plants in late spring. It is very dominant in flower, so plant this only where you want to draw attention to it. *Genista aetnensis* ♀, known as the Mount Etna broom, is a useful choice when a very tall, light shrub is needed for a sunny, dry site. Its habit is elegant, open and graceful, and the leafless shoots become a haze of yellow when the fragrant flowers appear in midsummer. The scent is delightful and may well perfume the whole garden. If it is in an exposed position, stake and support it well, as it has a habit of toppling over.

Members of the Protea family, the **grevilleas** are for the most part natives of Australia. Despite their hot-climate origins, some are exceptionally hardy, and thrive in open sun with good drainage. However, they dislike chalk. *Grevillea rosmarinifolia* ♀ is a lovely light, sprawling shrub, with long, soft shoots and narrow, rosemary-like leaves. These are deep green on top but silvery on the underside, and so they look very pretty when moved by the breeze. From winter through spring into summer, curly crimson flowers bloom at the end of the shoots. *Grevillea* 'Robyn Gordon' is a beautiful shrub for a warm spot, with fern-like foliage and striking bottlebrush-like flowers. Low-growing and not too vigorous, it is ideal for a small, sheltered garden. *Grevillea* 'Canberra Gem' ♀ is a much hardier, vigorous, rounded shrub that is good for coastal gardens, with waxy foliage and clusters of bright pink flowers. *Grevillea* 'Fireworks' is small, compact, with neat green foliage tinged red-green at the shoot tips; the plant is reminiscent of leptospermums. The flowers are deep pinkish-red, produced in clusters at the end of the shoots, in long succession from early spring into late summer. It is an excellent small shrub, particularly good for a pot on a sunny patio; plant in lime-free compost.

A hybrid between *Halimium* and *Cistus*, × *Halimiocistus* 'Ingwersenii', is a wide-spreading, low shrub with small, narrow, hairy dark green leaves and masses of pure white flowers over several weeks in late spring and early summer. It is very hardy and suitable for exposed sites. (See Good Companions, above right.) A better choice for a small space would be × *Halimiocistus sahucii* ♀, equally hardy, with shinier, less hairy foliage. White flowers appear intermittently throughout the summer. A beautiful plant but nowhere near as hardy, the hybrid × *Halimiocistus wintonensis* ♀ requires a warm and

× *Halimiocistus* 'Ingwersenii' (1) is good for low ground cover on a sunny site and combines well with *Ceanothus thyrsiflorus* var. *repens* (2).

Helianthemum 'Henfield Brilliant' (3) looks lovely with the blue foliage of *Festuca glauca* (4).

The pleasingly subtle colour of *Phlomis fruticosa* (5) combines well with the yellow *Helianthemum* 'Wisley Primrose' (6) and a white cistus, such as *Cistus* × *obtusifolius* 'Thrive' (see illus. page 83).

sheltered spot. The foliage is grey, the habit dwarf and compact, the flowers pearly white and beautifully marked with maroon and yellow.

Halimiums are low, spreading shrubs closely related to cistus. They thrive in full sun and a well-drained soil, but can be hit by severe frost. *Halimium lasianthum* ♀ has grey-green foliage and dark-eyed yellow flowers in late spring. *Halimium ocymoides* ♀ is similar but has smaller, grey leaves. The

hybrid between these two, *Halimium* 'Susan' ♀ is an excellent plant, compact and dwarf with rounded leaves. The flowers, yellow blotched with chocolate brown, are freely produced in late spring. Trim all halimiums after flowering to keep them compact and bushy.

Helianthemums (known as rock roses or sun roses) are close relatives of cistus and halimiums, and enjoy similar conditions. Usually found on sale in the alpines section of garden centres and

× *Halimiocistus sahucii*

× *Halimiocistus wintonensis*

Halimium lasianthum

85

nurseries, they are evergreen, very dwarf shrubs, suitable for paved areas, rock gardens, along paths and at the base of walls. The brilliant flowers are produced throughout summer.

There are countless hybrids, with flowers in various shades, from white to yellow, orange, pink, dark red and magenta-purple. Particularly good are: *Helianthemum* 'The Bride' ♥, creamy white flowers with yellow centres, silver-grey foliage; 'Henfield Brilliant', orange flowers, grey-green foliage (see Good Companions, page 85); 'Fire Dragon' ♥, with bright orange-scarlet flowers, grey-green foliage; 'Mrs C.W. Earle' ♥, double, scarlet flowers, dark green foliage; 'Rhodanthe Carneum' ♥, pale pink flowers with orange centres, grey foliage; and 'Wisley Primrose' ♥, primrose-yellow flowers with a darker centre, light grey-green foliage (see Good Companions, page 85).

Helianthemum 'The Bride'

Phlomis 'Edward Bowles'

Phlomis are both herbaceous and shrubby aromatic plants. The woody species are ideal for dry, sunny conditions. *Phlomis fruticosa* ♥ (Jerusalem sage) is a hardy, small, grey-green shrub, perfect for a sunny bank or border. Whorls of yellow-ochre flowers are produced in summer, reminiscent of a large dead-nettle. (See Good Companions, page 85.) *Phlomis chrysophylla* ♥ is similar but has narrower, smaller leaves, more like those of a sage. *Phlomis lanata* 'Pygmy' is a pretty, dwarf, compact plant with yellow woolly shoots, sage-green leaves and yellow flowers. *Phlomis longifolia* has darker green leaves carried on white woolly shoots and spikes of bright yellow flowers that appear throughout summer. *Phlomis* 'Edward Bowles' is one of the most spectacular of these plants, somewhere between a shrub and a herbaceous perennial. Huge heart-shaped leaves form clumps and clothe the woody stems. In summer the flower stems carry whorls of yellow-ochre flowers in candelabra fashion. It is a real statement

plant and, as the habit is open, it is good for bold foreground interest. It can be knocked back by frost but usually grows again from the base. *Phlomis italica* (see page 78) offers a lilac-pink alternative to the yellow flowers of most phlomis; the cultivar 'Pink Glory' is compact, and a better choice for small gardens.

The common rosemary, *Rosmarinus officinalis*, is an all-time favourite shrub. Cultivated in English gardens for at least 400 years, it is valued for its highly aromatic foliage and its versatile quality as a culinary herb. As a garden shrub it is invaluable for its soft, dark green and silver foliage and pretty growth habit. The flowers, usually pale blue, are a delight in early and mid-spring. The species has greyish-green leaves, white beneath, and a loose but upright habit to 2m (6ft). *Rosmarinus officinalis* 'Miss Jessopp's Upright' ♥ is probably the finest and most popular cultivar, vigorous and upright. 'Severn Sea' ♥, a dwarf form, has arching growth and brilliant blue flowers (illus. page 63). *Rosmarinus officinalis* Prostratus

TRIMMING HELIANTHEMUMS

Helianthemums need regular trimming after flowering to remove old flower stems and to keep the plants compact; on mature plants, shears are best for this operation. Examine closely before you cut: some varieties keep producing flowers on the old stems, in which case a decision has to be made – compact plant with good foliage or straggly plant with flowers? The choice is down to the gardener.

Lotus hirsutus ♥, sometimes known as *Dorycnium hirsutum*, is a pretty, fluffy, dwarf shrub with fairly upright growth and silver, hairy leaves shaped like clover. The pale pink flowers produced at the end of the stems in summer and autumn are followed by red-tinged fruit pods. *Lotus hirsutus* combines well with other soft aromatics, such as lavender and sage, and is very pretty with pink *Nerine bowdenii* against a sunny wall.

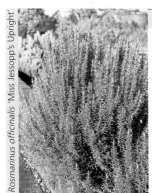

Rosmarinus officinalis 'Miss Jessopp's Upright'

GROWING AND USING ROSEMARY

Rosemary is the one herb that no garden should be without, however basic the skills of the resident cook. The young, woody stems of the upright forms can be used as fragrant skewers, superb to flavour meat. In addition to its culinary uses, rosemary makes excellent cut foliage, especially when it is in flower. The better the drainage and the poorer the soil, the greater will be the aromatic quality of the rosemary. Trimming for use in the house is generally enough to keep it in shape.

MORE SHRUBS FOR HOT, DRY, SUNNY SITES *Brachyglottis* • *Buddleja* • *Caryopteris* • *Ceratostigma* • *Cytisus* •

Group is not as hardy but its sprawling, almost trailing form is invaluable for walls and banks. It flowers freely, producing a mass of blue flowers. There are many more blue cultivars, as well as some with white and pink flowers – a less pleasing combination and nowhere near as useful in the garden.

The shrubby germander, *Teucrium fruticans*, is a delightful sprawling shrub with wiry silver stems and shiny green leaves, the underside of which are white and felt-like. The pale blue flowers, produced in the leaf axils and at the end of the shoots, appear throughout the summer. Although often described as dwarf, it spreads well in a dry, sunny spot and grows upwards against a wall. In a sheltered site it can even reach the upstairs windows of a house. The cultivar *Teucrium fruticans* 'Azureum' ♀ has sapphire-blue flowers but is not as hardy.

SPIKY SUN LOVERS

Hot summers and foreign travel have fired the imagination and increased our interest in palms and other hot, Mediterranean subjects. Phormiums, palms and cordylines have an exotic appearance, and are well suited to contemporary design, patios and bedding schemes. Yuccas are more familiar in mixed planting and have featured in our gardens for many years.

The hardiest of the **palms**, and the most reliable for general garden planting, is *Chamaerops humilis* ♀, a dwarf

Chamaerops humilis var. argentea

palm that rarely grows to more than 1.5m (5ft). It sometimes forms a small trunk but more usually makes a clump of long, woody-stemmed shoots. The leaves are stiff and spiky. *Chamaerops humilis* var. *argentea* is a striking, silver-blue form from the high Atlas mountains, very hardy and beautiful. Also very hardy is *Chamaerops humilis* 'Vulcano', an excellent compact form with leaves silvery beneath. All are good in pots or planted in scree with dry grasses and aromatics.

Cordyline australis ♀ (cabbage palm) has become so popular it is hard to find a garden without one – probably now towering over the house. Not strictly a shrub, but grown as one, it is related to the agaves. Architectural in quality from an early age, the dense heads of green, sword-shaped leaves provide relief from soft mounds of foliage. In a hot summer the plant may also produce huge sprays of fragrant flowers. *Cordyline australis* 'Torbay Dazzler' ♀ is softer, prettier and smaller than most cordylines, with green leaves edged creamy white (illus. pages 66, 124; see also page 55.)

Phormiums, more spiky sun-lovers, are described on pages 55, 66, 125.

Yuccas are related to cordylines, and produce rosettes of spiky, usually rigid leaves. The flowers, if they happen (often after a hot summer), are spectacular: tall, tropical-looking spikes of white, bell-shaped blooms. Yuccas are superb architectural foliage plants, excellent for pots and planting in gravel areas away from paths. *Yucca filamentosa* 'Bright Edge' ♀ is soft-leaved and stemless. Its leaves, normally turned down at the ends, have white threads hanging along their edges. The shape is semi-spherical, leaves upright in the centre and fanning progressively down to the horizontal. The narrow leaves have a bright gold margin; 'Variegata' ♀ is edged with creamy white. *Yucca flaccida* 'Golden Sword' ♀ is similar to *Yucca filamentosa*

Yucca gloriosa

Yucca gloriosa 'Variegata'

'Variegata' but its leaves are broader, with a central band of creamy yellow and green edges. The green-leaved *Yucca flaccida* 'Ivory' ♀ is more free-flowering than many, producing large panicles of white, green-stained flowers. *Yucca gloriosa* ♀ is a vicious character. Small and tree-like, it produces a stout stem; the leaves are straight, stiff and spine-pointed, gathered into a dense terminal head; the flowers are creamy white, often tinged red, on upright spikes up to 2m (6ft) high in summer. The creamy-yellow, striped foliage of *Yucca gloriosa* 'Variegata' ♀ fades to cream on older leaves.

PROTECTING CORDYLINES

Wet weather followed by frost sometimes damages the growing tip in the centre of the crown. In severe weather, it is advisable to draw the leaves gently together and wrap with horticultural fleece. Do not tie tightly as this will cause unsightly damage to the foliage in the coming year. Plants that lose the growing tip normally produce side shoots.

Shady sites

Shady areas in the garden should not be seen as inferior to sunnier spots. They will never be filled with colourful flowers, but they can be places of great foliage interest. Plants take on more definition in the shade: the foliage of shade-loving plants, unbleached by the sun, is lush and luxuriant. The native plants of woodland habitats need light shade. Some plants thrive in shade; others just tolerate it.

When it comes to large evergreen shrubs for shade, both aucuba and *Viburnum tinus* prove as versatile as ever. **Aucubas** (see pages 35, 57, 95, 98) exhibit good foliage colour and thrive in shade, however heavy, on almost any soil. They will withstand dry conditions, but in extreme drought may show blackening of the growth tips early in the year. *Viburnum tinus* (see pages 186–87) is one of the few shrubs that survives beneath the shade of oak trees, and is tolerant of any soil. In heavy shade, growth tends to be loose and flowers few.

On acid soils, **rhododendrons** and **camellias** are obvious options for dappled shade (see pages 101–107). Naturally woodland plants, they thrive,

Aucuba japonica 'Variegata'

and look right, under the drip-line of trees. Neither enjoys drought conditions; indeed, high temperatures and lack of water in summer can cause harm. The light, open habit of camellias suits mixed, informal planting. The denser, more upright varieties, with heavier flowers, are ideal for containers and more formal planting schemes. Varieties of **Camellia japonica** and **Camellia × williamsii** all grow well in light shade, though they flower more profusely where there is a reasonable amount of sunlight. Dwarf rhododendrons and the larger-growing, hardy hybrids grow well with some shade. Their flowers last longer and retain their colour better when they are away from strong sunlight.

Camellia × williamsii 'Saint Ewe'

Camellia japonica 'Alba Simplex'

ADDING COLOUR TO A SHADY BED

Yellow foliage tends to go lime-green in shade, but yellow variegations hold on to their colour and shine brightly. Yellow draws the eye and so makes a feature of a shady area: *Elaeagnus pungens* 'Maculata', *Ilex × altaclerensis* 'Golden King' ♡ and *Euonymus fortunei* 'Emerald 'n' Gold' ♡ are excellent choices for shade.

White-variegated foliage looks cool and sophisticated. It will lighten any dark area. The silver-variegated forms of box – for example, *Buxus sempervirens* 'Elegantissima' ♡ – are delightful in shade and combine well with larger-leaved subjects such as *Prunus lusitanica* 'Variegata' ♡.

Add colour with bulbs. *Narcissus* species, *Anemone blanda*, *Cyclamen hederifolium* (right), scilla, chionodoxa, galanthus and eranthis all bring seasonal colour to shady areas.

Pulmonarias are excellent alternatives to hostas for shady situations. They grow well on damp sites and the foliage is not as attractive to slugs and snails as that of hostas. Their mottled leaves look good throughout the season after early flowers have faded. They are particularly useful for bringing ground-cover colour to plain evergreens.

WHEN IS A SHADY SPOT NOT A SHADY SPOT?

Most plants tolerate some shade as long as there is good light and, ideally, a few hours of sunshine a day.

Deep shade means that there is no direct sunlight: the site is overhung by trees or buildings and light is poor.

Semi-shade, or partial shade, means that the position is shaded for part of the day. Perhaps there is direct sun in the morning or in the evening. The amount of shade varies according to the time of year. Most plants grow here, but those that prefer direct sun will not thrive.

In dappled shade direct sunlight is diffused through a light tree canopy.

Daphne pontica ♀ is a little gem for shade. A small, spreading evergreen with bright green, glossy leaves, it has clusters of spidery yellow-green flowers in mid- to late spring. Visually these are easily missed, but their fragrance is wonderful. This is a shrub for shade under trees, excellent on heavy soil, even alkaline clay.

Daphne pontica

× Fatshedera lizei 'Variegata'

GOOD COMPANIONS

Try placing the large-leaved *Hedera colchica* 'Sulphur Heart' ♀ (1) under an upright gold-variegated holly, such as *Ilex × altaclerensis* 'Golden King' ♀ (2).

In a large container or on open ground, the pretty, white-variegated *Hedera helix* 'Glacier' ♀ (3) looks good under *Fatsia japonica* ♀ (4).

The pink flowers and spotted leaves of *Pulmonaria saccharata* 'Leopard' (5) bring ground-cover colour to *Sarcococca confusa* ♀ (6) after its flowering season.

Vinca minor f. *alba* 'Gertrude Jekyll' ♀ (7), with white flowers, is pretty under the dark leaves of *Viburnum davidii* ♀ (8).

Shady situations demand bold foliage, and **Fatsia japonica** ♀ is a natural choice (see Good Companions, above; also 35–36). In shade it stays a rich, dark green, and the growth is luxuriant. It tolerates dry conditions. × **Fatshedera lizei**, the hybrid between fatsia and its close relative, hedera, is a tough character. It tolerates any soil, heavy shade, coastal exposure and pollution. Although widely grown as a houseplant, it is remarkably hardy and grows as a sprawling shrub, providing excellent ground cover. × **Fatshedera lizei** 'Variegata' ♀ has grey-green leaves with an irregular white margin.

Garrya elliptica 'James Roof' ♀ is a subdued shrub in summer and autumn but is luxuriously flamboyant in winter and early spring, draped with silky silver tassels (illus. page 182). If space is limited, prune to shape as the tassels start to fade and new growth begins. It looks best grown as a tall, top-heavy wall shrub, so that the tassels dangle and sway in the breeze. In light shade, a **Rhamnus alaternus** 'Argenteovariegata' ♀ will brighten the garrya during its quiet season (see page 65). In heavier shade, the white variegations of **Osmanthus heterophyllus** 'Variegatus' ♀ will set it off (see page 63). All osmanthus are

Gaultheria mucronata 'Bell's Seedling'

Hedera colchica 'Dendroides'

Mahonia aquifolium 'Apollo'

Ruscus aculeatus

good in shade, grow on any soil and, once established, tolerate dry conditions.

A South American native, and a shrub for acid soils, *Gaultheria mucronata* (*Pernettya mucronata*) cannot fail to attract attention with its marble-like berries carried on dense thickets of wiry stems. The berries are remarkable for their colours, ranging from white through shades of pink to deep burgundy red. For best effect, these shrubs should be planted in groups and with male plants (non-berrying) for pollination and fruit set. The variety **'Bell's Seedling'** ♀ is both male and female, with deep green foliage on reddish stems. Large, showy dark red berries follow the white flowers.

A shrubby form of the Persian ivy, *Hedera colchica* 'Dendroides' ('Arborescens') originated as a cutting of the adult, flowering growth of the trailing ivy. It is an excellent, rounded shrub and is most attractive in winter, when it fruits well. Once established, it is good in damp shade, but in the early stages it can be temperamental.

Mahonia japonica ♀ does well in light shade, as do many other mahonias (see pages 182–83). The most useful is **Mahonia aquifolium 'Apollo'** ♀. This is a very fine, vigorous form of the Oregon grape, forming a dense, low and spreading shrub. The leaves are deep green with red stalks, and tend to flush purple in the winter. The bright yellow flowers in large, dense clusters appear in early spring. It is one of the best flowering shrubs for shade, and makes a superb combination with

golden-variegated evergreens such as *Euonymus fortunei* 'Emerald 'n' Gold' ♀ and *Aucuba japonica* 'Marmorata'.

The tough and tolerant butcher's broom, *Ruscus aculeatus*, is similar in leaf shape to *Mahonia japonica*, but stiffer and a duller green. What appear to be the leaves are in fact flattened stems. In spring tiny white flowers appear in the middle of these; on female plants, these are followed by large red berries. This curious plant, a native of Europe and north Africa, forms dense upright clumps. It will grow in the driest, most inhospitable shade so, while it is not the most attractive shrub, it has its uses.

No shady garden should be without **Sarcococca confusa** ♀, Christmas box, with its shiny, evergreen leaves and stems and tiny white, deliciously fragrant flowers in winter. There are other sarcococcas; all are evergreen, and all succeed in shade but *Sarcococca confusa* is one of the glossiest, and has a pretty, arching growth habit. (See page 184; Good Companions, page 89.)

Skimmias are made for shade; in fact, their foliage discolours and goes yellow in full sun. They are especially good plants for shady town gardens,

tolerant of chalk and acid soils. Foliage, flowers and berries are all worthwhile features. Obvious choices are *Skimmia japonica* 'Rubella' ♀, with its red buds, and the female cultivars that berry, but the white-flowering male varieties are no less worthwhile. *Skimmia* × *confusa* 'Kew Green' ♀ has clusters of fragrant, white flowers against pretty, apple green foliage. *Skimmia japonica* 'Fragrans' ♀ is exceptionally fragrant – the white flowers smell of lily-of-the-valley. For smaller spaces or pots in shade, skimmia is a particularly good choice of evergreen shrub. (See pages 184–85.)

Snowberry, *Symphoricarpos albus*, tends to be disregarded in gardens because of its invasive qualities. A native of North America, this shrub is extremely hardy and grows in the poorest soils and in deep shade. It forms a thicket of fine, arching upright stems with small, light green leaves. It is a light and airy plant, and its leaves fall to reveal the fine frame and the round white berries. It suckers and spreads to form thickets. *Symphoricarpos alba* var. *laevigatus* grows to 2m (6ft) and always produces copious quantities of berries. *Symphoricarpos* × *chenaultii*

MORE SHRUBS FOR SHADY SITES *Berberis* • *Chaenomeles* • *Choisya ternata* • *Cornus alba* • *Cotoneaster* •

'Hancock' is dwarf and wide-spreading, and makes excellent ground cover under trees. The berries are heavily flushed pink, particularly when light is strong. *Symphoricarpos × doorenbosii* hybrids include the well-known **'Magic Berry'** and **'Mother of Pearl'** (illus. page 93)

Symphoricarpos are especially useful in country gardens where there are mature oak trees, under which they succeed. Their light, airy habit fits in well in the rural environment.

Symphoricarpos albus

Viburnum davidii ♀ is an extremely tolerant creature. It can make a large shrub but it is at its best when it is still young, forming a compact mound of perfect, deep raven-green, ribbed leaves. In the presence of a male pollinator, female plants produce blue-black berries in winter. (See Good Companions, page 89; see also pages 37, 123, 125.)

CLIMBERS AND GROUND COVER

Shady areas backed by a wall or fence need climbers and wall shrubs that perform without much light. The ivies offer some of our most decorative and useful climbers, but they are frequently overlooked and considered the 'thugs' of the garden. Use the small-leaved varieties, for example the white-variegated *Hedera helix* **'Glacier'** ♀, as a background for bold evergreens such as aucuba, and use the large-leaved varieties, for example the yellow-variegated *Hedera colchica* **'Sulphur Heart'** ♀, as a background for the neater, variegated evergreens such as osmanthus. (See Good Companions, page 89.) It is easy to forget that ivies will grow horizontally as well as vertically. In fact ivies make wonderful ground cover, filling gaps and extending the interest and effect of evergreen foliage shrubs.

On moist, shady sites *Pachysandra terminalis* is an excellent choice for ground cover. Although pachysandra looks like an evergreen herbaceous plant, it is in fact a close relative of box and belongs to the same family. It is not successful on shallow chalk, but grows well under most trees and spreads by suckering. Whorls of leaves at the end of short stems create an attractive evergreen effect. The variegated form, *Pachysandra terminalis* **'Variegata'** ♀, is particularly pleasing.

Pachysandra terminalis

Rubus tricolor

Of all the ground-cover plants suitable for shade, *Rubus tricolor* is perhaps the finest. Widely used in amenity planting, it is often overlooked in garden centres, probably because its trailing growth makes it untidy in a pot. It is evergreen, with dark green, shiny leaves carried on long, trailing stems covered in chestnut bristles. White flowers, sometimes followed by edible red fruits, are produced in July, but are of very secondary importance to the foliage. It is an incredibly efficient ground-cover plant, forming a dense carpet even on dry soil under beech trees.

The vincas, or periwinkles, are invaluable plants for ground cover in shade and on banks. The small-leaved forms of *Vinca minor* grow flatter and are less smothering than the larger-leaved forms of the greater periwinkle, *Vinca major*. *Vinca minor* **'Argenteovariegata'** ♀ has creamy-white variegated leaves and blue flowers, while *Vinca minor* f. *alba* **'Gertrude Jekyll'** ♀ has white flowers. It is pretty planted under *Osmanthus heterophyllus* 'Variegatus' (see also Good Companions, page 89).

Normally, variegated plants are less vigorous than plain green-leaved ones, but this is not true of the arching and rampant *Vinca major* **'Variegata'** ♀. Its creamy white-margined leaves and blue flowers shine light under laurels and quickly cover banks and rough ground on damp or dry sites.

Vinca major 'Variegata'

ESTABLISHING PLANTS UNDER TREES

It is often overhanging trees and other surrounding vegetation that create shade in a garden. In these situations new plants have a hard job getting established, as they compete not only for light but also for water and nutrients. To achieve the best results, be especially careful to prepare the ground well before planting and to water well after planting. In dry spells you will need to water throughout the growing season, when surrounding trees and shrubs are in full leaf.

Where soil is very poor, consider using shade-loving subjects in pots. This can be very useful close to the trunk of a tree, in a key spot in the garden. Use a large container and loam-based compost. Remember that regular watering will be necessary.

Fuchsia • Hydrangea • Itea • Kerria • Ligustrum • Lonicera • Prunus laurocerasus • Pyracantha •

Damp sites

Moist, fertile soil that has good drainage but does not dry out is the ideal growing environment. However, many soils are permanently damp and heavy, and plants may suffer from lack of oxygen around their roots. Clay soils, while very fertile, tend to have poor drainage and are therefore overly wet and heavy; poor drainage may also be the result of compaction. If you garden on a damp site, choose plants that are tolerant of such conditions.

Amelanchiers are hard-working shrubs, with pretty flowers, fine spring and autumn foliage, and fruit. *Amelanchier canadensis* (snowy mespilus) is a hardy deciduous, suckering shrub, native to North America. It is tall and erect, with upright sprays of white flowers and pretty, coppery new growth in mid-spring; in an open spot the foliage colours well in autumn. *Amelanchier lamarckii* ♀ is more spectacular, with larger, lax sprays of flowers, brighter new growth and better autumn colour.

Amelanchier lamarckii

All varieties of **Cornus alba** come into their own here, growing vigorously in wet conditions on virtually any soil. These versatile and useful plants are excellent for their deciduous foliage, autumn colour and winter stems (see pages 67, 170, 177–79).

Hippophae rhamnoides ♀, the sea buckthorn, is an easy-going plant, ideal

Hippophae rhamnoides

for sandy soil and coastal gardens, and tolerant of poor drainage and pollution. It often fruits well, retaining its yellow berries long after the silver, willow-like leaves have fallen. It is a useful plant where height is needed.

Physocarpus opulifolius is a hardy North American plant that thrives in open, moist conditions. *Physocarpus opulifolius* **'Dart's Gold'** ♀ has bright yellow foliage (see Good Companions, opposite); the leaves of *Physocarpus opulifolius* **'Diabolo'** ♀ are dark purple,

IMPROVING DAMP SOIL

Ground preparation is all important in a wet soil. Sometimes growing conditions on heavy soils can be improved by the addition of coarse washed grit. Some low-lying gardens are just naturally wet, so it is necessary to work with the conditions rather than trying to overcome them. Either choose tolerant plants or use raised beds to lift the level of the planting areas above the wet soil.

making it a very useful complementary shrub in almost any planting scheme.

Most **willows** (*Salix*) thrive on damp sites. Several varieties, which would ultimately grow into large trees if not contained, have attractively coloured stems in winter; they can be hard pruned in the same way as *Cornus alba* (see page 176), to encourage these, and to keep them to shrub proportions. The stems of *Salix alba* subsp. *vitellina* ♀ are bright yellow, while those of *Salix alba* subsp. *vitellina* **'Britzensis'** ♀ are brilliant orange-scarlet. The violet willow, *Salix daphnoides*, has purple-violet shoots, with a white bloom, and pretty, furry grey then yellow catkins in

Salix alba subsp. *vitellina* 'Britzensis'

Salix daphnoides

MORE SHRUBS FOR DAMP SITES *Calycanthus floridus* • *Cornus sericea* • *Gaultheria shallon* • *Myrica gale* •

Sambucus nigra f. porphyrophylla 'Gerda' ('Black Beauty')

Sorbaria tomentosa var. angustifolia

Symphoricarpos × doorenbosii 'Mother of Pearl'

spring. *Salix elaeagnos*, the hoary willow, is described on page 78.

The **elders** (*Sambucus*) are very accommodating plants and grow on dry and wet soils. All are deciduous. Choose the gold-leaved *Sambucus racemosa* 'Sutherland Gold' ⚑ (see page 47) for shade and the purple-leaved *Sambucus nigra* f. *porphyrophylla* 'Gerda' ⚑, ('Black Beauty') for sun. The cut-leaved *Sambucus nigra* f. *laciniata* ⚑, the fern-leaved elder, is a lovely plant, with finely cut foliage and heads of white flowers. (See Good Companions, right.)

Often taken for spiraeas, **Sorbarias** are big, vigorous deciduous shrubs with huge sprays of creamy white flowers, like large astilbes, in summer. *Sorbaria tomentosa* var. *angustifolia* ⚑ is a very elegant form, with spreading reddish branches, fern-like foliage and graceful flower stems.

Most spiraeas happily tolerate damp conditions but *Spiraea × vanhouttei* is one that excels on very damp soil. A vigorous, semi-evergreen shrub with arching branches, it is smothered in white hawthorn-like flowers in late spring. (See Good Companions, right.)

Symphoricarpos, the snowberries, thrive in damp and dry sites, producing lots of light, twiggy growth to a height of about 1m (3ft). White or pink berries add winter interest (see page 90).

Viburnum opulus and its cultivars are easy, deciduous shrubs that grow in any conditions. The native species is lovely for its flowers as well as its autumn colour (see page 172). *Viburnum opulus*

'Roseum' ⚑ ('Sterile'), the snowball bush, is a vigorous deciduous shrub that reaches 2m (6ft) or more. The 'snowballs' of sterile florets start lime green, progress through cream and then blush-

pink in late spring and early summer. (See Good Companions, below.)

Wet sites, especially near water, suit naturalistic planting; all the above look good in these surroundings.

GOOD COMPANIONS

Physocarpus opulifolius 'Dart's Gold' ⚑ (1) has bright yellow leaves and is effective with the yellow-variegated *Cornus alba* 'Spaethii' and bold-leaved herbaceous *Ligularia dentata* 'Desdemona' (2).

Sambucus nigra f. *lacinata* ⚑ (3), the fern-leaved elder, is useful with heavy, moisture-loving herbaceous plants such as *Gunnera manicata* (4) and *Rheum palmatum* 'Atropurpureum'.

The white flowers and fresh green foliage of *Spirea × vanhouttei* (5) combine prettily with the white-variegated leaves of *Cornus alba* 'Elegantissima' ⚑ (6).

Viburnum opulus 'Roseum' ⚑ (7) is lovely underplanted with *Alchemilla mollis* ⚑ (8), whose frothy green flowers are at their best when the heavy white blooms of the viburnum are in full flower.

Neillia thibetica • Photinia villosa • Prunus spinosa • Salix repens • Vaccinium corymbosum • Viburnum sargentii 'Onondaga' •

MOIST ACID SOILS

Plants that like moist acid soil do not tolerate drought; often, their natural, peaty habitat is moist all year.

The bog rosemary, *Andromeda polifolia*, is a natural choice. This dwarf evergreen shrub is a rare British native, with rosemary-like foliage and clusters of bell-shaped, pink flowers in late spring. *Andromeda polifolia* 'Alba' and *Andromeda polifolia* 'Compacta' ♀, bearing, respectively, white and pink flowers on compact plants, are the best choices for most gardens.

The aronia species *Aronia arbutifolia* and the hybrid *Aronia × prunifolia* do not have to be grown in acid soil but these deciduous shrubs do resent shallow chalk soils. Members of the rose family, they have hawthorn-like flowers in spring, red or purple fruits and – the main reason for growing them – exceptional autumn colour.

The sweet pepper bush, *Clethra alnifolia*, is an upright deciduous shrub, producing spikes of fragrant

Aronia arbutifolia

Waterside planting at Le Clos du Coudray, Normandy, France.

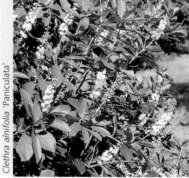

Clethra alnifolia 'Paniculata'

white flowers in late summer. A hardy character from North America, it is closely related to erica and must have lime-free soil. *Clethra alnifolia* 'Paniculata' ♀ is considered the best form.

Another very hardy native of North America, *Gaultheria shallon* is a useful evergreen for damp acid sites. It produces thickets of stems up to 2m (6ft) high. Leaves are thick and leathery, and the clusters of pinkish-white flowers are followed by dark purple fruits.

Rhododendrons hate drought, so damp acid soil is ideal for the hardy hybrids (see page 103). They do not like to be waterlogged but, given enough moisture, they grow and colour well.

SEASONAL CONTRAST

Wet sites offer wonderful possibilities when it comes to herbaceous perennials and deciduous shrubs and trees. Many moisture-lovers have bold foliage, and some grow at an incredible rate. Contrast is the appeal of damp areas: in the summer they are verdant, full, lush and leafy, while in winter a stark scene of stems and framework prevails. Evergreens are naturally adapted to resist desiccation; as a result, wet conditions are not their natural habitat and most look uncomfortable in damp sites.

Clay soils

Aralia elata 'Variegata'

A well-known gardener once said, 'If you have free-draining acid, sandy soil, plant rhododendrons; if you have chalk, plant clematis; if you have clay, move!' What he should have said was: 'If you have clay, you will have to make the best of it by choosing the right plants.' Clay soil can indeed be difficult to work but, on the plus side, it is very fertile and you can always improve its structure (see pages 16–17).

If you chose the right shrubs, cultivation of the soil is rarely required after planting, just the removal of weeds around the plants. If you use a glyphosate-based weedkiller to do this, ensure the herbicide does not splash the shrub's foliage. An occasional mulch of composted bark, garden compost or well-rotted manure will benefit the plants and gradually improve the soil structure. The level of nutrients in the soil means that supplementary feeding is rarely required for good flowering and strong performance.

Many plants grow well on clay soils, especially such deciduous flowering shrubs as deutzias, forsythias, ribes, philadelphus and weigelas, all of which are a natural choice for heavy clay.

For a striking architectural effect *Aralia elata* ♚, the Japanese angelica tree, is unbeatable. This is a large, suckering deciduous shrub whose upright stems grow to 3m (10ft) or more. The vast, green fern-like leaves, all at the top of the stems, give the shrub the look of a palm, and white flowers in huge sprays appear in autumn; the foliage can colour well at the same time. *Aralia elata* 'Variegata' ♚ has white-edged leaves, irregularly marked with creamy white. The flowers appear earlier and are less spectacular than on the green form. It is a choice and much sought-after plant.

All cornus do well on clay and are also valuable for wet sticky soils. Larger-growing varieties such as *Cornus alba* 'Elegantissima' ♚ (see page 178) are ideal for filling space and covering difficult ground.

The vigorous deciduous shrub *Leycesteria formosa* ♚ grows just about anywhere and succeeds well on clay, even on damp sites. The tall, arching, hollow stems are sea-green, and the flower clusters hang from the branches from early summer through to autumn, the claret-red bracts interspersed with small white flowers. These are followed by shiny purple fruits loved by pheasants, hence the common name, pheasant berry. When the leaves fall, remove any dead and twiggy growth, and cut out some of the old stems to ground level: this leaves the attractive green stems

EVERGREEN SHRUBS

When it comes to evergreens for clay soil, it is the hardy favourites that come to the fore: aucubas, choisyas and *Viburnum tinus*. All of these do well in sun as well as shade, and provide that all-important structure on the heaviest of soils. Mahonias also do well on clay, and provide cheery winter and early spring colour. (See Good Companions, page 96.)

The evergreen *Magnolia grandiflora* also grows on clay soils, but it dislikes wet conditions and resents being planted too deeply.

On clay soils that are slightly acid, the hardy hybrid rhododendrons grow surprisingly well. The larger-growing, later-flowering *Rhododendron catawbiense*, parent of many hybrids, is ideal for screening and background planting. 'Cunningham's White' is an old cultivar, with dark green foliage and prettily marked flowers in mauve, fading to white; it is incredibly hardy and will even tolerate slightly alkaline conditions. For dark red flowers, 'Nova Zembla' (right) takes some beating, a hardy plant of upright growth with deep red, weather-resistant blooms.

exposed to enjoy through winter. (See Good Companions, below.)

All deciduous magnolias grow well on clay (see pages 134–35). For smaller gardens, *Magnolia stellata* ♥ is the natural choice, performing reliably with a mass of starry, shiny blooms every spring. The grey, catkin-like buds are attractive in winter. Where space is not at a premium, choose one of the cultivars of *Magnolia* × *soulangeana*.

Even if the hardy hibiscus are late to break into leaf at the beginning of the season, you can depend on them for late-summer flowers. When hibiscus are flowering, **hypericums** and **potentillas** are still performing, both of which grow well in heavy soil conditions.

Magnolia × *soulangeana*

Roses (see pages 112–15) love clay soils, as do many other members of the rose family. For example, **cotoneasters** and **pyracanthas** require little attention and are excellent for smothering sites where cultivation is virtually impossible (see Good Companions, below).

Rosa 'Rosy Cushion'

Purple and yellow foliage effects are easy on clay soils: **berberis, cotinus,** ***Philadelphus coronarius* 'Aureus'** ♥, **spiraea** and ***Weigela florida* 'Foliis Purpureis'** ♥ all thrive under these conditions.

Clay soils are often too wet in winter to be ideal for silver-foliage plants, but *Brachyglottis* (Dunedin Group) 'Sunshine' ♥, formerly called *Senecio* 'Sunshine', copes with these conditions and, if pruned hard just before the flowers appear, retains its silver sheen throughout winter. (See page 79.)

GOOD COMPANIONS

A combination of *Leycesteria formosa* ♥ (1) with *Symphoricarpos orbiculatus* 'Foliis Variegatis' (2) and *Cornus alba* 'Gouchaultii' (3) is ideal where gardening is very difficult but some light shrub cover is needed – on a heavy clay bank, for example.

The yellow flowers of *Mahonia japonica* ♥ (4) combine well with the golden variegations of *Aucuba japonica* 'Marmorata' (5).

For ground cover on tough sites, use a larger-growing shrub rose such as 'Nevada' (6) with informal evergreens *Cotoneaster franchetii* (7) and *Pyracantha* 'Golden Charmer' ♥ (8).

PLANTING ON CLAY SOIL

Planting on clay can be difficult. It is really important to dig as large a planting hole as you can and to mix plenty of garden compost with the garden soil before you replace it around the plant, to help the roots to acclimatize to their new home. Clay soils can dry out and bake hard in the summer, so early autumn is the best time to plant in order to give the shrub longer to establish. Planting in spring may be difficult if the ground is wet and heavy.

Once established, shrubs grown on clay have great stability: the weight of the soil keeps the roots firm, and the plants rarely suffer from wind-rock. Provided planting is well established and good ground cover is achieved, little further maintenance or cultivation is needed.

MORE SHRUBS FOR CLAY SOILS *Abelia • Chaenomeles • Corylus • Cytisus • Deutzia • Escallonia • Garrya • Genista • Hamamelis • Leycesteria • Lonicera • Philadelphus • Potentilla • Sambucus • Skimmia • Syringa •*

Chalk soils

The depth of soils over chalk varies enormously. Where soils are deep, they can be adequately fertile and moisture-retentive to support most plants; only ericaceous plants, or lime-haters, are taboo. Shallow soils over chalk need more consideration; these are free-draining, and can lack nutrients and be quite dry in the summer, so you need to select plants that enjoy these conditions.

Deutzia × hybrida 'Magicien'

Soil pH has a profound effect on the availability of some nutrients to certain plants. Iron, essential for the growth of rhododendrons and other ericaceous plants, becomes locked up on chalky, alkaline soil: as a result, the leaves turn yellow and the plant suffers. Plants that thrive on chalk do so because they are adapted to cope with the conditions.

A vast range of plants can be grown on alkaline soil; in fact, more plants thrive on alkaline soils than in acid conditions.

The favourite hardy deciduous shrubs come to the fore on chalk: **deutzias** (see pages 151–52), **forsythias** (see pages 132–33), **philadelphus** (see page 160), lilacs (*syringa*; see page 145), **weigelas** (see page 162). All thrive and contribute colour and interest throughout spring. For summer colour, choose any buddleia or hibiscus. The hardy fuchsias, such as 'Mrs Popple' ♀ (see Good Companions, page 98) grow well in sun or shade and provide colour from midsummer on.

A close relative of weigela, *Dipelta floribunda* ♀ is an excellent, if less well-known, deciduous shrub. It is

Syringa 'Esther Staley'

Dipelta floribunda

Weigela florida 'Variegata'

Romneya coulteri

A WORD OF ENCOURAGEMENT

Chalk soil should never be seen as a disadvantage. Ericaceous plants, if craved, can be grown in pots; in that way the gardener gets the best of both worlds. Chalk soils can also be improved by the addition of bulky organic matter to increase the humus content of the soil; this improves texture as well as increasing the nutrient and water-holding capacity, thereby increasing the fertility.

lighter and more graceful in habit than many weigelas, with narrower leaves, often with a coppery tinge. The fragrant flowers are pink flushed yellow at the throat, profusely produced in late spring all along the upright, arching branches.

The Californian tree poppy, *Romneya coulteri* ♀, is somewhere between a shrub and a herbaceous perennial. It is

Cotoneaster simonsii

carrying shiny, dark green leaves and bright red berries in autumn (see Good Companions, below). *Cotoneaster simonsii* ♀ is upright in habit and semi-evergreen, with neat, glossy green leaves and large scarlet fruits. It makes an excellent hedge of around 1.5m (5ft) high. (See also Plant Profile, page 175.)

Ceanothus can succeed in chalk if plenty of organic matter is added, and are a natural choice for a sunny spot. **Cytisus** will grow on chalk, and partner the early-flowering evergreen *Ceanothus* 'Concha' ♀ well (see Good Companions below and pages 140, 146).

All euonymus grow very well on chalk and evergreen favourites such as the prostrate varieties of *Euonymus fortunei* BLONDY ('Interbolwi') and the more upright forms of *Euonymus japonicus* are useful in both sun and shade (see page 58).

a thicket-forming plant, spreading by underground stems. It can be difficult to establish, but on light, chalky soils it can become positively rampant, throwing up numerous hollow grey stems that will easily reach 2m (6ft) in height. The deeply cut, grey-blue leaves are a delightful background to the huge, tissue-paper white blooms with their yellow-stamened centres. This is a plant for a warm, sunny spot – alongside a wall perhaps.

Spiraeas also grow well on chalk. The golden-leaved varieties of *Spiraea japonica* (see page 46) are invaluable for their colourful foliage throughout summer. *Spiraea japonica* 'Anthony Waterer', with its bright crimson, fluffy, flat flowerheads, is a good shrub for the front of a border, and its colourful flowers are much loved by bees and butterflies. The foliage is sometimes variegated pink and green, unlike the newer *Spiraea japonica* 'Dart's Red' ♀, which has plain green foliage. (See Good Companions, page 99.)

EVERGREEN SHRUBS

Evergreens for chalk are not a problem. The ever-tolerant **aucubas** are always a good choice, as are the versatile **cotoneasters**. The latter suit both town and country gardens. Their white flowers

attract pollinating insects and butterflies in spring. Birds appreciate their showy and appetizing fruit in autumn. There is a cotoneaster for virtually any situation, from the lowest ground-cover plant to the largest shrub. *Cotoneaster dammeri* ♀ has long trailing shoots

---

GOOD COMPANIONS

The sapphire clouds of *Ceanothus* 'Concha' ♀ (1) in full bloom alongside the cream wands of *Cytisus* × *praecox* 'Warminster' (2) make a breathtaking sight.

For covering chalky banks, *Cotoneaster dammeri* ♀ (3) is a natural partner for *Vinca minor* 'Argenteovariegata' ♀ (4).

To prolong the season of interest, plant the hardy fuchsia 'Mrs Popple' (5) or 'Riccartonii' alongside early-blooming deutzias such as *Deutzia* × *rosea* 'Carminea' (6).

MORE SHRUBS FOR CHALK SOILS *Brachyglottis* • *Choisya* • *Cornus mas* • *Hypericum* • *Ligustrum* • *Lonicera* •

Hebes (see pages 52, 76, 154) are happier on chalk soils than on acid ones – the drier conditions in winter reduce the incidence of leafspot diseases caused by damp conditions.

For shady situations on chalk, the best dwarf evergreen is **Sarcococca confusa**♀ (see page 90; illus. page 184).

Photinia × fraseri 'Red Robin'♀ and **Laurus nobilis**♀ (see pages 123 and 31) are large structural evergreens that thrive on chalk. Both are excellent screening shrubs, achieving a height of several metres if left unchecked. They also respond well to either pruning or trimming. For a lower, more compact structural evergreen, consider a **Buxus sempervirens**♀ cultivar (see page 29).

The Spanish broom, **Spartium junceum**♀, is a member of the pea family, similar to cytisus and genista in appearance, with large showy, fragrant, yellow flowers. This is a shrub that looks poor as a young plant in a pot and can be leggy and awkward as an elderly shrub. The habit is loose and upright,

GOOD COMPANIONS

An ideal plant for coastal gardens, *Spartium junceum*♀ (1) works well planted against the silver-green foliage of *Elaeagnus × ebbingei*♀ (2).

On a sunny site *Spiraea japonica* 'Dart's' Red'♀ (3) combines well with the silver foliage of santolina and the purple-pink branches of *Berberis thunbergii* f. *atropurpurea* 'Rose Glow'♀ (4).

with green, sedge-like stems that appear devoid of leaves. The flowers bloom along the upper part of the stems, throughout summer and early autumn. The bush will reach 3m (10ft) or more if left unchecked, but is best pruned in spring from an early age to keep it compact. Never cut back into old wood as new growth is unlikely to regenerate. (See Good Companions, above.)

Many Mediterranean natives, notably **cistus** and **helianthemums**, are very happy on shallow, dry chalk soils, while **rosemary** is more aromatic than ever in a dry, sunny spot, on soil of low fertility. (See pages 83, 150; 85–86; 86–87.)

Rosemary and lavender grace a sunny terrace at Hestercombe, Somerset.

Mahonia aquifolium • Olearia • Potentilla • Pyracantha • Ribes • Sambucus • Symphoricarpos • Tamarix • Viburnum • Yucca •

Acid soils

The range of plants that need an acid soil includes some of our most beautiful spring-flowering shrubs, as well as some of the finest for autumn colour. No wonder acid soils are the envy of many who garden on chalk. However, now that container gardening is so popular, growing acid-lovers in pots, using ericaceous compost, is an easy option for those who garden on alkaline soil.

Azaleas and rhododendrons at Trewithen, Cornwall.

There is a complex relationship between soil pH (the measure of acidity and alkalinity) and the availability of certain nutrients to certain plants. Soil pH is measured on a scale of 1 (extremely acid) to 14 (extremely alkaline). Neutral soil has a pH value of 7.0. This, or just below, is the ideal for gardening as it allows the cultivation of the widest range of plants.

Acid soils, whether sandy or peaty, are normally low in nutrients, and most acid-loving plants are adapted to a soil of relatively low fertility. However, there are certain micronutrients that they must have; it is these that become unavailable to them when grown on an alkaline soil. Sometimes, neutral soil can be made more acid by the addition of sulphur chips and moss peat. However, an alkaline soil is so because of the underlying rock: add vast quantities of acidic ingredients to a chalk soil and the chalk will still come through – it is not worth the battle. Instead, grow plants that are suited to the site.

Although the term ericaceous strictly refers to those plants that belong to the family Ericaceae, it is used generally for plants that need acid soil.

All the plants in this section are acid loving, and need a pH of less than 7.0. Most can be grown in containers as long as ericaceous compost is used.

GROWING ACID-LOVING PLANTS

Most acid-lovers originate from open heathland or woodland conditions and you should bear this in mind when positioning them in the garden, in the open or in pots. Most are from cool climates, and dislike drought and high temperatures: a hot, sunny spot and no water can prove fatal. They are shallow-rooting plants and have a very fibrous root system, which is dense and difficult to rewet once dry. Pay good attention to watering at all times, even in winter.

Acid-loving plants are not heavy feeders, so use a slow-release, lime-free fertilizer sparingly. Mulch plants with leaf mould or lime-free compost in spring, when the soil is moist. Keep the mulch away from the main stems, but use it generously around the drip-line of the plant (where the foliage extends on to the soil surface) – this is where root activity is at its maximum.

PLANTING IN POTS

Rhododendrons (see pages 101–105), camellias (see pages 106–107) and pieris (see page 109) make excellent subjects for pots. Choose a large pot at least 40cm (16in) in diameter and no less than 30cm (12in) deep. Put plenty of drainage in the form of broken crocks in the bottom, and plant in ericaceous, loam-based compost for best results. This holds water and nutrients better than soil-less composts, prevents drying out and is less attractive to vine weevil (see box, page 103). Raise the pot slightly off the ground using pot feet, or pieces of tile, to prevent waterlogging.

Plants in containers appreciate an occasional drenching in summer with a liquid fertilizer and growth stimulant containing sequestered iron. The same treatment can be used for sickly yellow specimens growing in the open ground.

Rhododendrons and azaleas

In many ways, the rhododendron offers the qualities that constitute the perfect garden plant: evergreen foliage, reliability of flowering, showy blooms, no pruning requirements and few pests. The only drawback, for some gardeners, is that most will grow only on acid soil. The name suggests 'red tree', but the rhododendron spectrum is much broader, their jewel colours lighting up our gardens through late spring and early summer.

Rhododendron 'Praecox'

The rhododendrons, a vast and diverse group, vary in stature from compact shrubs just a few centimetres high to trees. For garden purposes, the rhododendrons fall into three principal categories: dwarf rhododendrons, compact hybrids and hardy hybrids. The genus also includes deciduous and evergreen azaleas.

DWARF RHODODENDRONS

This group includes the small-leaved, compact species and hybrids that are frequently grown as rock garden subjects and early-flowering plants for pots. They combine well with heathers and conifers, and suit small gardens. In height they range from 30cm (1ft) to 1m (3ft).

Rhododendron 'Bengal' is hardy and compact, with glossy dark green foliage; loose trusses of deep red flowers are reliably produced. *Rhododendron* **Blue Tit Group** are excellent to plant with heathers; they form a dense, round bush, up to 1m (3ft), but usually smaller; tiny, funnel-shaped flowers appear in clusters at the end of the branches in mid-spring, opening lavender-blue but darkening with age. **'Ginny Gee'** ✿ is a dwarf, but spreading, compact shrub with neat foliage; the flowers are widely funnel-shaped, opening to pale pink and fading to white edged with pink (see Good Companions, right). **'Patty Bee'** ✿ is strong-growing but very compact, with attractive, small, mid-green leaves and brown, felty stems and buds, opening to primrose flowers, produced in profusion in early spring and adding interest to evergreen planting; it looks good with yellow-spotted aucuba. **'Praecox'** ✿ is a loose, open shrub with small, often bronzy leaves that are aromatic when crushed. The pretty flowers, which are produced in twos and threes at the end of the shoots, open in early spring; they are pale rosy purple, almost translucent. Put it under light tree cover to prevent frost damage. It looks delightful underplanted with *Primula vulgaris* (primrose).

Rhododendron **'Ramapo'** ✿ is a very hardy, compact and reliable shrub with blue-grey young foliage; the blue-violet flowers appear in clusters, all over the bush in early spring if grown in full sun. **'Scarlet Wonder'** ✿ is a tough, hardy subject that succeeds on any site with acid soil. It has attractive, rounded leaves of dark green and grows to form a dense mound; the bright ruby flowers are carried in loose trusses at the end of the shoots in late spring (see Good Companions, below). **'Shamrock'** is a compact, spreading dwarf shrub with glossy, dark green foliage and lime-green buds that open to pale yellow flowers in early spring. **'Snipe'** is dwarf, dense and compact, with pale green foliage; its flowers are a pastel mix of pale pink, violet and purple with deeper spots.

GOOD COMPANIONS

Rhododendron 'Scarlet Wonder' ✿ (1), flowering in late spring, provides good ground cover with *Ceanothus thyrsiflorus* var. *repens* (2).

Rhododendron 'Ginny Gee' ✿ (3) is a very pretty plant, blooming at the end of the winter-flowering heather season; it is useful for revitalizing pink and white *Erica carnea* (4).

COMPACT HYBRIDS

These are smaller-growing varieties of the typical, large-growing rhododendron hardy hybrids, and as such they have more typical rhododendron flowers and foliage than the dwarf rhododendrons. The compact habit is often the result of hybridizing vigorous varieties with *Rhododendron yakushimanum*. They are hardy plants and range in size from 60cm (2ft) to 1.5m (5ft).

The *Rhododendron yakushimanum* hybrids are excellent plants, but with a very solid habit. They are a suitable choice for pots, where they can stand alone. In the garden, plant them singly, with lighter plants around them – heathers in sun, ferns or pulmonarias in shade; if planted in groups, they create a solid, heavy mass. Compact hybrids with *Rhododendron yakushimanum* in the parentage include the following. 'Dreamland' ♀ is a small, domed shrub with silvery young foliage, becoming dark green, and large, very pale pink flowers with darker edges in loose trusses. 'Fantastica' ♀ is very hardy, small and spreading, with dark green leaves that are white and woolly beneath. The flowers, which are carried

Rhododendron 'Dreamland'

Rhododendron 'Percy Wiseman'

Rhododendron 'Sneezy'

Rhododendron 'Hotei'

in large trusses, are pale pink, shading to white, but with deep pink wavy edges. 'Golden Torch' ♀ has neat foliage and a particularly solid growth habit. The flower buds are salmon-pink, opening to bell-shaped blooms of pale yellow in tight trusses. 'Percy Wiseman' ♀ is a lovely hybrid, with dark green foliage and round trusses of

large, funnel-shaped flowers, which open apricot, fading to cream flushed with apricot-pink. 'Sneezy' is very hardy and vigorous, with dark green leaves that are silvery when young; the flowers, which are produced in large, dense trusses in late spring, are deep pink, paler in the centre with red spots.

Some other compact rhododendrons are as follows. 'Golden Gate' is a dome-shaped shrub with reddish-pink flowers with an orange-yellow centre, carried in clusters of five or six. 'Hotei' ♀ has rounded, narrow leaves and deep yellow, bell-shaped flowers; 'Kokardia' has magnificent trusses of rich purple flowers. 'Mrs Furnivall' ♀ is a larger hardy hybrid but has a dense habit; it has trusses of wide, funnel-shaped flowers that are a light rose-pink, conspicuously blotched with brown and crimson in the throat. 'Nancy Evans' ♀ is a small shrub, with rounded, glossy, dark green leaves that are bronze when young. Orange-red buds open to pretty, frilled, amber-yellow flowers in rounded trusses (see Good Companions, left).

GOOD COMPANIONS

Plant *Rhododendron* 'Nancy Evans' ♀ (1) with *Euphorbia griffithii* 'Fireglow' (2) for a glowing combination.

Pink rhododendrons, such as the compact hybrid 'Rocket' (3), combine well with *Hyacinthoides non-scripta* (bluebells) (4).

HARDY HYBRIDS

This group includes large, stately shrubs that produce showy flowers in big trusses. Their hardiness varies according to parentage; generally, these are plants that withstand exposed situations and are easy to grow. They range in size from 1.5m (5ft) to 3m (10ft).

The first hybrids appeared around 1825, when *Rhododendron arboreum* flowered for the first time in the British Isles. During the 75 years that followed, many hybrids were raised from this plant, as well as from *Rhododendron catawbiense* and *Rhododendron maximum*, hailing from North America, and *Rhododendron ponticum*, from Turkey. As new species were introduced from China and the Himalayas, other characteristics in flower shape, colour, growth habit and foliage emerged.

'Albert Schweitzer' ♥ is a large, upright shrub, with conical trusses of deep pink flowers with a darker blotch. 'Gomer Waterer' ♥, one of the best hardy hybrids, is a medium-sized shrub with healthy, leathery leaves and red-brown buds; the large flowers, which are carried in dense, round trusses, are deeply frilled, white, flushed mauve, with a mustard-yellow blotch in the throat. 'Halfdan Lem' is a vigorous, medium-sized shrub with dark green,

Rhododendron 'Mrs T.H. Lowinsky'

slightly waved foliage and bright red leaf stalks; the bright red flowers are carried in large trusses. 'Horizon Monarch' ♥ is a medium-sized shrub with excellent foliage. The flowers, which are produced earlier in the year than on most varieties, in large, upright trusses, are pinkish-orange in bud, opening to wide, lightly frilled blooms of creamy yellow, marked red in the throat. 'Lord Roberts' ♥ is an old hybrid but it still has the best flower colour of all the reds; it produces dense round trusses of funnel-shaped flowers, deep crimson with black markings. 'Mrs T.H. Lowinsky' ♥ is vigorous and tall, with broad, healthy leaves. The lilac

Rhododendron 'Horizon Monarch'

flowers, which are paler in the centre, are heavily spotted orange-brown. 'Van' is a healthy and vigorous but compact grower, with large, loose trusses of vivid deep pink flowers.

CARING FOR RHODODENDRONS

Regular watering of rhododendrons is essential. Since the roots are fibrous and compact, it is difficult for water to penetrate a dry rootball; if a plant does dry out, a dripping hose is better than a deluge. Removing fading flowers from the plant stimulates the production of the new growth next season.

Bud blast is a fungal disease that causes the buds to die on the plants before opening. The buds usually grow brown and sooty, as black fungal spore carriers appear on the buds in spring, before they develop. This fungal infection is spread the previous summer by leaf hoppers. Treatment is by controlling the leaf hoppers with a systemic insecticide spray, applied in mid- and late summer. Spraying with a copper-based fungicide in autumn and early spring also gives some control of the fungus if present. Infected buds must be removed and destroyed, not left on the plants.

VINE WEEVIL

Vine weevil can be a problem to evergreen acid-loving plants particularly camellias and rhododendrons. To treat, apply a soil and foliar drench of a systemic insecticide recommended for this purpose. Alternatively, a biological control can be used. A solution containing a parasitic nematode is watered on in early spring or autumn; the nematodes attack the vine weevil larvae that are feeding on the roots at this time.

DECIDUOUS AZALEAS

Botanically belonging to the same genus as rhododendrons, but as aesthetically and atmospherically different as frost from fire, deciduous azaleas display maturity at an early age. The deciduous quality displays a changing profile with the seasons; leaf loss reveals, and accentuates, a graceful and expressive frame, a style and deportment possessed only by the most sophisticated of shrubs. Layered branches carry elegant foliage, and graceful clusters of long-lasting, exotic blooms, which are decorative even in bud, have an oriental air. The elegant form of deciduous azaleas is an excellent contrast to the solid, heavy form of most evergreens. Autumn colour is a feature of many varieties. All flower in late spring.

The range of flower colours covers almost everything conceivable, with the exception of blue and purple shades. Some groups are fragrant, and where this quality is possessed it could be regarded as one of the most delicious fragrances in the plant world. *Rhododendron luteum* ♥, the yellow-flowering species, has a fresh honeysuckle scent that has been imparted to many hybrids.

Rhododendron 'Fireball' ♥ is also fragrant, with copper young foliage and

Rhododendron luteum

Rhododendron 'Fireball'

Rhododendron 'Irene Koster'

CARING FOR DECIDUOUS AZALEAS

After flowering, deciduous azaleas enjoy a shower of liquid fertilizer with sequestered iron. This fortifies the plant for the growing season and strengthens the foliage for the colourful days of autumn ahead. There is no need to dead-head deciduous azaleas. The open structure of the plant is part of its character. However, deciduous azaleas respond well to pruning after flowering, if a more compact plant is required.

WHERE TO PLANT DECIDUOUS AZALEAS

Deciduous azaleas grow well in full sun or partial shade, and associate well with most schemes. Many early spring subjects team up well with them to prolong the season of interest, for example narcissi, crocus, chionodoxa, puschkinia, and dwarf iris. Early woodland herbaceous plants, such as pulmonaria, helleborus, primula and spring- and autumn-flowering hardy cyclamen, sit naturally beneath their elegant frames. In woodland situations, they are excellent to line a path or act as a focus in a dell or clearing, the fragrance being accentuated by still air.

Deciduous azaleas also make stately, elegant architectural features when grown in pots. Positioned close to the house, the form of the plant is light enough to give foreground interest, without blocking the view of the garden beyond. In addition, they look good near water, their oriental frame and brilliant colours reflecting hauntingly in still pools and slow streams.

deep orange-red flowers. 'Cannon's Double' ♥ has double, creamy flowers opening from apricot flushed red buds, and long-lasting, rich bronze-purple tints in autumn. 'Glowing Embers' is a vivid reddish-orange with an orange blotch. 'Homebush' ♥ has small, spiky, deep pink flowers in dense round trusses, quite unlike any other azalea; it is a lovely shrub that mixes well with other plants. 'Irene Koster' ♥ is a favourite fragrant garden hybrid, with pale rose-pink flowers with a small yellow blotch, an exotic cast mark emphasizing the beauty of the orchid-like flowers. 'Klondyke' ♥ displays bronze leaf colour for the entire growing season. 'Mount Saint Helens' is a good pink. 'Northern Hi-Lights' is creamy yellow, pretty and fragrant. 'White Lights' ♥ is a hardy, rounded, fragrant shrub with profuse white flowers with yellow centres opening from pink buds.

EVERGREEN AZALEAS

Evergreen azaleas vary in stature from compact, upright dwarf shrubs with tiny leaves and profuse small flowers, to spreading low shrubs with bolder foliage and large, ruffled blooms. All are free-flowering; indeed, a well-grown plant will obscure all traces of foliage when in full bloom. Vast numbers of hybrids have arisen in the US and Europe as well as Japan, home of the azalea and from where Ernest Wilson introduced the Kurume azaleas in 1920.

The garden evergreen azaleas are hardy plants that require moisture around the roots and shelter from cold winds. Winter winds can cause leaf drop in exposed positions, and heavy rain and frost can spoil the flowers of the early-blooming varieties. Partially shaded, woodland conditions are ideal, and if planted in drifts in a woodland garden they are breathtaking in bloom, as long as attention is paid to colour combinations. However, when they are struggling against the odds on the

Rhododendron 'Blue Danube'

Rhododendron 'Kermesinum'

wrong soil in a suburban back garden these azaleas have little appeal.

The hardy types are often confused with the hybrids of *Azalea indica*, widely grown as houseplants. Although these can survive outside in the mildest localities, they are not generally regarded as garden plants.

Some attractive garden evergreen azalea varieties include *Rhododendron* **'Blue Danube'**, which is one of the best when in full flower with its striking blue-violet blooms. **'Geisha Orange'**, like all of the Geisha varieties, is an extremely hardy, mound-forming shrub with small, neat foliage and soft orange flowers. **'Hinomayo'** is a taller shrub, reaching 1.5m (5ft), with graceful,

shocking pink flowers; originally from the emperor's garden in Tokyo, Japan. **'Johanna'** has bronze foliage through autumn and winter and good red flowers (see Good Companions, below). **'Kermesinum'** is compact and low with masses of small, vivid purplish-red flowers. **'Kermesinum Rosé'** is similar in habit but has white-edged, rose-pink flowers. **'Palestrina'** has an abundance of pretty, white flowers with a hint of light green. **'Rose Greeley'** has 'hose-in-hose' flowers of white, blotched green; it is one of the few scented varieties of evergreen azaleas. **'Vuyk's Scarlet'** has large, bright red flowers with wavy petals and a loose, flowing growth habit.

CARING FOR EVERGREEN AZALEAS

Evergreen azaleas require no pruning. Bushiness can be encouraged on straggly plants by cutting back after flowering. Follow up with a light feed and plenty of water.

Evergreen azaleas are generally pest-free. Azalea gall is occasionally a problem, resulting in individual leaves becoming severely distorted, pale green and waxy; remove infected leaves. Old evergreen azaleas are particularly susceptible to colonization by lichen. Grey-green, moss-like lichen clothes the branches, inhibiting the plant's growth. Although lichen is not directly harmful, it is usually a sign that the plant is not growing vigorously; feeding and mulching will help.

GOOD COMPANIONS

Evergreen azaleas (1) are highly suitable for shaded scree areas and fit any oriental design. They associate well with dwarf pines and bamboos, such as *Pleioblastus viridistriatus* (2).

Add ground cover to evergreen *Rhododendron* 'Johanna' (3) (deep red flowers) with *Leucothoe fontanesiana* SCARLETTA 'Zeblid' (4) – its elegant green, red-tinged foliage turns bronze in winter.

Camellias

Camellias are woodland plants by origin, widespread across Asia from India through China to Japan and Korea. When introduced into England in 1740, they were cosseted and suffocated in the stifling 'stove houses' of the day, because they came from Asia. Eventually, gardeners realized that these were not delicate hothouse plants but sturdy creatures that were happiest in cold conservatories and orangeries. Today, they are plants for the garden, but their beginnings as pot subjects underline their suitability for growing in containers – which is much appreciated by those living on chalky soils.

Camellia 'Cornish Snow'

Camellias may flower only once a year, but they are very worthwhile plants to grow, particularly since their glorious blooms appear at a time when many shrubs are just sticks. The flowers are produced over a long period from winter into late spring. They will usually tolerate the cold as long as early sun does not damage the frozen blooms: to prevent this, choose a position that does not get morning sun. The foliage is perhaps the most handsome of the plain evergreens, and the growth habit is usually tidy and compact.

Gardens with acid soil and semi-shade welcome camellias in the open ground. They require no special treatment, just adequate watering, particularly when the plants are young.

There are numerous camellia varieties to choose from. It is a good idea to buy container-grown plants in flower, so you can see exactly what the flower looks like. Here are a few good ones:

Camellia 'Cornish Snow'♛ is a very early- and profuse-flowering camellia, with single white flowers and small leaves. It is a strong-growing bush, loose in habit, and eventually forms a large shrub; good for a woodland setting. Camellia 'Inspiration'♛ is a medium-sized shrub with neat foliage and large, semi-double, glowing rich pink flowers.

Camellia japonica cultivars are among the most popular of camellias. As a rule, they have broad, glossy dark green leaves and most have strong,

Camellia 'Inspiration'

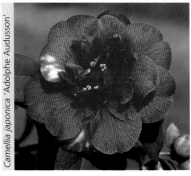

Camellia japonica 'Adolphe Audusson'

upright growth. *Camellia japonica* 'Adolphe Audusson'♛ has semi-double, blood-red flowers with showy yellow stamens; it is vigorous, compact and good for formal situations. 'Alba Plena'♛ has an upright, bushy habit and large, double white flowers, while 'Alba Simplex' bears single white flowers with prominent yellow stamens. 'Lavinia Maggi'♛ produces large white or pale pink, double flowers, with deep pink stripes. *Camellia japonica*

A mature camellia – exotic blooms in early spring.

'Masayoshi' ♥, sometimes known as 'Donckelaeri', is a bushy, compact shrub with large, semi-double, soft red flowers, marbled white; it is a good, hardy camellia and rarely shows any frost damage.

For general planting *Camellia* × *williamsii* is regarded as the best camellia. The parents are *Camellia japonica* and *Camellia saluensis*. The × *williamsii* cultivars are free-flowering, graceful shrubs. The foliage is similar to

Camellia japonica 'Alba Simplex'

Camellia japonica 'Masayoshi'

Camellia japonica 'Lavinia Maggi'

Camellia × williamsii 'Anticipation'

that of *Camellia japonica* but often the leaves are narrower and the growth habit is looser. In the majority of cases, the whole flower drops to the ground as it fades, instead of remaining dead on the plant; as the flowering season progresses, this proves to be a real bonus as far as the overall look of the shrub is concerned.

Good cultivars of *Camellia* × *williamsii* include the upright *Camellia* × *williamsii* 'Anticipation' ♥, which has large, peony-like blooms of deep pink. **'Debbie'** ♥ has similar flowers, of clear pink. **'Donation'** ♥, the best-known camellia of them all, has large, semi-double, orchid-pink blooms and is very free-flowering; it has an upright, but loose, habit, especially when young. **'Les Jury'** ♥ produces double red flowers on a compact, upright plant with bronze young foliage. **'Saint Ewe'** ♥ has single, cupped blooms and open, graceful growth. This is a very pretty plant that is not too overpowering and therefore mixes well with other shrubs.

CARING FOR CAMELLIAS

Watering is vital, ideally with rainwater; camellias will not tolerate drought. Let a camellia dry out during late summer and it will respond by dropping first its buds and then its leaves. Camellias require no pruning; if you must trim to shape, then do so immediately after the flowers have fallen.

The commonest problem with camellias is brown scale; this manifests itself as black sooty deposits on the leaves, taking away all vitality and gloss. The sooty mould is a secondary infection of the sticky excretion of scale insects, which are found lurking as tiny brown bumps along the underside of the leaf midrib. Because of their tough outer coat, and strong attachment to the leaf, they are difficult to dispose of. A modern systemic insecticide applied as a spray to the upper and lower surface of the foliage is the most effective solution. Apply at the first sign of scale.

Heathers

Although they are not great in stature, heathers contribute long-lasting flower colour as well as evergreen foliage that often changes colour and texture with the seasons. Versatile plants, they make excellent ground-cover shrubs and combine well with conifers for all-year-round effect.

Ericas and callunas

Daboecia cantabrica 'Bicolor'

Calluna vulgaris, the European heather or ling, is a hardy evergreen plant of heathland habitat. It requires lime-free soil, but is otherwise easy to grow, being tolerant of moist or quite dry conditions and shade, although it flowers better and retains a more compact habit in sun. There are many varieties, varying in flower colour, foliage colour, and height – from flat mats to low mounds (see box right, Attractive foliage and Outstanding flowers). The bud-blooming heathers (see box right, Decorative buds) are now very popular, not only for permanent planting but also as winter colour for containers. The flower buds are pointed and show colour from an early age; the habit is fine and graceful.

Daboecia cantabrica, Connemara heath or St Dabeoc's heath, is often also thought of as a heather or ling. An evergreen, it is closely related to *Erica* but likes the same growing conditions as *Calluna* (see box, Growing heathers). The large, round, bell-shaped, rose-purple flowers are produced from early summer to late autumn. There are also a number of good cultivars, including: *Daboecia cantabrica* 'Bicolor', with white and pink-purple flowers, some striped, often on the same spike; *Daboecia cantabrica* subsp. *scotica* 'Jack Drake', which has ruby red flowers; *Daboecia cantabrica* subsp. *scotica* 'Silverwells', with white flowers; *Daboecia cantabrica* subsp. *scotica* 'William Buchanan', a deep purple, and *Daboecia cantabrica* subsp. *scotica* 'Waley's Red', with flowers of a deep magenta.

For the lime-tolerant *Erica carnea*, *Erica* × *darleyensis* varieties, and the tree heaths, see pages 131–32.

GROWING HEATHERS

Groups of three or five small, pot-grown heathers produce better results than single, more mature plants. Heathers should be trimmed after flowering to promote bushy plants. Those that look good during winter because of their dried flowers, and those with coloured foliage, can be left until early spring before trimming. After trimming, mulch with moss peat or leaf mould. Although heathers cope with quite dry conditions, they dislike long periods of hot, dry weather. Watering is necessary to keep plants in good condition.

CALLUNA VULGARIS CULTIVARS

Below are some of the best *Calluna vulgaris* cultivars. All of them flower in summer, apart from the bud-bloomers ('Decorative buds'). Foliage is mid-green unless otherwise stated.

Attractive foliage
'Joy Vanstone' ♀: Golden foliage, rich orange in winter; pink flowers.
'Kerstin' ♀: Upright with dark mauve-grey foliage tipped with pale red and yellow tips in spring; mauve flowers.
'Robert Chapman' ♀: Golden foliage in spring turning to orange, then red; soft purple flowers.
'Spring Cream' ♀: Vigorous, with dark green foliage, tipped with cream in spring; long spikes of white flowers.
'Wickwar Flame' ♀: Bright orange and yellow summer foliage turning copper-gold in winter; mauve flowers.
'Winter Chocolate': Greenish-yellow foliage; lilac pink flowers.

Outstanding flowers
'Annemarie' ♀: Double flowers opening light purple, deepening to pink-purple; compact with dark green foliage.
'Beoley Gold' ♀: Strong-growing, white-flowered variety with yellow foliage.
'County Wicklow' ♀: Dwarf and spreading, with pale pink double flowers.
'Dark Beauty' ♀: Compact, with double, deep pink flowers darkening with age; dark green foliage.
'Darkness' ♀: Deep purple-pink flowers in short, dense spikes and dense bright green foliage.
'Gold Haze' ♀: Bright golden foliage with white flowers.
'H.E. Beale': Very long spikes of double bright pink flowers; good for cutting.
'Mair's Variety' ♀: Tall with white flowers, good for cutting.

Decorative buds
'Alexandra' ♀: Compact and upright with dark green foliage; red and white buds turn to deep crimson.
'Alicia' ♀: Similar in habit to 'Alexandra', with large white buds.
'Anette' ♀: Clear pink buds, good for cutting and drying.

Pieris

Also known as lily-of-the-valley bush, or flame of the forest, pieris were one of the most sought-after shrubs in the 1960s. Recently, they have become less popular, perhaps simply because they were such a garden centre spring staple for 20 years or more that we tired of them. Nonetheless, they are desirable evergreen shrubs, mostly of neat and graceful habit, and are due for a revival.

Pieris japonica 'Katsura'

Pieris japonica 'Valley Valentine'

Pieris 'Forest Flame'

The flower buds appear in the autumn in beaded sprays; those with red buds are particularly attractive during early winter and midwinter, the buds set against the dark green foliage. The white or pink flowers, which are similar in character to the bells of heather but are borne in sprays like lily-of-the-valley, open any time from early spring onwards. Many pieris have attractive bronze, salmon or red young growth, which is spectacular but soft and susceptible to frost damage. They are therefore best suited to a sheltered spot, ideally under trees, where the branches will cast dappled shade, and where other shrubs will protect them from scorching wind.

Pieris also make excellent subjects for pots. The more compact ones lend themselves to containers for semi-shade and shelter on the patio.

Pieris formosa 'Wakehurst' ♡ is strong and vigorous, with short, broad leaves and deep, bright red new growth; it has white flowers.

GOOD COMPANIONS

Pieris are superb planting companions for heaths and heathers. The glossy, evergreen foliage of the pieris is an excellent contrast to the fine, conifer-like foliage of the heathers.

PROTECTING NEW GROWTH

Do not be put off by the risk of frost damage to the new foliage of pieris; scorched foliage is easily pinched off the plant, and a new flush of growth soon follows. In very cold weather, the diligent gardener may protect the new growth from frost damage with horticultural fleece.

The cultivars of *Pieris japonica*, from Japan, eastern China and Taiwan, are the most popular pieris in gardens of today because of their hardiness and compact habit. *Pieris japonica* 'Debutante' ♡ is a mound-forming dwarf shrub that was collected in the wild on the Japanese island of Yaku-Shima as recently as 1980; this has short, white flower panicles carried in an upright manner. *Pieris japonica* 'Katsura', compact and good for pots, is grown mainly for the new foliage, which is deep red, turning chestnut-brown as it ages; the mature leaves are glossy dark green, the flowers white, the overall appearance rich and healthy. *Pieris japonica* 'Prelude' ♡ has a similar habit, with less shiny foliage that shows off white flowers to advantage.

Pieris japonica 'Variegata' is one of the oldest variegated forms, with dark green leaves with a narrow creamy margin and white flowers. It is smaller and more compact than some, so good for pots. *Pieris japonica* 'Little Heath' ♡ has dainty leaves, similarly variegated. It is not free-flowering in shade, but in a sunny position produces pretty pink buds that open to white flowers.

There are also many pink-flowered varieties. *Pieris japonica* 'Blush' ♡, *Pieris japonica* 'Flamingo' and *Pieris japonica* 'Valley Valentine' ♡ are all lovely in bud as well as flower, but perhaps lack the appealing simplicity of the white-flowered forms.

Pieris 'Forest Flame' ♡ is the best known of all the pieris; it is a hybrid between *Pieris japonica* and *Pieris formosa* 'Wakehurst'. This combines the hardiness of *Pieris japonica* with the brilliant red young growth that is so much a feature of its other parent. The white flowers are carried in large, drooping panicles; often branched, their mass weighs down the branches. *Pieris* 'Flaming Silver' ♡ is a sport of *Pieris* 'Forest Flame', with the same bright red new growth that develops a silvery white margin as it matures.

Other acid-loving plants

Gardeners on acid soils can choose from some of our most beautiful ornamental shrubs, quite apart from the obvious options of camellias, rhododendrons, heathers and pieris. Most are woodland plants by nature, so the dappled shade of trees is the perfect setting in a garden. Conifers are natural planting partners as they enjoy the same conditions and come into their own on acid soils.

Crinodendron hookerianum

Crinodendron hookerianum♀, from Chile, is not the hardiest of plants and is limited to milder areas. It needs partial shade, so suits an acid woodland garden or a sheltered wall facing the afternoon sun. Dark, raven-green glossy evergreen foliage, and an upright dense frame, provide the perfect backdrop for the waxy crimson, lantern-shaped flowers, which hang along the branches on long stalks in late spring.

Desfontainia spinosa♀, a native of South America, resembles a small-leaved holly when it is not in flower. Dark, spiny evergreen leaves provide the ideal setting for the tubular, scarlet, yellow-mouthed flowers that appear all over the bush in late summer. This is a slow-growing shrub that is not fully hardy and needs a sheltered site, ideally in dappled shade.

Originally hailing from Asia, from the Himalayas to Japan, **enkianthus** bring an oriental touch to the garden. They

flower in the late spring, when their drooping, porcelain-like flowers in the shape of Chinese lanterns hang along the branches. This is not their only season of glory: their autumn colour is some of the finest in the garden. *Enkianthus campanulatus*♀ is an upright-growing deciduous shrub, reaching a height of 2–3m (6–10ft). The branches are attractively tiered, light copper in colour, creating a pleasing winter frame even after the leaves have fallen. The cup-shaped flowers vary from pale yellow to rich bronze, and are attractively veined; they are long-lasting, as is the autumn display of yellow, copper and red. *Enkianthus cernuus* f.

Enkianthus campanulatus

rubens♀ is a slightly smaller shrub, with deep red, fringed flowers and rich reddish-purple autumn colour. Seen less commonly, *Enkianthus perulatus*♀ is a slower-growing and more compact deciduous shrub, slowly achieving 2m (6ft). The flowers are white and urn-shaped, like individual lily-of-the-valley flowers; the autumn colour is scarlet.

The narrow form of enkianthus makes them highly suitable to under-plant with acid-loving, ground-cover subjects such as gaultheria.

The **eucryphias** are magnificent evergreen and deciduous shrubs, mostly with a stately, upright habit and exquisite late-summer flowers, which are white with conspicuous stamens and resemble the blooms of a single philadelphus. Eucryphias like a sheltered position on a moist, lime-free soil but are not as lime-intolerant as most of the plants in this section. They prefer to have their roots shaded by nearby shrubs.

The most successful of the plants in this group is *Eucryphia glutinosa*♀. Although deciduous, this is still one of the most desirable forms. It is upright in habit, and has pretty, divided foliage that displays beautiful autumn colour;

Enkianthus perulatus

MORE PLANTS FOR ACID SOILS *Andromeda polifolia* 'Compacta' *(for wet soil)* • *Leucothoe fontanesiana* 'RAINBOW' •

Eucryphia lucida 'Pink Cloud'

Eucryphia glutinosa

Eucryphia × nymansensis 'Nymansay'

Fothergilla major

the blooms are 6cm (2½in) across and cover the plant in midsummer and late summer. *Eucryphia × intermedia* 'Rostrevor' ♥ is a fast-growing hybrid with evergreen simple and trifoliate leaves on the same plant. It forms a dark green, broad column, so is an excellent structure plant. The flowers, smaller than those of *Eucryphia glutinosa*, are white and fragrant and crowd the branches in late summer and early autumn. *Eucryphia lucida* is a native of Tasmania, with upright growth and small evergreen foliage. The fragrant flowers, which are produced earlier than most other eucryphias in early summer and midsummer, hang from the branches and are particularly pleasing on mature shrubs, where they can be viewed from below. *Eucryphia lucida* 'Pink Cloud' is a popular cultivar with pink-edged petals. *Eucryphia × nymansensis* 'Nymansay' ♥ is the most popular and reliable eucryphia, growing rapidly to form a dense column. Dark evergreen foliage is the perfect setting for the large white flowers that cover the branches in late summer and early autumn.

Fothergilla major ♥ is related to hamamelis (see page 181) but, unlike hamamelis, must have acid soil. Native to the south-eastern USA, it is a deciduous, slow-growing, horizontally branched shrub with hamamelis-like leaves. The creamy-white, bottlebrush flowers appear before the leaves in spring; the brilliant autumn colour is long-lasting. It is a good plant for a woodland garden.

Kalmia latifolia ♥, the calico bush, is a beautiful, rhododendron-like shrub, with glossy, mid-green foliage and clusters of pretty, bright pink flowers in early summer. The flower buds look like piped blobs of icing, and even the open, cup-shaped flowers seem to have an icing-sugar frosting. It does not do well in a container, so is rarely offered for sale in garden centres; it can also be a difficult shrub to get started, but it is glorious when established. It is wise to anchor even small plants after planting with a stake; the roots take time to establish. There are many cultivars on offer, although few have the charm and pretty disposition of the species. *Kalmia latifolia* 'Ostbo Red' is easier to grow and is more often available, but it is not such a pleasing colour and the foliage is smaller and darker.

Apart from the splendour of spring, the finest display of autumn colour is seen on plants that thrive on acid soils. **Nyssa**, one of the most spectacular shrubs for autumn display, will grow on acid soil. All **hamamelis** and *Acer palmatum*, both somewhat lime-tolerant, colour better on soils with low pH. Evergreens grown for autumn and winter foliage colour such as **leucothoe** (see page 173) are acid-lovers. See also Autumn on acid soil, page 172.

Kalmia latifolia

Lindera benzoin • Myrica gale • Nyssa sylvatica • Pseudowintera colorata • Styrax japonicus • Trochodendron aralioides •

Roses in mixed plantings

Roses are ideal for mixed plantings: they offer a spectacular range of flower form, colour and fragrance, and occasionally attractive foliage and hips, all of which complement a wide variety of other shrubs and herbaceous plants. Repeat-flowering varieties extend the season of interest, producing a good opening flush in early summer, a few blooms in midsummer and another good flush of flowers in late summer and early autumn.

Le Jardin d'Angelique, Normandy, France.

Beds planted exclusively with roses have been popular at times throughout history, latterly during the great rose boom of the 1960s. At that time, large numbers of Hybrid Tea and Floribunda rose varieties were introduced, and these frequently did not combine well with other subjects except for summer bedding. Twenty years later, the trend changed in favour of the softer shades of the old roses, which work better in borders combined with other plants. Below is a selection of the best roses to grow in mixed plantings.

OLD SHRUB ROSES

The old roses are garden classics, loved for the beauty of their flowers and for their exquisite fragrance; however, they often perform only once in the season. Old roses generally associate well with herbaceous plants and lavender.

The **Gallicas** are the oldest garden roses, descended from those grown by the Romans and Greeks. *Rosa gallica* **var. officinalis**♀, the apothecary's rose, produces tough, disease-resistant foliage on an upright, stocky shrub reaching 1m (3ft). It is highly fragrant, with semi-double blooms of light crimson, arranged around a bunch of golden stamens. The petals dry to ruby velvet, if gathered fresh, and retain their fragrance; they are wonderful for pot pourri. *Rosa gallica* 'Versicolor'♀ (Rosa mundi) is equally good and fragrant, but has pink flowers irregularly brushed and striped with crimson. (See Good Companions, opposite). Both

these roses are now officially classified as Species roses.

The **Albas** date back to the Middle Ages. They have a large, free-branching habit, and their disease-resistant, light blue-green foliage contributes as much as the flowers. They require little care, and grow on poor soil. *Rosa × alba* 'Alba Semiplena'♀ has large, flat, nearly single, soft white flowers, with yellow stamens, followed by red hips; the flowers have a fabulous fragrance, and the foliage is also very attractive. (See Good Companions, opposite). *Rosa* 'Maiden's Blush'♀ is vigorous with lovely grey-green foliage and flat, loosely double, blush-pink blooms with a delicious scent. It looks good planted with pale blue delphiniums.

The **Moss roses** were popular in Victorian times. These are lax shrub roses that produce flower buds with a moss-like growth on the sepals, conspicuous before the flower opens and a feature of the shrub. *Rosa* 'William Lobb'♀, old velvet moss, is richly fragrant, with dark crimson flowers fading to a softer grey-violet. (See Good Companions, opposite).

The **Hybrid Musks** were more popular before the advent of David

Rosa gallica var. officinalis

Rosa 'Felicia'

Austin's English roses (see page 115). Not unlike Floribunda roses, but with more grace, they are repeat-flowering, have a loose, open habit and are effective in mixed plantings. *Rosa* 'Buff Beauty' ♀ has full blooms of soft, warm apricot with a delicious Tea-rose scent, set against dark green foliage. *Rosa* 'Cornelia' ♀ is small, with large clusters of very fragrant, double, coppery pink flowers with richer tones, dark green foliage and vigorous growth. One of the best Hybrid Musks is the highly aromatic *Rosa* 'Felicia' ♀. A strong-growing and profuse-flowering rose, it is very pale pink around the edge of the blooms, darkening towards the centre.

There are a number of **large shrub roses** belonging to various groups that are used extensively in mixed plantings because of their attractive, informal, well-branched habit (see also page

Rosa 'Complicata'

Rosa glauca

Rosa × odorata 'Mutabilis'

144). One such example is the highly fragrant *Rosa* 'Complicata' ♀, which forms a large, healthy, resilient shrub that can be grown as a climber into a tree and is particularly suited to a country garden. The foliage is bright green and matt, and the large, single pink flowers are paler towards the central mass of golden stamens. Although it is officially classified as a Gallica owing to its parentage (probably a hybrid between *Rosa canina*, the British native dog rose, and a Gallica), it is quite different from other Gallicas in having large flowers and a lax, arching habit. *Rosa glauca* ♀ (*Rosa rubrifolia*) is a superb foliage plant, with fine arching growth and dark mahogany stems that carry blue-mauve foliage (grey-green in shade). The single flowers are clear pink, white in the centre, and followed by red hips. Officially, this is classified as a Species rose. *Rosa × odorata* 'Mutabilis' ♀ is a vigorous, slender, shrubby China rose with fine dark foliage, copper when young, and Tea-rose scented, long-flowering blooms. Slender buds open buff, the flowers turning to copper, through rose-pink to crimson. All colours appear on the plant at the same time, like a mass of delicate butterflies or a bouquet of sweet peas. Avoid planting in cold, exposed sites.

MODERN SHRUB ROSES

In the context of this book, the term 'modern shrub roses' covers a multitude of different shrubs, often hybrids between bush roses and stronger species or climbers. They are useful for their continuous flowering qualities and robust habits.

Rosa 'Ballerina' ♀, a Polyantha rose, has a graceful habit and produces large heads of dainty, small, pretty pink flowers; it is a wonderful shrub for mixed planting, as it flowers continuously and is lightly fragrant. *Rosa* 'The Fairy' ♀ , also a Polyantha rose, is a small, tough, disease-resistant shrub of spreading habit; it produces tiny pink pom-pom flowers in sprays. *Rosa* 'White Pet' ♀

GOOD COMPANIONS

Rosa gallica 'Versicolor' (Rosa mundi) ♀ (1), a pink rose brushed and striped with crimson, looks delightful with silver *Artemisia* 'Powis Castle' ♀ (2).

The white *Rosa × alba* 'Alba Semiplena' ♀ (3) combines beautifully with silver shrubs such as *Elaeagnus* 'Quicksilver' ♀ (4).

The tall, vigorous, dark crimson *Rosa* 'William Lobb' ♀ (5), old velvet moss, is a good choice for the back of a border with silver- or plum-foliage shrubs such as *Physocarpus opulifolius* 'Diabolo' ♀ (6).

has small white pom-pom flowers on a vigorous, spreading mound. Delicately fragrant, this is a deservedly popular Polyantha rose.

Rosa BONICA ('Meidomonac') ♛, a Shrub rose, produces sprays of double pink flowers, with a hint of salmon, and shiny green foliage; it has a spreading habit and is hardy and disease-resistant.

Rosa ICEBERG ('Korbin') ♛ is the definitive white Floribunda, with an upright bushy habit and ample clusters of pure white blooms and fresh green foliage; it is good in any context.

The **Rugosas** are the easiest roses to grow. They are very hardy, vigorous and disease-resistant, with fresh apple-green foliage, and they flower continuously through the season. Most produce excellent hips that last well into winter (see page 174). *Rosa rugosa* is a native of Japan, where it is found growing on sandy shores; it therefore suits the coast and light sandy soils, although it is tolerant of most conditions. *Rosa* 'Blanc Double de Coubert' ♛ has large fragrant, open, semi-double, tissue-paper white flowers that bloom from

Rosa 'Blanc Double de Coubert'
Rosa 'Roseraie de l'Haÿ'
Rosa BONICA
Rosa 'Ballerina'
Rosa ICEBERG

late spring on. *Rosa* 'Roseraie de l'Haÿ' ♛ has huge, wine-purple flowers with a delicious scent; it is almost a true old rose but requires less care.

Ground-cover roses are particularly useful on sunny banks of heavy soil. Some of these, including *Rosa* GROUSE ('Korimro') ♛ and *Rosa* PARTRIDGE ('Korweirim'), are very vigorous plants, producing long, trailing growth more like that of a climber. Others, such as the County Series roses, for example *Rosa* LANCASHIRE ('Korstesgli') ♛ and *Rosa* SUFFOLK ('Kormixal'), form low mounds and can be planted in groups or combined with other ground-cover shrubs. *Rosa* FLOWER CARPET WHITE ('Noaschnee') ♛ and *Rosa* PINK FLOWER CARPET ('Noatraum') ♛ are particularly useful, as they are reliable and disease-resistant. They produce fresh green foliage and semi-double flowers, in white or bright pink respectively, throughout summer. Their wide use in amenity planting endorses their ease of cultivation. Since the colours are somewhat hard, it is best diluted with plenty of foliage planting. Other colours are available, but they do not perform as well as these two shrubs.

GROWING ROSES

Many gardeners are put off roses, believing that they require a lot of care and they are a problem when it comes to pests and diseases. Disease is best controlled at the time of purchase by buying resistant varieties. Most roses benefit from annual feeding and like a good fertile soil, although some thrive on poor soil; it is all a matter of selecting the right kinds for the site.

Situation: Roses do not need full sun but they will not thrive in shade. Do not attempt to grow them on sites that do not get a few hours of sunshine each day – there are other shrubs that will be more successful. Roses are good on heavy clay soils, because of their fertility; they are not the first choice for peaty acid soils, and need plenty of organic matter on thin, sandy soils.

Pruning: Repeat-flowering shrub roses should be cut back by between one-third and two-thirds in winter. Remember: the harder you cut, the more vigorous the growth and the later the flowers. Non-repeat-flowering varieties should be lightly pruned in winter by no more than one-third. Tidying the shrub, by removing weak and diseased growth and old flowerheads, is all that is required. In the case of mature shrub roses, whether repeat- or non-repeat-flowering, you may need to cut dead or old stems to the ground periodically. When pruning David Austin's English roses, leave all the twiggy branches on the plant for more prolific flowering.

Feeding: Roses like plenty of nutrients and moisture. Apply a balanced rose feed, containing magnesium and iron, in early spring and again in midsummer after the first flush of flowers. Mulch in spring with garden compost or well-rotted manure.

Pests and diseases: A healthy rose is a disease-resistant rose, so feeding is the first step in control. Where diseases such as black spot, mildew and rust are a problem, prevention is better than cure; start spraying when the first foliage appears and continue at fortnightly intervals throughout the season. If insect pests are not a problem, use only a fungicide. A combined insecticide and fungicide in the absence of pests is not only wasteful but may result in resistance to its effects at a later date. The foliage of *Rosa rugosa* can be sensitive to some sprays, so take care when spraying neighbouring roses with pesticides. If deer are a problem, grow climbers and ramblers only.

DAVID AUSTIN'S ENGLISH ROSES

The rose breeder David Austin brought the beauty, fragrance and fine qualities of the old roses together with the repeat-flowering qualities and more manageable growth habits of modern varieties. It is no wonder, therefore, that his English roses have become the most popular roses in our gardens.

Because of his dedicated and extensive breeding programme, David Austin is constantly introducing new English roses with refined qualities. Many of the original favourites have been superseded by new varieties with more compact habit, superior disease resistance, longer flowering season and better weather resistance, to name but a few improvements. Because English roses are grown in many countries with varying climates, different varieties excel in local conditions.

Rosa ABRAHAM DARBY ('Auscot') is a bushy shrub producing sumptuously huge blooms of pink, apricot and yellow throughout the summer; it has a delicious fruity fragrance. *Rosa* COTTAGE ROSE ('Ausglisten') retains the character of a true old rose, and is one of the best in the group; its cupped flowers of warm pink, with a delicate fragrance, bloom freely throughout the summer.

An excellent choice for the back of the border, *Rosa* CROWN PRINCESS MARGARETA ('Auswinter') is a tall, arching shrub, with apricot-orange blooms that have a strong, fruity fragrance. Another tall, vigorous rose for the back of the border is *Rosa* GERTRUDE JEKYLL ('Ausbord') ♥, whose delicate buds open to large, flat, fragrant, rich pink blooms (see Good Companions, right). *Rosa* GOLDEN CELEBRATION ('Ausgold') ♥ is one of the largest, most flamboyant English roses. It has giant, cup-shaped, rich golden-yellow blooms, which are

Rosa ABRAHAM DARBY / *Rosa* WINCHESTER CATHEDRAL / *Rosa* CROWN PRINCESS MARGARETA / *Rosa* GRACE / *Rosa* GRAHAM THOMAS

wonderfully fragrant and very reliable. The superb *Rosa* GRACE ('Auskeppy') produces deliciously scented, pretty, many-petalled flowers of pure apricot, paler at the edges and deeper in the centre, and fresh, apple-green foliage; it has a tidy growth habit and is a good alternative to *Rosa* 'Buff Beauty'.

One of the most widely planted roses in this group is *Rosa* GRAHAM THOMAS ('Ausmas') ♥, with upright habit and golden-yellow blooms. However, a better yellow for the English climate is *Rosa* MOLINEUX ('Ausmol') ♥. Another popular and reliable shrub is *Rosa* MARY ROSE ('Ausmary') ♥, which has

exquisite rose-pink, loose-petalled, lightly fragrant blooms. For a small garden, the dark-leaved *Rosa* NOBLE ANTONY ('Ausway'), with its scented magenta-crimson flowers, is a good choice. (See Good Companions, below.)

Rosa THE MAYFLOWER ('Austilly') is a small, compact, disease-resistant shrub whose deep, rose-pink, old rose blooms have a strong fragrance; it is rarely without flowers throughout the summer. *Rosa* WINCHESTER CATHEDRAL ('Auscat') is the white form of Rosa MARY ROSE ('Ausmary'). A beautiful, reliable shrub, it has delicate fragrant flowers of porcelain white.

GOOD COMPANIONS

Plant *Rosa* GERTRUDE JEKYLL ('Ausbord') ♥ (1) with *Clematis* PETIT FAUCON ('Evisix') ♥ (2); the dark purple-blue velvet clematis blooms complement and extend the flowering season of the rich pink rose.

The magenta-crimson *Rosa* NOBLE ANTONY ('Ausway') ♥ (3) planted with *Nepeta* × *faassenii* ♥ (4) is a stunning sight.

Walls and fences

Walls and fences, used to mark a boundary or to divide a garden into different areas, are the ideal way to add vertical interest to the garden. They may be attractive features in their own right, but most importantly they provide a backdrop for planting, presenting the opportunity for growing a variety of shrubs, thus contributing to diversity in the garden without demanding intensive maintenance.

A wall or fence, however tall, provides shelter – and the perfect opportunity to grow plants that may not survive in an open area of the garden. Wind chill, in the depths of winter, vastly reduces temperature, but the barrier of a wall or fence lessens the effect of the wind. Walls offer more protection and shelter than fences, and therefore tend to support more tender subjects.

Climbers are the obvious choice for a vertical surface. However, there are also many woody shrubs that benefit from the additional support provided by a solid structure. Tall, leggy shrubs can be used to fill the higher space, while those that need shelter, and some support, can grow beneath them.

CHOOSING PLANTS

Before selecting plants for a wall or fence, establish the aspect. In the northern hemisphere, south (that is, south-facing) and west (west-facing) walls are warmest, the ideal spot for sun lovers. South-facing walls can get very hot in midsummer, so choose plants that will relish the heat. North (north-facing) and east (east-facing) walls are colder and shadier; high north walls get little sun. Shady walls are not necessarily a disadvantage – you just have to choose the right plants.

When selecting climbers and wall shrubs, always choose plants that are

Trained pyracantha at Bourton House Garden, Gloucestershire.

appropriate to the height of the support. You can train most plants, but a vigorous wall shrub, such as *Cytisus battandieri* ♀ or *Fremontodendron californicum*, is not suitable for a 2m (6ft) fence. When the plant gets too large, and you cut it back, it will just grow all the more vigorously above the top of the support, leaving bare branches against the fence that you wanted to cover.

If you are lucky enough to have beautiful old stone or brick walls, you should choose plants that complement rather than conceal them. Colour is an important consideration: a dark red flowering shrub may be appealing but it can be lost against a dark red brick wall. More likely, you are faced with bare fencing all around the edge of your plot. In this case, you are looking for shrubs that will cover the fence well.

ESTABLISHING PLANTS

Walls and fences are often dry at the base, partly because the height of the structure keeps off some of the rainfall. Also, many walls are constructed in such a way that rainwater drains away from them, which creates even drier conditions. Adding plenty of organic matter at the time of planting helps to retain moisture. Do not plant too close to a wall – ideally, at least 60cm (2ft) away. This gives the shrub space to develop, and is also important in terms of support. Shrubs that have been planted too close to a wall tend to grow away from it, and eventually overbalance. Water regularly until the plants are fully established. Covering the ground with a layer of gravel will keep the roots cool and also conserve moisture.

MORE SHRUBS FOR SHADY WALLS *Azara microphylla* • *Cotoneaster franchetii* • *Cotoneaster horizontalis* •

SHADY WALLS AND FENCES OVER 3m (10ft)

Drimys winteri ♀ (winter's bark) is a tall shrub with large shiny, leathery leaves. Clusters of fragrant white flowers are produced at the ends of the branches in late spring. Mature specimens develop very attractive bark. A native of Chile, winter's bark can grow as a freestanding shrub or small tree in a sheltered woodland garden in mild localities. It is, however, ideal for a sheltered, lightly shaded wall in a position where it can grow freely without its potential height being inhibited.

Drimys winteri

Eriobotrya japonica

Eriobotrya japonica ♀ (loquat) is the most striking evergreen that can be grown outdoors in the British Isles. The large leathery, corrugated leaves, felty brown underneath and silvery green above, can easily reach 30cm (12in) long. As the plant matures, the branches take an angular stance, giving the plant a wonderful stature. A member of the rose family, it may produce clusters of hawthorn-like flowers during winter and spring, but

normally only when the previous summer has been a hot one; the yellow, edible fruits are rarely produced in cooler climates. Eriobotrya always creates a dramatic effect and is superb against an old stone or brick wall. It is also stunning with modern architecture.

Garrya elliptica can easily achieve 3m (10ft) or more on a high, shady wall. Its top-heavy habit shows off the silver-grey catkins that hang from the branches in winter. *Garrya elliptica* 'James Roof' ♀ is the best variety, with exceptionally long silver tassels. At other times of the year, the garryas' dark green foliage can look sombre, so plant them in front of silver-variegated ivy or with *Euonymus fortunei* 'Silver Queen' ♀ at their feet. (See also pages 89, 180, 182.)

Itea ilicifolia ♀ is a member of the escallonia family, but in appearance it resembles a holly. The dark green, softly spiny leaves are carried on lax branches. In late summer the shrub is draped with soft green, catkin-like flowers, reminiscent of a garrya. It is a fairly hardy and easy shrub to grow and suits shady town gardens. Underplant it with ferns and pulmonarias.

If you have acid soil, both *Eucryphia* × *nymansensis* and *Crinodendron hookerianum* ♀ (see pages 110, 111) make superb wall shrubs for high walls

Itea ilicifolia

out of direct sun. Both enjoy sheltered woodland conditions, so adequate moisture at the roots is essential if these plants are to thrive.

SHADY WALLS AND FENCES UNDER 3m (10ft)

Camellias (see pages 106–107) are ideal for lightly shaded walls, provided they do not get the morning sun. Some of the less hardy varieties of tall, spreading habit can be trained onto the wall.

Chaenomeles

Camellia sasanqua is a beautiful plant for a sheltered wall in a mild district. Very early blooming, from midwinter onwards, it has smaller, more delicate flowers than most camellias, with the added attraction of a delightful scent. It may need protection when young, but mature plants withstand most winters.

Chaenomeles (see page 130) are ideal grown against a low wall or·fence, either trained in to wires or allowed to lean against a wall for support. The plant's spreading growth quickly makes an impact and, if the right variety is chosen to show up against the background, it will make a striking splash of colour from early spring for several weeks. The glossy foliage is good throughout the summer.

For a mound-forming evergreen at the base of a shaded wall, look no further than *Choisya ternata* ♀, the

× *Fatshedera lizei* • *Forsythia suspensa* • *Kerria japonica* • *Mahonia japonica* • *Photinia* × *fraseri* 'Red Robin' •

Mexican orange blossom. Although it blooms more prolifically when given some sun, it will flower in shade; the foliage is always excellent (see page 33).

Most *Euonymus fortunei* varieties readily climb if grown against a wall; some reach a height of 2–3m (6–10ft). They provide a bushier alternative to ivy for low, shady walls and fences and thrive in the most difficult conditions. *Euonymus fortunei* 'Emerald 'n' Gold' ♀ is particularly happy against a wall, as is *Euonymus fortunei* 'Silver Queen' ♀. The latter can be slow to start, but once it gets going will lighten

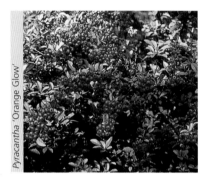

Pyracantha 'Orange Glow'

the darkest corner with its wonderful creamy-variegated foliage. *Euonymus japonicus* varieties are excellent grown in sun or shade, in towns or by the sea.

Pyracanthas (see also page 174) are among the most popular wall shrubs, with shiny, evergreen foliage, white flowers in spring and colourful red or orange berries in autumn and winter. Either grow them as loose, trimmed shrubs against a wall or fence, or train them as espaliers on wires. The latter can be very effective in formal situations and town gardens, particularly as an attractive backdrop for other trimmed and trained evergreens. Pyracanthas cope with most soils and situations, and are particularly useful for a draughty, shady wall where other plants fail. Trim the current season's growth back to the berry clusters in late summer to show off the ripening fruit. Pyracanthas are also suitable for walls over 3m (10ft).

SUNNY WALLS AND FENCES OVER 3m (10ft)

Cytisus battandieri ♀, the Moroccan broom or pineapple broom, is a very tall shrub with grey-green stems and silky grey leaves that resemble those of a large clover. The flowers appear in early summer – cones of rich yellow, tightly packed, pea-like blooms, which are deliciously pineapple-scented. A native of Morocco, it thrives in full sun and poor, dry soil. It will grow in the open but has a very gangly habit and often grows too tall and overbalances. It is

Cytisus battandieri

excellent against a wall, but it must be a high one as it can quickly reach the top of a two-storey house. Seed-raised plants can take time to flower. The cultivar *Cytisus battandieri* 'Yellow Tail' ♀, with exceptionally large flower spikes, is reliable and free-flowering. Never prune later than summer, as you reduce the chance of flowers the following year; hard pruning stimulates very vigorous growth.

Fremontodendron californicum is another extremely tall-growing shrub, suitable only for growing against a high, sunny wall. It has grey, scaly stems and leathery leaves, which are also covered with fine, waxy scales (these protect the plant against desiccation). Spectacularly large rich-yellow flowers are produced throughout summer and autumn. Fremontodendron likes full sun and good drainage, and is excellent on chalk. It is a good choice for the sunny

gable end of a house. Anchor it to the wall carefully with vine-eyes and wires; otherwise, as it matures, it can fall away. *Fremontodendron* 'California Glory' ♀ is popular for its exceptional flowers and free-flowering quality. Fremontodendrons are not plants for cold areas. Take care when cutting back or pruning, as the waxy scales can irritate the eyes and nose.

Ceanothus are natural choices for high sunny walls. Because of their bushy habit, they are suitable for growing against a tall fence where they are able to grow on above their support. Choose

Fremontodendron 'California Glory'

the tall evergreen varieties. They grow quickly and make an impact in the first season after planting. They cope well with hot, dry situations. Most are good on chalk.

Ceanothus do not need to be trained, but if you wish to do so, choose a dense, compact grower, such as *Ceanothus* 'Puget Blue' ♀, and start training in the early stages of growth. The best varieties for growing against walls and fences are the following: *Ceanothus* 'Concha' ♀, *Ceanothus griseus* var. *horizontalis* 'Yankee Point' and *Ceanothus* 'Italian Skies'. (See also page 140.)

Ficus carica, the fig, is a handsome, fast-growing shrub with impact. It needs plenty of space. The plant has special character from an early age, and increases greatly in size when the large, distinctive leaves unfurl in spring. Named varieties such as *Ficus carica* 'Brown Turkey' ♀ reliably produce a

MORE SHRUBS FOR SUNNY WALLS *Abeliophyllum distichum* • *Callistemon citrinus* 'Splendens' •

Ficus carica 'Brown Turkey'

Abutilon megapotamicum

Clianthus puniceus

Carpenteria californica

Coronilla valentina subsp. glauca 'Variegata'

good crop of fruit as they mature. Figs are more manageable when their roots are restricted, so plant them in a large container sunk in the ground. In colder districts, remove all embryo fruits that have overwintered in late winter. The fruits that are produced from then on should grow to maturity the same autumn. Figs are also suitable for high walls and fences in shade.

SUNNY WALLS AND FENCES UNDER 3m (10ft)

Abutilon megapotamicum ♀ has more lax growth than most other abutilons, so is ideally suited to growing as a wall shrub. The fine arching green stems, with narrow, maple-like leaves, need wires for support; the plant grows quickly in a sheltered situation. The flowers hang from the branches like tiny lanterns in summer and autumn: orange-red calyces with a soft yellow skirt of petals and purple anthers. *Abutilon megapotamicum* 'Variegatum' has pretty, yellow-mottled foliage, but is less vigorous than *Abutilon megapotamicum*. *Abutilon* × *milleri* ♀ is more upright in growth habit, with broader leaves. The flowers are bell-shaped and orange with crimson stamens. It flowers continuously through summer and autumn and, in a favoured location, at any time of the year. *Abutilon* × *milleri* 'Variegatum' has yellow mottled foliage.

Carpenteria californica ♀, another beautiful Californian evergreen shrub, is reminiscent of a large, graceful cistus. Narrow, mid-green leaves are well spaced on upright branches. The spectacular flowers are produced in loose upright clusters at the end of the branches in midsummer. The individual blooms are clear and white, with golden stamens. It does not need a wall for support, but grows best at the base of a sunny wall, where it will reach 3m (10ft). *Carpenteria californica* 'Bodnant' is an excellent form, with larger flowers.

Clianthus puniceus ♀, the parrot's bill or lobster's claw, is an exotic member of the pea family, a native of New Zealand. It is semi-evergreen and strong-growing but will thrive outside only in mild areas. The growth habit is sprawling; the leaves, with many leaflets, are like those of a large vetch. The flowers are spectacular, red and claw-like with black eyes, carried in hanging clusters in early summer. *Clianthus puniceus* 'Albus' ♀ has white flowers.

Another member of the pea family, *Coronilla valentina* subsp. *glauca*, is also a good choice for the base of a sunny wall or fence. The blue-green foliage is the perfect background to the rich yellow flowers produced year-round, but mostly in spring. *Coronilla valentina* subsp. *glauca* 'Citrina' ♀ bears pale yellow flowers; *Coronilla valentina* subsp. *glauca* 'Variegata' has pretty, cream-variegated foliage.

Any of the Mediterranean shrubs that feature on pages 82–87 will be happy against a low wall or fence in full sun. The taller, more tender varieties of cistus, such as **Cistus** × **cyprius** var. **ellipticus** f. **bicolor** 'Elma' ♀, and the upright varieties of rosemary, are natural choices.

Magnolia grandiflora at Lanhydrock, Cornwall

Grevillea rosmarinifolia • *Luma apiculata* • *Magnolia grandiflora* • *Punica granatum* • *Sophora* SUN KING ('Hilsop') •

Hedges and screens

Berberis thunbergii f. atropurpurea 'Atropurpurea Nana' at The Garden House, Devon.

Hedges and screens are used for the demarcation and fortification of boundaries, the division of larger plots into smaller areas, for privacy, and for concealing unsightly views. Sadly, their decorative contribution is often of secondary importance to their physical presence. Before planting a hedge or screen, there are some important points to consider, any of which, if overlooked, can be the beginning of major problems in the future.

Hedges can serve many very useful purposes, and can be highly decorative, but an important point to bear in mind is that they take up room, and when a shrub gains height it also gains width. Go out and measure the width of a hedge that you are considering planting before you decide – it is quite likely that the hedge that you thought was 30cm (12in) wide is in fact over 1m (3ft) wide. A large evergreen hedge, such as *Prunus laurocerasus*, can easily take 2m (6ft) or more off your garden. In addition, hedges are greedy; they take a lot of water and

nutrients from the soil, so in most cases you will not be able to plant close to them; access for maintenance is also needed. Hedges need cutting at least once a year, and a tall, broad hedge is a challenge to cut and may require power equipment; you may have to hire a professional contractor. You need to ask yourself if that is something you are prepared to take on before you get planting.

In a small garden, if privacy is the main objective and you don't have space for a hedge, instead use a fence, trellis or wire screen, clad with climbers

or wall shrubs (see pages 116–19); these are more economical on space and may give a more instant effect than a hedge.

Where space is not an issue, large evergreen shrubs can be used as screens, to block out unsightly views and to provide privacy (see page 123). Alternatively, consider providing more foreground interest to draw attention away from the object to be screened. Light deciduous trees, such as birch and sorbus, are often more effective in hiding a neighbouring building than a solid evergreen hedge.

TIPS FOR CHOOSING HEDGING PLANTS

- Any shrub that has dense, branched growth and short internodes (the lengths of stem between the leaves) should be suitable for a hedge.

- Ideally, select an evergreen or, in the case of deciduous shrubs, a plant with enough twiggy growth to maintain the structure when the leaves have fallen.

- A shrub that responds to pruning by producing new side shoots from young or old wood is usually good.

- Choose a shrub that retains good leaf cover to ground level and does not go leggy with age.

- Do not skimp on cost. A hedge is a long-term investment, and it is much better to get it right than compromise on cost.

- Plant the best stock you can find. Healthy, vigorous plants will give you the effect you are looking for more quickly.

- Bigger is not always better. Large plants may take longer to establish and grow on.

GROWING HEDGES

When planting a hedge, you need to pay as much attention to preparation and planting technique as you would with other shrubs (see pages 16–17).

Start to clip the hedge from an early age, and long before it gets to the eventual height you want it to be. The best time is just after a flush of growth. Most are clipped after the spring flush, and again in late summer, to allow time for some new growth before the onset of winter. Some hedges will need more frequent clipping, for example the shrubby honeysuckle *Lonicera nitida*; others, such as beech (*Fagus sylvatica*), are cut only once a year, in late summer.

PLANTS FOR HEDGES OVER 1m (3ft) HIGH *Griselinia littoralis* • *Hydrangea macrophylla* • *Hypericum* 'Hidcote' •

DECIDUOUS HEDGES

Some of the most popular hedging shrubs lose their leaves in winter. *Fagus sylvatica* ♀ (beech) and *Fagus sylvatica* **Atropurpurea Group** (purple beech), although deciduous, are unusual in holding on to their coppery brown dry leaves through the winter, dropping them only when the lime-green new leaves open in spring. Beeches make a wonderful formal hedge up to 5m (16ft) high, and if well maintained will enhance any garden; a good choice on chalk.

Carpinus betulus ♀, the hornbeam, is similar to beech in leaf, but without the coppery twigs and retention of

Fagus sylvatica varieties

HEDGE PLANTING DISTANCE (HPD)

For deciduous hedges in towns and evergreen hedges, plants are usually container-grown and may be planted any time. Approximate hedge planting distances (HPD) are given in the plant descriptions. The distances are taken from the centre of one plant to the centre of the next.

Beech, hornbeam and deciduous hedges in rural areas are normally planted as young, bare-root plants (whips) during the dormant season. Plant in two parallel rows. The rows should be 30–45cm (12–18in) apart, and in each row the plants should be 90cm (3ft) apart. Make a zigzag with the plants.

Hydrangea macrophylla

leaves in winter. It is faster to grow and establish, and thrives on any site or soil.

Hydrangea macrophylla cultivars make good hedges, often by the coast.

Hedges for rural areas

Hedges in country gardens need careful consideration, as cultivated plants can look out of place. A hedge of indigenous plants is more in keeping, and can give interest year-round, as well as providing a haven for wildlife and nesting birds.

Crataegus monogyna (hawthorn or quickthorn) is the most popular choice, as it is easy to establish, fast-growing, and tolerant of the most severe, indiscriminate trimming. *Prunus spinosa* (blackthorn or sloe) is not the most attractive plant when it comes to foliage, but it forms an impenetrable barrier and is lovely when smothered with white blossom in spring.

A backbone of hawthorns and blackthorns can be supplemented with the following plants: *Acer campestre* ♀ (field maple), *Cornus mas* ♀ (Cornelian cherry), *Corylus avellana* (hazel), *Euonymus europaeus* (spindle), *Lonicera periclymenum* (honeysuckle), *Rosa canina* (dog rose) and *Rosa rubiginosa* (sweet briar), perhaps with the evergreen *Ilex aquifolium* ♀ (holly).

Hedges for town gardens

In early spring hedges of *Forsythia* × *intermedia* set our streets ablaze with yellow. If trimmed after flowering and

again in late summer to shorten the new wood, it can be kept as a formal hedge, solid with flowers in spring. The foliage is healthy and trouble-free; the bare stems are a pleasing tan in winter (HPD – see box, left – 75cm/30in).

Prunus × *cistena* ♀ is a light, pretty hedge, up to 1.5m (5ft) in height, with wine-red leaves on dark stems and dark-eyed, white flowers in spring; it looks good with low palisade fencing (HPD 60cm/2ft).

Many roses make excellent informal hedges for town gardens, including *Rosa gallica* var. *officinalis*, but *Rosa rugosa* is the best of them all. It is disease-free, with fresh green foliage and strong, upright, spiny stems, which make an attractive and effective barrier. Its flowering period is relatively long, the blooms are fragrant and weather-resistant, and the hips that follow the flowers keep the hedge looking good into the autumn. This hedging plant is particularly useful as it tolerates poor, sandy soils (HPD 75cm/30in).

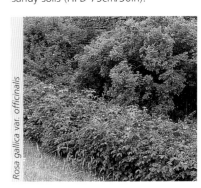

Rosa gallica var. *officinalis*

Prunus cerasifera 'Nigra' • *Prunus lusitanica* • *Pyracantha* 'Teton' • *Rhododendron ponticum* • *Rosa* 'Felicia' •

EVERGREEN HEDGES

Aucuba japonica is an extremely versatile plant. With its large glossy leaves and dense habit, it makes a good alternative to the cherry laurel (*Prunus laurocerasus*, see opposite) for a hedge to 2m (6ft). Particularly useful in shade, the light variegation is excellent to brighten a dark corner. It is very useful where traffic pollution is a problem (HPD 90cm/3ft). For sunnier positions, and on the coast, the best choice for a glossy

Buxus sempervirens

Aucuba japonica

Euonymus japonicus 'Aureus'

yellow-variegated hedge is *Euonymus japonicus* 'Aureus'. Although it is liable to revert, the appearance of plain green and yellow areas in the hedge is not unattractive (HPD 75cm/30in).

Box hedges offer the widest possible diversity in scale of any hedging plant, from *Buxus sempervirens* ♀, common box, which can easily make a broad hedge of 3m (10ft) or more high (HPD 60cm/2ft), to *Buxus sempervirens* 'Suffruticosa' ♀, used to create dwarf edges in parterres and around flower beds (HPD 25cm/10in). Box hedges can be formal or informal; where space permits, the 'cloud' hedge, a high,

A 'cloud' hedge

wide hedge clipped in an undulating, irregular shape, is increasingly popular.

Elaeagnus × *ebbingei* tends to be more commonly used as a screening shrub than a hedge, but it is an excellent choice for either use and suits exposed coastal conditions as well as urban sites. The silvery-green foliage is attractive throughout the year, and the inconspicuous fragrant flowers are a delight in early winter (HPD 90cm/3ft).

Escallonias are among the finest hedging plants for mild coastal situations. They are drought-tolerant plants, with dark green, very glossy leaves and lovely pink or red flowers in summer. Trim in late summer to remove old flower stems or, if heavier pruning is required, do this in early spring before the flush of new spring growth. Good varieties for hedges up to 2m (6ft) high include *Escallonia* 'Red Hedger', a medium to large shrub with crimson flowers; it is wind-resistant and responds well to trimming, and *Escallonia rubra*

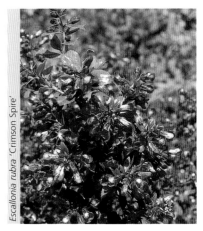

Escallonia rubra 'Crimson Spire'

'Crimson Spire' ♀, a strong and upright shrub with large leaves and bright crimson flowers. For taller hedges or screens, recommended shrubs include *Escallonia rubra* 'Ingramii', with rose-pink flowers and large aromatic leaves, and the wind-resistant *Escallonia rubra* var. *macrantha*, with large glossy leaves and pinkish-red flowers (all escallonia HPD 90cm/3ft).

Ligustrum ovalifolium, the oval-leaf privet, was once the most widely planted hedging shrub, but has been less so in recent years. It is very tolerant of just about any soil or aspect, and is evergreen except in cold, exposed situations. Easy to cut, it regenerates even after rough treatment. Old privet hedges can be susceptible to honey fungus (*Armillaria*); this is one of the factors that have led to the demise of their popularity (HPD 60cm/2ft).

Lonicera nitida, with its straight twigs and tiny evergreen leaves, has long been used for hedging, and offers a faster-growing alternative to box. With regular clipping, it can be kept as a very narrow hedge, so is less greedy of space than many other evergreen shrubs (HPD 60cm/2ft).

Olearia × *haastii* is a rounded, medium-sized shrub with small leathery, oval leaves, which are white and felty beneath, and fragrant white, daisy-like flowers in summer. It makes a good

PLANTS FOR HEDGES UNDER 1m (3ft) HIGH *Berberis atropurpurea* 'Nana' • *Lavandula angustifolia* 'Hidcote' •

LOW DECORATIVE EVERGREEN HEDGES

Some hedges are used within the structure of the garden to emphasize paths, to demarcate areas, or simply as decorative divisions. Box is a natural choice (see opposite), but there are other dwarf evergreens that do the job just as well. *Ilex crenata* 'Convexa' ♀ is a superb alternative to box, and *Viburnum davidii* ♀ is an unusual bold-leaved alternative. Many of the small-leaved hebes also make excellent low decorative hedges, for example *Hebe albicans* ♀.

In sunny, dry situations, choose the aromatics: lavenders, upright varieties of rosemary, and even sage all make excellent low hedges. The finest choice of all for a low hedge in sun is *Santolina chamaecyparissus* ♀ (cotton lavender). Its dense silver foliage will stay looking good all year round if clipped regularly and if not allowed to flower (HPD 50cm/18in). (See also pages 78–79.)

All screening shrubs should be thought of in conjunction with other good screening plants such as **bamboos** and **conifers**. A combination of the different types of screening plants perhaps offers the most pleasing solution for a garden boundary, and is the most natural continuation of the planting within the garden.

Berberis julianae

hedge, up to 2m (6ft) high, for both town and coastal gardens (HPD 75cm/30in).

Olearia macrodonta ♀ (New Zealand holly) is one of the best screening and hedging plants for exposed coastal gardens. It is a strong-growing, pliable shrub, which quickly attains 2m (6ft), eventually 3m (10ft). The sage-green, holly-like leaves, with silvery undersides, provide a soft background for pastel colours. The shrub produces heads of fragrant, daisy-like flowers in early summer (HPD 90cm/3ft).

Photinia × *fraseri* is unbeatable for wherever a bright, cheerful effect is

Olearia macrodonta

Photinia × *fraseri*

needed, and where the hedge will be a feature rather than a background. It is unmissable in spring, when the new shoots of bright scarlet appear like flames all over the top and sides of the hedge. Photinia also makes an excellent large screening shrub (HPD 90cm/3ft). (See also page 34.)

Prunus laurocerasus ♀ (the cherry laurel) is one of the most popular of all hedging plants, and forms an excellent background to other shrubs. Large dark, glossy leaves and a dense habit create a good-looking hedge, particularly useful where a tall, solid barrier is required. Its biggest disadvantage is disfigurement of the leaves when cutting. For this reason, trim the shrub early in the season, so that the new flush of growth quickly covers the partially cut leaves. *Prunus laurocerasus* ETNA ('Anbri') has copper new growth (HPD 90cm/3ft).

Evergreen screening shrubs

Most of the structure shrubs mentioned in the first section of this book (pages 29–37) make excellent screening shrubs, both for privacy and for shelter. A mixed screen of large evergreens provides a low-maintenance barrier, and is effective when it comes to absorbing noise and dust and providing shelter from wind; however, you need to allow plenty of space for them.

Some of the large-growing berberis are particularly worthy of mention here for their tough character and ability to overcome the most hostile conditions: *Berberis darwinii* ♀, with its fine dark green foliage and stunning orange flowers in spring, makes a good hedge. If left unclipped, it is also an excellent evergreen screening shrub. *Berberis julianae* ♀ is one of the best. Dense and spiny, with clusters of prickly dark green leaves, which are copper-tinted when young, it forms a large, round bush up to 3m (10ft). Dense clusters of scented yellow flowers appear in the leaf axils in spring. The elegant *Berberis* × *stenophylla* ♀, with its graceful arching stems and dark leaves, is a haze of soft orange flowers in late spring.

TALL, RELATIVELY FAST-GROWING SCREENING SHRUBS

Elaeagnus × *ebbingei* (see opposite)
Griselinia littoralis ♀ (see page 33)
Laurus nobilis ♀ (see page 31)
Photinia × *fraseri* (see left)
Pittosporum tenuifolium ♀ (see page 34)
Prunus laurocerasus ♀ (see left)

Lonicera nitida 'Baggesen's Gold' • *Osmanthus* × *burkwoodii* • *Osmanthus heterophyllus* • *Rosa gallica* var. *officinalis* •

Pots and containers

As gardens have become smaller, patios, decks and courtyards have become an essential element of the 'outdoor room', and container planting now plays a key role in garden design. Pots allow plants to be positioned where cultivation in the ground would be difficult or even impossible: perhaps where there is no soil, or because certain plants do not grow on your soil type. They also offer ultimate flexibility, as they can be moved around at any time.

The union of plant and pot is an art form in its own right. Choose containers carefully. Appropriateness is the most important factor: a well-chosen pot looks at home in the garden all year round, so beware of bright-coloured glazes in traditional settings. Think big. Small pots and large plants are a poor combination, from an aesthetic and a practical point of view, as they dry out quickly and can blow over. If plants are going to need repotting, choose a container with a shape that allows this: avoid those that narrow at the neck.

Shrubs are a natural choice. Flowering time and colour are secondary to foliage form, plant habit and character.

BOLD EVERGREENS

Architectural evergreens lend themselves to pots, ideally positioned so they make a statement. **Cordylines** and **palms** are excellent for hot, sunny situations and near the house. They suit pots in outdoor living areas but elsewhere in traditional gardens may be out of place. The light, spiky forms create foreground height and interest. (See pages 55, 66, 87.)

Fatsia japonica ♥ makes an impact wherever it is sited, and can be cut back hard if it grows too large; it is excellent for a shady position against a wall that gets no sun, or to add a tropical feel to a shady courtyard. (See pages 35–36.)

Cordyline 'Torbay Dazzler'

Osmanthus also make excellent plants for pots: their compact growth and tolerance of difficult growing conditions are a success story for any container gardener. *Osmanthus heterophyllus* 'Goshiki', with mottled yellow-bronze and green foliage, is bright and cheerful without being brash: it looks lovely in a dark green, glazed pot. The silver-edged leaves of *Osmanthus heterophyllus* 'Variegatus' ♥ are holly-like, bright and clean, and it is a good choice for a stone container, perhaps set against grey paving. (See page 63.)

Phormiums provide spiky form and colour contrast. Some of the exotically colourful ones are not the hardiest, but are excellent for containers in sunny, sheltered positions. *Phormium* 'Maori

---

CLIPPED SHAPES

Clipped shapes suit formal situations, and can bring structure to informal schemes when used as exclamation marks. The choice of container is particularly important: the shape of the container must balance that of the plant.

Buxus sempervirens 'Suffruticosa'

Clipped box (*Buxus*) and bay (*Laurus nobilis*) are traditional choices. The privet *Ligustrum delavayanum* is a faster-growing and less expensive option, often sold as shaped balls, cones and standards. It is dense and dark, with tiny dark green leaves and clusters of white flowers, followed by black berries. Since it dislikes cold, it is not suitable for exposed gardens, where it loses its leaves.

Lavender and rosemary offer softer alternatives for sunny, Mediterranean schemes, and both look good in terracotta. Regular clipping is the secret of success. If you are growing lavender as a shaped plant, do not allow it to flower; if it is cut back hard, patches of bare wood will be the result.

MORE SHRUBS FOR CONTAINERS *Convolvulus cneorum* • *Euonymus japonicus* 'Microphyllus Aureovariegatus' • *Hebe* 'Red Edge' • *Hebe* 'Pascal' • *Hydrangea macrophylla* 'Ami Pasquier' • *Ilex crenata* 'Convexa' •

Fatsia japonica and Pittosporum tenuifolium 'Tom Thumb'

Chief' bears upright leaves variegated with scarlet, crimson and bronze. For a real statement, choose the much larger *Phormium tenax* Purpureum Group ♀, with large, upright, bronze-purple leaves and architectural flower stems. (See also pages 55, 66.)

Smaller pittosporums are excellent in pots. *Pittosporum tenuifolium* 'Gold Star' is a good plant for containers; the growth is upright and compact and the leaves are yellow-green. *Pittosporum tenuifolium* 'Tom Thumb' ♀ is also a natural choice, with shiny, deep purple foliage in winter, and bright green spring growth. It looks good in any situation, and the unusual colour suits unusual containers: lead, steel, purple glazes and slate-grey all look superb with this plant. (See pages 64; 49.)

Viburnum davidii ♀ bears such strongly formed leaves they look as if they could have been fired with the pot; they complement strong oriental glazes. (See page 37.)

ACID-LOVING PLANTS

Containers are the obvious solution for those who wish to grow ericaceous plants but have alkaline soil. Most acid-loving plants are suitable for growing in pots. (See pages 100–111.)

Camellias are excellent in containers. Growth habits vary according to variety, from lax to compact, and they can create a formal or informal effect depending on the choice of plant. The glossy evergreen foliage looks good all year round, and the early spring blooms are a delight. Site

---

CULTIVATION TIPS

• Always use a properly formulated potting compost. Loam-based composts are best for permanent plantings. Use loam-based ericaceous compost for lime-haters.

• Good drainage is essential. A generous layer of broken crocks in the bottom of the pot is ideal. Also, add extra grit to the compost for plants requiring good drainage.

• Raise pots slightly to facilitate drainage and prevent earthworms making their home in the pot; beneficial in the open ground, they cause problems in containers.

• Pots need watering, even in winter. Dehydration can cause bud drop on early bloomers such as camellias.

• Rather than repotting larger subjects, scrape away the top 2cm (¾in) of compost and refresh with new loam-based compost and a handful of controlled-release fertilizer.

---

pots where the early morning sun cannot damage frozen blooms.

Some good camellia varieties with a particularly compact habit include *Camellia japonica* cultivars, especially 'Mercury' ♀, with large, semi-double, deep crimson flowers; and 'Nuccio's Gem' ♀, which has superb, double white blooms. **Camellia × williamsii** cultivars are also good, including 'Jury's Yellow' ♀, for creamy flowers with a creamy-yellow centre; and 'Donation', which, though vigorous and speading, is free-flowering and highly suitable .

Variegated pieris are excellent in pots, particularly *Pieris japonica* 'Little Heath' ♀; it has pretty, silver-variegated leaves, pinkish new growth and flower buds, and a light, frothy habit.

The more compact rhododendrons are good choices for larger containers. *Rhododendron* 'Nancy Evans' ♀ is a favourite, with apricot-yellow blooms in loose clusters and healthy dark green foliage; the habit is relatively loose.

Deciduous **azaleas** give good autumn colour, interesting branch framework and glorious flowers in late spring, offering a changing picture throughout the year. One of the loveliest is rose-pink *Rhododendron* 'Irene Koster' ♀, which is also fragrant and colours well in autumn. Evergreen azaleas, with a short season of interest, are not ideal for pots.

Rhododendron 'Nancy Evans'

125

SEASONS

There is no such thing as a dead season in the garden; every season has its particular character. The fresh, cool blooms of early spring blossom into the riotous colour of late spring, an exuberance that softens into the richness of summer. Autumn brings the warm shades of changing leaves, illuminated with the sapphire and amber of late flowers. The hardy, fragile beauty of winter draws one year to a close, yet it also heralds the start of the next. When it comes to the interest and colour provided by hardy shrubs, the seasons never end.

RIGHT: *Hamamelis* × *intermedia* 'Pallida'

Early spring

As the days start to lengthen, temperatures rise and some of our loveliest plants awaken, particularly the deciduous shrubs that produce their flowers on bare stems, before the leaves appear. Early spring is an unpredictable time of year, as a flower's life can be cut short by a spell of overly warm or cold weather. However, it is perhaps precisely that fragile quality, combined with the expectation of treats to come, that makes this season all the more magical.

Whichever season we may favour, all of us are moved by the awakening of spring. As we venture out for the first gardening forays of the year, it is uplifting to see how quickly the garden changes, often daily, as buds burst open and shoots and flowers emerge. The unpredictability of the weather in spring creates variability in flowering season: warm weather can entice the buds of deciduous shrubs to open overnight, while a cold snap keeps them tightly closed. When the season starts late, early- and late-spring flowers perform together in one great spring celebration.

Some winter-flowering shrubs are still blooming in early spring: *Daphne odora* goes on producing its deliciously fragrant flowers, and *Viburnum tinus* is still performing, its blooms resembling powdery elderflowers against the dark green foliage. Around now, the white candles of *Prunus laurocerasus* (cherry laurel) appear along the branches and the flesh-pink buds of fragrant, spring-flowering evergreen **viburnums** are

Fresh young foliage and fragile flowers herald the start of spring.

ready to open when warmed by the late-spring sun. **Rosemary** also delights, with its sky-blue blooms among spiky branches of soft grey-green.

Spring gardens on acid soil certainly steal the variety show at this time. **Camellias** (see pages 106–107, 125) are stars of early spring – rich, gorgeous and delicate, they are great favourites. The blooms and new growth of **pieris** (see page 109), one of the most spectacular displays of this season, joins the early **rhododendrons** (see pages 101–105). **Magnolias** (see Plant Profile, pages

134–35) begin a lavish but fragile display that can last for weeks or may be extinguished overnight by severe frost.

Plants that flower early are often of woodland origin; they need to perform before the leaf canopy robs them of sunlight and water. The bulbs hold centre stage and, as one leading light is extinguished, another takes over. Spring hues are generally pale and fresh, but with some highlights; vivid yellow **forsythias**, for example, compete with the early pink **cherries** (*Prunus*) and **flowering currants** (*Ribes*).

USEFUL BULBS TO UNDERPLANT SHRUBS

Anemone blanda ♔
Crocus chrysanthus 'Snow Bunting' ♔
Crocus tommasinianus 'Whitewell Purple'
Muscari armeniacum ♔
Ornithogalum nutans ♔
Scilla siberica ♔

Amelanchier lamarckii

Azara lanceolata

Amelanchiers, or snowy mespilus, are lovely light, frothy deciduous shrubs or small trees, with delicate sprays of white starry flowers in early spring. There are a number of good species, most of which prefer acid soil and a moist site. They are accommodating plants, and are frequently seen growing happily on chalk, although they are not generally recommended for shallow chalk soils.

Amelanchier canadensis is an upright suckering shrub with erect sprays of flowers; an extremely hardy, easy-to-grow plant, it is ideal on wet ground. *Amelanchier lamarckii*♀, often incorrectly sold as *Amelanchier canadensis*, is a broad, spreading shrub or small tree, with arching sprays of white flowers produced at the same time as the delicate, coppery new leaves emerge; the leaves colour brilliantly in autumn on acid soil. It is an easy plant to grow. (See Good Companions, right.) *Amelanchier laevis* is similar, and is also often confused with *Amelanchier canadensis*. *Amelanchier* x *grandiflora* 'Ballerina'♀ is an excellent selection, with a more vigorous habit and slightly larger flowers.

Azaras are light, pretty evergreens from South America. All species need a sheltered spot, and are ideal grown against a wall. The yellow, mimosa-like flowers are fragrant and produced in early spring. For mild areas, *Azara lanceolata* is a lovely tall, elegantly flowering shrub with attractive pointed, bright green leaves and yellow-orange flowers garlanded along the branches. *Azara microphylla*♀ is hardier, with small leaves, which resemble shiny box foliage but are larger, spread along fine, arching branches. The tiny yellow flowers are scented and appear on the underside of the stems. This is a lovely shrub to bring height and lightness to plantings with gold-variegated evergreens.

Berberis are extremely useful and resilient plants: they tolerate poor soil, they are resistant to wildlife damage and pests and diseases, and they do not require any pruning; with their prickly foliage, they are an excellent choice for security planting. Some berberis are deciduous, while others are evergreen. The evergreen berberis are transformed when their bright, jewel-like flowers appear against the solid background of their rigid foliage in early spring. Those with unattractive growth are ideal to plant alongside ceanothus, where the latter are useful in providing foliage bulk and continuity of flower. All the berberis described below are evergreen.

Berberis darwinii♀ is commonly thought of as a hedging plant, but it is really one of the most wonderful evergreen flowering shrubs. It is an excellent structure plant, with its shiny, prickly, dark green foliage. In early and mid-spring, the blood-orange buds appear, opening into drooping clusters of exquisite, pure orange flowers. A good screening and security plant, it is glorious with springtime blues such as pulmonarias, scillas and muscari, and will keep flowering into bluebell time. (See Good Companions, below.)

GOOD COMPANIONS

Amelanchier lamarckii♀ (1) is pretty underplanted with *Pulmonaria* 'Roy Davidson' (2).

The orange and blue flowers of *Berberis darwinii*♀ (3) and *Muscari armeniacum*♀ are a striking combination (4).

Berberis 'Goldilocks' is a vigorous large evergreen, with spiny dark green leaves and yellow flowers in large, hanging clusters. For larger flowers and an upright form, the evergreen *Berberis linearifolia* (*Berberis trigona*) is an excellent choice. Although it has an ungainly habit, it is exquisite in flower, with gem-like blooms hanging from the branches in early spring, straight stems and narrow, spiny leaves. *Berberis linearifolia* 'Jewel' bears scarlet buds opening to bright orange; *Berberis linearifolia* 'Orange King' has large, rich orange flowers.

Berberis × *lologensis* is a naturally occurring hybrid with variable, spiny leaves. An excellent cultivar is *Berberis* × *lologensis* 'Apricot Queen'♀, with attractive rich apricot-orange flowers.

Berberis × *stenophylla*♀ is an underrated large shrub. Few evergreens have the grace of its arching branches of small, dark green leaves; in early spring, it is covered with soft orange-yellow flowers. There are many cultivars, including the dwarf *Berberis* × *stenophylla* 'Corallina Compacta'♀ which rarely grows over 30cm (12in).

Berberis × lologensis 'Apricot Queen'

Berberis stenophylla

Chaenomeles, known as japonica or ornamental quince, and previously called *Cydonia*, is easy to grow on any soil. *Chaenomeles speciosa* and *Chaenomeles* × *superba* are delightful early-flowering deciduous shrubs that can be grown in the open or against a wall. Their angular twigs and exquisite blossoms, which open on the bare wood, bring an oriental air to the garden. All have an open, spreading habit, so they are not for tidy gardeners.

Chaenomeles speciosa 'Geisha Girl'♀ bears lovely double, rich peach flowers. Another beautiful cultivar is *Chaenomeles speciosa* 'Moerloosei'♀ ('Apple Blossom'), with delicate pink and white blooms in abundant clusters. *Chaenomeles speciosa* 'Nivalis' is an exquisite white variant, with large flowers. However, white is not the best choice, as the flowers are spoiled in a poor spring.

PLANTING AND PRUNING CHAENOMELES

Chaenomeles need careful siting. Plant dark colours against a light background, otherwise the flowers are lost without the backdrop of leaves to show them off. The lighter red varieties are wasted against brick walls. If pruning is required, then do this straight after flowering. This is important for those trained against walls; in other situations, if a lot of pruning and control are required perhaps this is the wrong shrub.

Chaenomeles × *superba* 'Crimson and Gold'♀, one of the most popular of the ornamental quinces, has crimson blooms with wonderful gold anthers. Where pink is preferred, *Chaenomeles* × *superba* 'Pink Lady'♀ produces beautiful deep pink buds opening to clear pink flowers. *Chaenomeles* × *superba* 'Rowallane'♀ is a glorious dark red colour.

Chaenomeles × superba 'Pink Lady'

Chaenomeles speciosa 'Moerloosei'

Corylopsis pauciflora

Corylopsis are delightful deciduous shrubs that are closely related to witch hazel (*Hamamelis*) (see page 181).

Corylopsis pauciflora♀ is a small, spreading shrub that can eventually reach 2m (6ft), although such large ones are rare. The tiny, hazel-like leaves, which are pink when young, normally appear after the flowers. The blooms are extremely pale, primrose-yellow, and borne in hanging, translucent clusters; they are cowslip-scented. Normally a low shrub in gardens, it is important to underplant this with evergreen ground cover, such as a small dark-leaved ivy, to show off the flowers to best effect. *Corylopsis pauciflora* needs neutral to acid soil.

The considerably larger *Corylopsis sinensis* var. *sinensis* 'Spring Purple' is upright in habit, with larger hanging clusters of pale lemon-yellow flowers. The new foliage is plum-purple before it turns to green in summer. The leaves emerge at the same time as the flowers, creating a pleasing effect. *Corylopsis sinensis* var. *sinensis* 'Spring Purple' prefers neutral to acid soil, although it will also grow successfully on good soil over chalk.

Winter-flowering heathers (*Erica*) are evergreen and a valuable source of very early colour. Most varieties, such as *Erica carnea* and *Erica × darleyensis*, are in full flower in late winter and early spring. They suit alpine planting and gravel areas and are a wonderful choice for early containers. On a larger scale, the tree heaths come into their own from early spring onwards (see page 132). The cultivars of *Erica carnea*, *Erica × darleyensis* and *Erica erigena* are all lime-tolerant, but none are at their best on shallow chalk.

Erica carnea originates in the Alps of central Europe, so it is extremely hardy. As the most widely planted of all small shrubs, it has many cultivars; most grow into dense hummocks, about 15cm (6in) high, smothered in flowers. In early winter, the swelling buds are cheery and full of promise; the flowers start to open in early spring. The bristling mats of pink, white and deep purple-red are at their best with the early spring bulbs, such as crocus, scillas and dwarf irises. Some cultivars have bright gold foliage.

Some of the best *Erica carnea* cultivars are as follows: the slow-growing 'Ann Sparkes' ♛, with golden foliage, bronze-tinged in winter, and purple flowers; 'Foxhollow' ♛, which has yellow-green foliage, tinged red in winter, and pale pink flowers; 'Golden Starlet' ♛, with lime-yellow foliage and white flowers; 'Myretoun Ruby' ♛, which produces dark green foliage and deep pink flowers; the popular 'Pink Spangles' ♛, with its profusion of pink

Erica carnea 'Myretoun Ruby'

Erica carnea 'Foxhollow'

Erica × darleyensis 'Arthur Johnson'

Erica × darleyensis 'White Perfection'

flowers; 'Rosalie' ♛, with bronze-green foliage and pink flowers; the strong, trailing 'Springwood White' ♛, the best white-flowering heath, with bright green foliage (see Good Companions, page 133); 'Vivellii' ♛, with bronze-red winter foliage and vivid carmine flowers.

Erica × darleyensis, a hybrid between *Erica carnea* and *Erica erigena*, is a taller-growing shrub than *Erica carnea*. The garden cultivars of *Erica × darleyensis* have inherited this taller character, growing to about 25–30cm (10–12in) high, and producing an altogether bigger, looser-growing plant – one that is useful to bring colour at a greater height to mixed plantings of heathers, conifers and dwarf evergreens.

Some of the best *Erica × darleyensis* cultivars include: 'Arthur Johnson' ♛, with tall stems bearing long sprays of magenta flowers, excellent for cutting; 'J.W. Porter' ♛, with pink flowers, dark green foliage and reddish new shoots in spring; 'Kramer's Rote' ♛, with bronze-green foliage and magenta flowers; 'Silberschmelze', with dark green leaves tinged red in winter and sweetly scented white flowers over a long period; 'White Perfection' ♛, with bright green foliage and white flowers.

Erica erigena is another lime-tolerant winter-flowering heath that forms a dense, small to medium-sized shrub. 'Golden Lady' ♛ has golden-yellow foliage and white flowers, and is a good, compact alternative to a dwarf yellow conifer, growing to some 30cm (12in) high; 'Irish Dusk' ♛ is one of the best-known and loveliest of the winter-flowering heathers, growing to about 50cm (18in) high with healthy dark foliage and salmon-pink flowers, an unusual shade for a heather; 'W.T. Rackliff' ♛ is extremely dense and compact, and makes an excellent low hedge up to 75cm (30in) in height; it produces dark green foliage and white flowers with brown anthers.

PLANTING AND CARING FOR WINTER HEATHERS

Winter-flowering heathers are offered for sale in several sizes. Where space permits, buy smaller plants and plant one variety in groups of three or five – this will produce a better overall effect. Follow the general advice on planting on pages 16–19.

Ericas should be trimmed after flowering to remove faded blooms and promote bushy growth; use hand shears or sheep shears for this. Mulch after trimming with organic, lime-free compost and slow-release, lime-free fertilizer.

Erica arborea var. 'Alpina'

Forsythia × intermedia

The **tree heaths (*Erica*)** are lovely large evergreen shrubs with fragrant, pollen-laden flowers that are a delight in early spring. All those described here are recommended for neutral to acid soils; however, they will grow on clay soils and are not totally intolerant of lime. Tree heaths associate well with rocks and stone, and tolerate dry conditions. They can be hard-pruned back to the old wood after they have finished flowering, in order to promote long, straight, floriferous growth.

Erica arborea is an attractive, soft evergreen that in mixed plantings offers a contrast in foliage form; it is also a good shrub to cut for floral decoration. It can grow to 5m (16ft), but is normally seen at half this height in gardens. A mountain plant, it produces extremely hard root nodules, which are fire-resistant and used to make briar pipes. The medium-sized *Erica arborea* var. *alpina* ♈ is more commonly grown and is hardier and more upright. Foliage is bright green and flowers are white with brown anthers. (See also page 41.)

Another very hardy, medium-sized tree heath is *Erica australis* ♈, the Spanish heath, which is later-flowering and has rosy-purple flowers.

Erica lusitanica ♈, the Portuguese heath, is earlier-flowering than *Erica arborea* and continues over a long period from winter into spring. The fine, plume-like green stems are crowded with white tubular flowers.

Erica × *veitchii* is a hybrid between *Erica arborea* and *Erica lusitanica*. The cultivar *Erica* × *veitchii* 'Exeter' ♈ is a superb shrub, growing to around 2m (6ft). The foliage is bright green and the flowers white and fragrant, produced profusely in early spring. Although not good on cold, exposed sites it is an easy shrub to grow. *Erica* × *veitchii* 'Gold Tips' ♈ has bright yellow young foliage, becoming dark green.

Like them or loathe them, there is no denying the impact of **forsythias** in our gardens in early spring – the eruption of bright yellow seems to be everywhere. Members of the olive family, forsythias arrived in our gardens in the mid-19th

century. Since then, they have been widely planted as freestanding shrubs, wall shrubs and hedges. They are very easy to grow, and are a good choice on difficult sites and poor soil.

Forsythias look good planted as a screen or structure plant at the back of a border, where the mid-green leaves will provide a good summer backdrop. To extend the season of interest, plant *Clematis viticella* or perennial sweet peas to grow through the forsythia's branches. Forsythias should be pruned after flowering, cutting out some of the flowered wood, allowing vigorous new shoots to develop. Most of the commonly grown varieties root easily from cuttings.

Forsythia suspensa was the earliest forsythia to be introduced. A rambling, deciduous shrub, it is a lovely plant to grow over a wall, where it will grow to 3m (10ft) or more. The yellow flowers are well spaced, dainty and graceful in appearance. Hybridized with *Forsythia viridissima*, a late-flowering variety with an upright habit, *Forsythia suspensa* has

Forsythia × intermedia WEEKEND ('Courtalyn')

Kerria japonica 'Golden Guinea'

Kerria japonica 'Pleniflora'

given rise to *Forsythia × intermedia*, a vigorous, medium to large, upright deciduous shrub, our familiar garden forsythia. There are numerous cultivars: *Forsythia × intermedia* 'Lynwood Variety' ♀, the best and most widely planted, has broader petals and profuse flowers; *Forsythia × intermedia* 'Spectabilis', one of the original selections, is very free-flowering – the whole shrub is a mass of yellow when in flower (see Good Companions, right); *Forsythia × intermedia* WEEK-END ('Courtalyn') ♀ is a mutation of *Forsythia × intermedia* 'Lynwood Variety', it retains its excellent qualities but has a smaller, more compact habit and so is better for small gardens.

Other colourful deciduous shrubs that dominate the garden in early spring are kerrias, which have been resident in our gardens since Victorian times. Their upright green stems form a clump, arching when mature. They look good in winter, and the mid-green, well-spaced foliage has a light, airy quality. Kerrias are excellent flowering shrubs for shade and thrive on any soil. They are lovely when used to lighten dark evergreens, and to plant against green ivy if grown against a wall. Prune by cutting out selected older stems after the flowers have faded in order to keep the plant open and graceful and to prevent unattractive, bushy growth. *Kerria japonica*, which is not often seen, has single, pale orange buttercup flowers all along the branches in spring. *Kerria japonica* 'Golden Guinea' ♀ is the widely grown cultivar, with large, single flowers. However, it is *Kerria japonica* 'Pleniflora' ♀ ('Flore Pleno') that is the favourite: the double, pale orange flowers are scattered, like loose pom-poms, over the plant from early spring onwards; it is more upright than the single-flowered form.

Osmanthus delavayi ♀ is a very beautiful, small evergreen shrub of rigid but graceful growth. The stiff, arching stems are tan-brown with small, matt, extremely dark green leaves. It is slow-growing, but from an early age produces exquisite, tiny white tubular flowers, which are wonderfully fragrant. For those gardeners who look forward to the scent of jasmine, this is an early fillip. This shrub is easy to grow, and tolerant of most soils and some shade. Plant near to a path, where the fragrance can be enjoyed. (See Good Companions, below.)

GOOD COMPANIONS

The white flowers of *Erica carnea* 'Springwood White' ♀ (1) complement the white bark of *Betula utilis* var. *jacquemontii* 'Silver Shadow' ♀ (2).

Let a *Clematis* 'Kermesina' (3) scramble through *Forsythia × intermedia* 'Spectabilis' (4) to extend its season of interest.

Osmanthus delavayi ♀ (5) is delightful with the pure white, fragile *Pulmonaria* 'Sissinghurst White' ♀ (6) and a small-leaved, silver-variegated ivy such as *Hedera helix* 'Glacier' ♀.

Magnolias

Perhaps the most magnificent of all hardy trees and shrubs, magnolias are a stunning sight in full bloom in early spring. Their flowers, almost other-worldly in appearance, seem all the more miraculous when they burst from bare branches, before the leaves appear.

Magnolias are mostly deciduous, although there are also evergreen varieties (all the magnolias described and illustrated on these pages are deciduous). They are easy to grow and are tolerant of heavy clay, and although they prefer acid to neutral soils, most are reasonably tolerant of lime. Many magnolias are too large for the average garden, and some tree magnolias can take several years to flower, so you need to select the species carefully. When planting, consider the ultimate size and shape of the shrub; most magnolias are beautiful specimen shrubs that need space around them and are not seen at their best overcrowded by surrounding planting. The early-flowering magnolias are susceptible to frost and wind damage to the flowers, so choose a sheltered site to avoid damage.

Magnolias need no pruning. If pruning is done to control size, care is needed not to ruin the shape. The larger magnolias, such as *Magnolia* × *soulangeana*, respond to pruning by producing vigorous upright growth, which is not desirable; selective removal of whole branches is better than cutting half-way.

Magnolia liliiflora 'Nigra' ♀ is a good choice for a small garden. It forms a wide, spreading, large shrub, usually about 2m (6ft) high, but can grow to 4m (13ft). The flowers are carried upright on the branches, like waxy, deep purple candles, retaining their slender tulip form as they open to reveal a creamy white interior. They are produced from early spring through to summer, never with the same profusion as some magnolias but with supreme sophistication.

Magnolia × *loebneri* is a hybrid of *Magnolia stellata* with *Magnolia kobus*. It is usually grown as a large shrub

A *Magnolia stellata*'s starry white flowers sing in the spring sunshine.

and flowers freely from an early age. The flowers are fragrant, with long, strap-like petals, and a more open and starry bloom than *Magnolia stellata*. *Magnolia* × *loebneri* is the best choice for chalk.

Among the most well known of all magnolias is the wide-spreading *Magnolia* × *soulangeana*, known as the tulip tree. A heart-stopper in bloom, this glorious shrub produces a profusion of large, pointed buds that open to goblet-shaped, creamy white blooms, flushed pink at the base. The flowers start to appear before the leaves, but continue until the young lime-green leaves start to unfurl. This magnolia copes with atmospheric pollution and so is often seen in urban situations. There are many cultivars, all of which flower at an early age.

Unless you have plenty of space, the best magnolia is undoubtedly *Magnolia stellata* ♀. A slow-growing shrub from Japan, it forms a compact, broad shrub, eventually reaching 3m (10ft) high. The winter buds on the bare branches are grey and hairy, resembling large pussy willows, and are an attractive feature in their own right. The fragrant white flowers, which are borne profusely in early spring, have narrow petals, rounded at the tips, and are sweetly scented; they are much more weather-resistant than most magnolias. There are many cultivars.

Magnolia 'Heaven Scent' ♀ is a large shrub or small tree, with highly fragrant, narrow, cup-shaped flowers with pink petals flushed darker at the base, and a darker stripe on the back of the petals.

Magnolia × *loebneri* 'Leonard Messel' ♀ (left) is the best-known × *loebneri* cultivar, with pale lilac-pink flowers. Upright in growth and open in habit, it is suitable for mixed plantings and combines well with other shrubs in a large border. The cultivar 'Merrill' has white flowers.

Magnolia stellata 'Centennial' is a superb cultivar, vigorous and free-flowering, with many-petalled flowers that are incurved at the petal tips.

OTHER GOOD MAGNOLIAS

Magnolia × *soulangeana* 'Lennei' ♀ has large leaves and flowers, rose-purple outside and creamy-white stained pink-purple inside.

Magnolia × *soulangeana* 'Alba' has scented, pure white flowers, without the pinkish flush of other soulangeanas.

Magnolia × *soulangeana* 'Brozzonii' ♀ bears large white flowers, shaded purple at the base, and blooms later than other soulangeanas.

Magnolia × *soulangeana* 'Rustica Rubra' ♀ is vigorous, with cup-shaped, rich rosy-red flowers.

Magnolia stellata 'Rosea' bears white, pink-flushed flowers.

 Magnolia stellata 'Waterlily' ♀ (left) has large white, waterlily-like flowers.

Magnolia 'Susan' ♀ is an upright, medium-sized shrub, ideal for the smaller garden. The elegant, candle-like flowers are dark red-purple in bud, opening to soft reddish purple. It is lovely planted with honesty (*Lunaria annua*).

Magnolia × *soulangeana* is the most popular magnolia of them all.

Prunus incisa 'Kojo-no-mai'

The **bush cherries (*Prunus*)** offer a spectacular display when in flower in early spring, although the season is generally short-lived. They are plants for large gardens, where they need not occupy key positions. All of the bush cherries described here are deciduous.

Prunus cerasifera 'Nigra' ♔ and *Prunus cerasifera* 'Pissardii' are often seen as trees, but both can be grown as large shrubs. Delightful in early spring, when they explode in a cloud of tiny, single blossoms of pale pink or white, they are useful for their deep plum foliage that follows later on dark twigs. However, they are rarely perfect, owing to shot-hole virus and fungal disease, so they are not plants that should be viewed at close quarters.

As a shrub, the purple-leaf sand cherry, *Prunus × cistena* ♔, is a better choice. Light and dainty in growth, it is upright in habit, slowly reaching 2m (6ft). Red-purple leaves on burgundy stems follow the shower of white flowers in spring. It is an excellent, if rarely used, hedging plant.

Prunus incisa 'Kojo-no-mai' is an exquisite variety of the Fuji cherry, and flowers for longer than the other bush cherries. It is a small, slow-growing shrub, with wonderful zig-zag twigs and a bonsai-like habit. In early spring, the branches are loaded with pretty, delicate pale pink, paper-thin blossoms (the Japanese name means 'flight of butterflies', an appropriate description). The leaves colour beautifully in autumn. This is a delightful plant to grow in a gravel garden with scree and rocks, or is perfect for a pot on the terrace. It grows on any soil, in sun or semi-shade.

The other bush cherries are certainly not as popular as they were. All have their problems in terms of disease, often suffering from die-back caused by

Prunus glandulosa 'Alba Plena'

bacterial canker. Warm, wet winters do not help these conditions, and their decline in popularity is partially due to climate change. Although the early spring flowers are delightful, the shrubs are not attractive for the rest of the year and do need some attention.

Prunus glandulosa is a small shrub, with slender, erect stems carrying flowers before the leaves in early spring. It needs a warm, sunny position and is lovely for cutting for the house; it has long been cultivated in Japan for just this purpose. *Prunus glandulosa* 'Alba Plena' has large, double white flowers; those of *Prunus glandulosa* 'Sinensis' are also double, but bright pink. Both can be forced into flower early, and may be grown in a pot to be brought into a cool conservatory in midwinter for early flowers.

Prunus triloba 'Multiplex' is a larger version of *Prunus glandulosa*, with double, sugar-pink flowers like crumpled balls of tissue paper along the branches in early spring. The dark twigs are the ideal setting for the perfectly spaced blooms, and a plant in flower is a real delight. The flowering shoots should be carefully pruned once the flowers have faded, to encourage strong, straight stems to flower the following year.

Prunus triloba 'Multiplex'

Ribes sanguineum 'Koja'

Sophora microphylla SUN KING ('Hilsop')

Another good, reliable deciduous spring favourite is the flowering currant *Ribes sanguineum*. It is extremely useful in the garden as it is medium-sized, up to 2m (6ft), very hardy, easy to grow and is tolerant of any conditions. Perhaps cast aside because of its ubiquitous planting in the middle of the last century, it has a certain nostalgic charm as a reminder of 1960s gardens. Poor positioning often spoils this plant: it is nearly always teamed up with forsythia, and the two are not a pleasant combination. The currant fragrance of the foliage and wood is a feature of the plant; if you do not appreciate it, avoid planting this shrub close to a path.

The flowering currant should be pruned after flowering. Some of the old flowered stems can be cut back hard to ground level as soon as the flowers have faded; later pruning can result in poor, weak growth.

Ribes sanguineum 'King Edward VII' is a compact bush with crimson flowers; *Ribes sanguineum* 'Koja' is a newer, red-flowering variety with large flower clusters and healthy foliage. A softer alternative to the red-flowered cultivars is *Ribes sanguineum* 'Poky's Pink', with pink flowers flushed white; the strong, upright *Ribes sanguineum* 'Pulborough Scarlet' ♀ has flowers of a deep pink-red; *Ribes sanguineum* WHITE ICICLE ('Ubric') ♀ produces large, drooping clusters of pure white flowers that open early.

A relative newcomer to our gardens is the hardy *Sophora microphylla* SUN KING ('Hilsop') ♀. A Chilean plant, it arose as a chance seedling in a batch of nothofagus seedlings. The original plant grew on in the Sir Harold Hillier Gardens for several years, surviving hard winters and performing reliably, before it was introduced as a garden plant. It is a vigorous shrub of rather angular growth with dark green, usually evergreen, pinnate leaves. Severe cold can cause leaf-fall but the foliage is soon replaced in spring. The hanging, bright yellow flowers are produced over a long period in late winter and early spring. This sophora can be grown as a freestanding shrub or it can be trained on a wall. It flowers reliably even as a young plant. (See Good Companions, below.)

Stachyurus praecox is an extremely beautiful shrub with reddish-brown stems growing upright, then arching. For most of the year it is an ordinary green deciduous shrub, not unlike *Leycesteria* (pheasant berry) in habit (see page 96). Once the leaves have fallen, dark reddish-brown buds appear at the nodes. These remain over winter and start to open in very early spring, gradually developing into stiff, pendent flower clusters of palest yellow, hanging like drop earrings all along the branches. Stachyurus will grow in any fertile soil, in sun or partial shade, although it does not thrive on shallow chalk. It needs a dark background to show off the flowers, and is perfect in oriental garden settings, with bamboos and ferns, or sited arching over water. (See Good Companions, below.)

GOOD COMPANIONS

For a pretty, sunny spring combination, underplant *Sophora microphylla* SUN KING ('Hilsop') ♀ with blue muscari, which flower at the same time (1).

Stachyurus praecox ♀ (2), *Phyllostachys nigra* ♀ (3) and *Polystichum setiferum* ♀ (4) make an attractive grouping of contrasting shapes and foliage.

Late spring

As the garden heads towards summer, flowers abound, and wave after wave of colour rolls through the borders. Bare earth disappears as the borders fill out, fresh green foliage unfurls, and the colours become stronger and the production bolder. Cherries are at their most floriferous, the apple trees draw the bees, and the irises, euphorbias and primulas start to bloom.

Some of the most beautiful **abutilons** start to flower in late spring and continue into summer. Members of the mallow family, they are fast-growing deciduous shrubs, ideal for a warm, sunny, sheltered site, such as against a wall (see p.119), on well-drained soil. They grow well on chalk, and tolerate soil of low fertility, but dislike heavy wet soil. Abutilons are useful shrubs where height is required quickly, growing 1m (3ft) or more a year.

Abutilon vitifolium, which bears downy leaves like a vine, grows quickly to 4m (12ft). The growth is upright and

Abutilon × suntense 'Jermyns'

Azara serrata

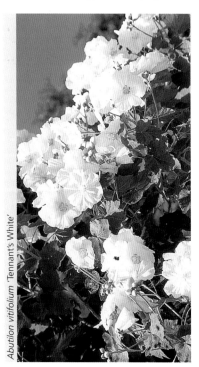

Abutilon vitifolium 'Tennant's White'

ABUTILON AFTERCARE

Abutilons become leggy and woody as they age. From the first year after planting, they should be pruned in midsummer, straight after flowering, cutting back by one-third. Abutilons are not long-lived plants and should be replaced after five years or so in most situations; sometimes whole branches die out at the end of winter, particularly in wet conditions. They are best staked, except in very sheltered sites, as they can quickly become top-heavy.

spreading, the shoots pale green. The saucer-shaped flowers are paper-thin, and a delightful watery mauve colour. A lovely cultivar is *Abutilon vitifolium* **'Veronica Tennant'** ♀, which bears large mauve flowers in a deeper shade than the species. *Abutilon vitifolium* **'Tennant's White'** ♀ is slightly more upright and pure, shimmering white.

Abutilon × suntense, a hybrid of *Abutilon vitifolium*, is a beautiful, large

and fast-growing shrub, with less downy foliage and clusters of smaller, saucer-shaped flowers that open in succession, ranging from white in some cultivars to violet-blue in others. *Abutilon × suntense* 'Jermyns' ♀ is the original Hillier form, with clear mauve-blue flowers. It starts to flower any time from mid-spring onwards, and puts on an amazing show for many weeks. It is a superb plant and is surprisingly hardy.

Azara serrata ♀ is one of the hardiest azaras. It is a large, narrow shrub, ideal for growing against a wall in a sheltered position. The oval, bright evergreen leaves shelter the orange-yellow flowers, which explode from buds formed the previous season. Often likened to an orange ceanothus, a plant in flower has a wonderful mimosa-like quality. The fine stems and glossy foliage make this shrub an attractive evergreen throughout the year. Plant it with other dark evergreens to show off the flowers.

Choisya 'Aztec Pearl'

Choisya 'Aztec Pearl' ♀ is a reliable, easy, compact shrub, reaching 2m (6ft). The evergreen palmate leaves have very narrow leaflets, giving a delightful light foliage effect offered by few other evergreens. The fragrant flowers appear from knobbly buds in late spring and again in autumn. They are pink-flushed in bud, opening to white, and are produced in such profusion that the foliage can be totally obscured when the shrub is in full flower. Like other choisyas, growth can be slow for the first two years. Shelter from cold winter winds to prevent leaf drop.

Choisya ternata ♀ (the Mexican orange blossom) is one of the evergreen mainstays of the English garden (see page 33). Neatly rounded and medium-sized, it can start to produce its fragrant white flowers any time from midwinter, but the main flush comes with warmer days at the end of spring.

Cytisus × *praecox* is the most popular of the brooms, a small shrub, with fine, arching, leafless green shoots that have a light, grass-like quality and offer a useful contrast to other broad-leaved shrubs. It can begin to bloom anytime from mid-spring onwards: tiny buds appear all the way along the stems, each one opening into a very fragrant, pea-like flower. *Cytisus* × *praecox* 'Albus' has white flowers;

Cytisus × *praecox* 'Allgold' ♀ bears long-lasting, strong yellow flowers; *Cytisus* × *praecox* 'Lilac Lady' is a new cultivar, with pale green stems and small, dainty lilac flowers; *Cytisus* × *praecox* 'Warminster' ♀ is the original form, and still the best. Usually growing to 1.5m (5ft) and no more, in flower it is a rich, beautiful cream cascade. (See Good Companions, page 143.)

There are many hybrid brooms, all deciduous, some with exceptionally showy larger flowers. A few favourites are *Cytisus* 'Boskoop Ruby' ♀, which

Cytisus 'Boskoop Ruby'

is small and rounded in habit, with deep crimson flowers, and is one of the best reds; *Cytisus* 'Burkwoodii' ♀, which is larger-growing and more vigorous, and has cerise flowers with deep crimson 'wings' edged with yellow; *Cytisus* 'Hollandia' ♀ produces pale cream and cerise flowers on arching branches; *Cytisus* 'Lena' ♀, a compact, spreading shrub, produces showy deep red and yellow flowers; *Cytisus* 'Luna' has large flowers and is available in shades of yellow, tinged with red; *Cytisus* 'Minstead' has small flowers in white, flushed with lilac; it is a subtle plant, useful for a frothy pink effect in mixed plantings; *Cytisus* 'Zeelandia' ♀ is a neat bush with flowers of lilac, pink and cream; it is lovely with blue ceanothus.

There are also two good dwarf deciduous brooms. They are useful shrubs for areas alongside walls and paving in a sunny position. *Cytisus* × *beanii* ♀ only grows to 30cm (12in) high; neat and compact, it is smothered with golden-yellow flowers in late spring and makes a good alternative to *Genista lydia*; *Cytisus* × *kewensis* ♀, of similar height, has horizontal growth when established, creating a sheet of pretty cream flowers in late spring. (See Good Companions, page 142.)

HEALTHY BROOMS

Brooms prefer a neutral soil, not too acid and not too alkaline. They can be pruned to encourage bushiness by trimming immediately after flowering and from an early age; hard-pruning later in life is often fatal. Never cut back into bare wood, as they do not regenerate. Crowded among other shrubs, brooms can become leggy and woody at the base. There is no way of reversing this, and replacement is the only solution.

Brooms are short-lived plants, particularly on shallow chalk soils, and normally need replacing after a few years. Never try to move an established broom; instead, replace it with new stock.

Cytisus 'Minstead'

Ceanothus

The Californian lilacs, or *Ceanothus*, are extremely distinctive shrubs. When they burst into bloom, the colour of summer skies erupts from our gardens, lifting our spirits with the promise of sunny days ahead.

Late spring is just the beginning of the season for these lovely plants. Some ceanothus bloom in summer, others in autumn (see pages 82–83, 118, 150). They are very versatile plants, and offer just about everything a gardener could wish for in a shrub: they are free-flowering, have attractive foliage, are easy to cultivate and are fast-growing – a young ceanothus can, depending on the variety, put on up to 1m (3ft) of growth in a year. In addition, many are evergreen.

Ceanothus are excellent in seaside gardens, and the upright varieties are ideal for growing against a wall. They like full sun and good drainage; most are lime-tolerant, but they are not good on shallow chalk. They may be pruned lightly after flowering, but never cut back into old wood, as they rarely regrow. This does depend on the variety, but if new shoots are emerging from the wood it is usually safe to cut back to this point.

Most ceanothus are not long-lived plants. Ten years is an average lifespan, so be prepared to replace them after that time. There are white-flowered varieties, but why bother with these when there are so many beautiful blue ones available?

Ceanothus 'Blue Mound' ♀ is a superb hardy ceanothus that forms a mound of stiff, arching branches smothered with small, fluffy heads of bright blue flowers in late spring, and often again in early autumn. It is an excellent structure shrub, but needs a lot of space – it can reach 2m (6ft) across, by nearly the same high.

OTHER GOOD CEANOTHUS

Ceanothus arboreus 'Trewithen Blue' ♀ is large and vigorous, with deep blue arching sprays of flowers.

Ceanothus 'Cascade' ♀ has bright blue flowers in clusters on cascading green stems.

Ceanothus 'Dark Star' ♀, an arching shrub, has tiny dark green leaves and small clusters of deep purple-blue flowers.

Ceanothus griseus var. *horizontalis* 'Yankee Point' has a sprawling habit and deep purple-blue flowers.

Ceanothus 'Italian Skies' ♀ is vigorous and spreading, with deep blue flowers.

Ceanothus 'Concha' ♀ is a glorious, hardy, reliable shrub. It is fairly upright in habit, but with strong, arching stems and rich dark green foliage. The red-brown flower buds explode like an exotic firework into a cloud of sapphire-blue in spring. (See Good Companions, pages 98, 146.)

Ceanothus 'Puget Blue' ♀, a beautiful shrub, was once the most popular of the dark sapphire ceanothus, being hardy and flowering over a long period. The growth habit is stiff and upright, with rather rigid branches and small, tight foliage.

Flowering dogwoods (Cornus)

The flowering dogwoods are the real heart-stoppers of late spring. They are hardy, deciduous plants and, although not totally intolerant of lime, they prefer a neutral or slightly acid soil with plenty of depth and organic matter. A sheltered open woodland situation is the ideal, although they can also thrive in town gardens, and fine specimens are to be seen on reasonable soil over chalk.

Cornus florida, the North American dogwood, is a large shrub or bushy small tree of elegant stature, normally upright. The flowers consist of four slightly wavy, petal-like bracts, with a round boss in the centre that is a tight cluster of the true flowers. The branches arch gracefully when the shrub is in full bloom in late spring. In addition to the spring display, the leaves colour beautifully in autumn.

Cornus kousa comes from Japan and Korea and its oriental origins are a distinct characteristic. It is a large shrub, with attractive pointed mid-green leaves that colour richly on neutral or acid soils in autumn. In spring, the horizontal, arching branches are covered with delicate white, four-bracted flowers that sit daintily above the leaves like white butterflies. Strawberry-like fruits follow in autumn. *Cornus kousa* needs to be well established before it flowers freely.

Cornus 'Norman Hadden' and *Cornus* 'Porlock' are two very similar hybrids, equally beautiful, originating from the same garden in Devon. They are both semi-evergreen, large shrubs or small trees of graceful, spreading habit, and are excellent plants for a smaller garden, to bring height to mixed plantings. Both grow well in a tub of lime-free, loam-based compost.

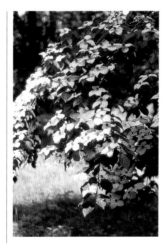

Cornus florida 'Cherokee Chief' ♀ has beautiful, deep rose-pink bracts. The round buds appear on the branches during winter, opening in late spring.

Cornus 'Norman Hadden' ♀ (left) has four-bracted flowerheads, creamy with a dark eye, held on short stalks above the leaves. The flowers grow larger as they mature and blush pink in early summer. In autumn some of the foliage turns soft red at the same time as the hanging, strawberry-like fruits are produced. *Cornus* 'Porlock' is very similar. (See Good Companions, page 142.)

Cornus kousa 'Satomi' ♀ is a Japanese variety, with deep salmon-pink bracts and an open, arching habit as it matures. The leaves turn rich purple-red in autumn.

OTHER GOOD FLOWERING DOGWOODS

Cornus kousa 'Gold Star' has large white bracts and yellow-blotched variegated foliage.

Cornus florida 'White Cloud' has bronze-green foliage and large white bracts.

Cornus kousa var. *chinensis* ♀ has an open, graceful habit with creamy bracts turning pink. 'China Girl' is a vigorous form with a mass of large flowerheads.

Exochorda × macrantha 'The Bride'

Olearia × scilloniensis

Aptly called the pearlbush, *Exochorda × macrantha* **'The Bride'** ♥ is one of the gems of the spring garden. A loose, spreading bush, with arching branches and pale green leaves, it is transformed in late spring when round white buds break into open, pure white, apple-blossom flowers. At its peak, a mature plant is a large mound of shimmering white. Exochorda is easy to grow, but it needs feeding on shallow chalk. It also requires plenty of space, and is not best placed immediately alongside a path or packed in among other shrubs. Ideally, plant it at the end of a border or to cascade over the edge of a terrace. (See Good Companions, page 143.)

The Tasmanian daisy bush, *Olearia phlogopappa*, is a pretty, tender shrub for a sunny, warm, sheltered spot. It has upright branches and narrow aromatic leaves, clustered densely on the stems. The Splendens Group consists of various coloured cultivars, including *Olearia phlogopappa* **'Comber's Blue'** and *Olearia phlogopappa* **'Comber's Pink'**, both with Michaelmas daisy-like flowers in late spring. Growing to 1.5m (5ft), they are ideal to plant at the base of a wall with lavenders and grey foliage plants.

Olearia × scilloniensis, a hybrid of *Olearia phlogopappa*, is an outstanding tall but compact shrub, also with upright growth and neat grey foliage. The white daisy-like flowers, with silver-white centres, are so freely produced that they smother the plant completely when it is in full bloom. (See Good Companions, page 146.)

Peonies are mostly thought of as herbaceous perennials. However, the woody species – the tree peonies – are among the most spectacular deciduous shrubs in both flower and foliage. Native to China and Tibet, the tree peonies are hardy, although the new growth of some may be susceptible to frost damage, so a sheltered spot is preferred. They like full sun and good drainage; most are good on chalk, especially *Paeonia delavayi*. All are tall and upright, with few stems.

Paeonia delavayi ♥ is a suckering shrub, with upright brown stems with peeling bark up to 2m (6ft) high. Even a small plant is an impressive sight when the large, deeply cut architectural leaves unfurl. They are as much a feature of the plant as the single ruby flowers with golden anthers; these are followed by large black-seeded fruits shaped like a

GOOD COMPANIONS

Cornus 'Norman Hadden' ♥ (1) sits well with *Cotinus coggygria* 'Royal Purple' ♥ (2) and *Rosa* 'Geranium' ♥ (3).

The cream-coloured blooms of *Cytisus × kewensis* ♥ (4) make it a good partner for the blue-flowered *Ceanothus* 'Centennial' (5).

Paeonia delavayi var. lutea

Paeonia suffruticosa 'Double Deep Pink'

Paeonia suffruticosa 'Rock's Variety'

PLANTING TREE PEONIES
AND AFTERCARE

Tree peonies are not attractive in winter when the leaves fall, exposing a few rough, upright stems; for this reason, plant them against an evergreen background that will take over to provide winter interest. They require no pruning – if you cut them back when the leaves fall, you will remove the flower buds. Protect new growth and flower buds with horticultural fleece in early spring.

jester's hat. *Paeonia delavayi* var. *lutea* produces similar foliage, but the flowers, which are produced at the ends of the branches, are yellow, resembling large kingcups.

Paeonia × lemoinei is a hybrid of *Paeonia delavayi* var. *lutea* and *Paeonia suffruticosa*. This results in cultivars with very large yellow or bicoloured flowers. *Paeonia × lemoinei* 'Souvenir de Maxime Cornu' has bright yellow blooms edged with carmine.

Paeonia ludlowii is similar to *Paeonia delavayi*, with larger, saucer-shaped flowers.

Paeonia suffruticosa, the Moutan peony, is the most spectacular of all tree peonies, growing to 2m (6ft) high. The flowers are very large, usually well in excess of 15cm (6in) across. In the wild,

the flowers are white but the cultivars include some of the most gorgeously coloured, extravagant blossoms.

Prostanthera (the mint bush) is a genus of very aromatic, small evergreen shrubs suitable for a warm, sunny position. They have become increasingly popular in recent years. *Prostanthera cuneata* ♥ is the most popular species. A native of south-eastern Australia and Tasmania, it is surprisingly hardy. It has small leaves, which are crowded on the stems of a low, spreading bush and are sweetly aromatic when brushed against. The tiny flowers, which are produced in profusion in late spring, are

lilac-white. It looks very pretty planted with silver foliage and purple sage. (See Good Companions, page 146.)

Although fairly rare, **rhaphiolepis** are worthy of a mention. These members of the rose family have attractive leathery evergreen foliage and pretty clusters of apple-blossom flowers in late spring. They are not the hardiest of plants but, in a sheltered position, they remain unscathed through all but the coldest winters. Rhaphiolepis like well-drained, fertile, acid or alkaline soil, and a position in full sun. The cultivars of *Rhaphiolepis × delacourii* are lovely shrubs for a warm, sheltered garden: *Rhaphiolepis*

GOOD COMPANIONS

Cytisus × praecox (1) is lovely with purple honesty and deep burgundy tulips such as *Tulipa* 'Queen of Night' (2).

The arching branches of *Exochorda × macrantha* 'The Bride' ♥ (3) are perfect for showing off the flowers of *Clematis* 'Alba Luxurians' ♥ (4) in late summer.

× *delacourii* 'Coates' Crimson' has rose-crimson blooms, and *Rhaphiolepis* × *delacourii* 'Spring Song' bears pale pink flowers over a relatively long period. *Rhaphiolepis umbellata* is the toughest species of all; it is a low evergreen, only growing to 1m (3ft) or so in height; the flowers are white-pink and produced at the tips of the branches in late spring.

On acid soils, it is undoubtedly the **rhododendrons** and **azaleas** that steal the late-spring show as the dense evergreen mounds are transformed with blooms of translucent pastels and rich silk shades. See pages 101–105.

Ceanothus 'Blue Mound' and Rosa 'Nevada'

Rhaphiolepis 'Spring Song'

Rosa xanthina 'Canary Bird'

As spring finally heads towards summer the early **roses** start to bloom (see also pages 112–115). Some of the large shrub roses, such as *Rosa* 'Frühlingsgold' ♔, display their large open blooms on upright stems. With its big, single or semi-double creamy-yellow flowers, this is a lovely shrub to use as a screening plant in combination with gold-variegated shrubs.

Rosa 'Nevada' ♔ is a tall shrub with a mass of large creamy flowers, with golden stamens, in late spring and early summer. It is an easy shrub to grow where space needs filling. Prune out some older shoots after flowering, right to the base. It may flower again later.

Several cultivars of the Scotch rose or Burnet rose, *Rosa pimpinellifolia* (*Rosa spinosissima*), deserve much wider and more frequent planting in the garden.

The twiggy, prickly stems are covered with small, neat leaves, and maroon-black fruits often follow the pretty, early flowers that stud the compact bush. *Rosa pimpinellifolia* 'Andrewsii' ♔ produces pink and cream, semi-double flowers with yellow stamens, and sometimes repeats in autumn; *Rosa pimpinellifolia* 'Glory of Edzell' has clear pink, lemon-centred flowers; *Rosa pimpinellifolia* 'William III' is short and dense, with red-purple flowers and black fruits.

The **rugosa** hybrids will already be clothed in their apple-green pleated foliage by late spring and, in warm situations, they are also in flower at this time. They repeat-flower throughout the season and are perhaps the best choice for those gardeners who prefer steady flowering to the delights of an

ephemeral seasonal display. Their hips are an autumn highlight (see page 174).

Rosa xanthina 'Canary Bird' ♔ is a delightful shrub rose. In late spring, it opens its large buttercup-yellow blooms along the arching wands of emerging fern-like foliage; the display of flowers may not be a long one, but it is a prominent signal that summer is on its way. The single, creamy-yellow blooms of *Rosa xanthina* f. *hugonis* ♔ clothe the arching stems of this graceful shrub while the first ceanothus are in flower.

As gardens have become smaller, and shrubs have to work harder to earn their place, some of the larger shrub roses that bloom only once have become less popular. However, they are easy to grow and reliably produce a superb display, becoming the most outstanding plants in the garden, if only for a few days.

Lilacs (Syringa)

Late spring is lilac time. Members of the olive family, lilacs (or syringas) are some of our most popular deciduous garden shrubs. The fragrance of lilac is one of the definitive floral perfumes.

Syringa vulgaris, the species from which our garden, or common, lilacs are descended, is a native of the mountains of eastern Europe, introduced to British gardens in the 16th century. The garden lilacs (hybrids and cultivars of *Syringa vulgaris*) are large shrubs and need space. This, combined with the fact that their flowering season is relatively short and they are not the most attractive of plants for the rest of the year, means that there are better flowering shrubs for small gardens. So familiar are the garden lilacs, other syringas are often forgotten; in fact, some of these, including *Syringa × prestoniae* hybrids, and *Syringa pubescens* subspecies, are far more useful shrubs, with a longer season of interest and a more attractive growth habit.

Lilacs are generally easy to grow, thriving on most well-drained soils, especially chalk; they prefer full sun. Although lilacs flower from an early age, the flower size is usually small for the first few years.

Prune lilacs immediately after flowering, cutting back the wood that has flowered. Some gardeners cut the whole plant back to about 1m (3ft) each year, to stimulate the production of straight flowering shoots and for an even distribution of flowers. Old lilacs can be rejuvenated by sawing old branches to ground level.

Syringa vulgaris 'Andenken an Ludwig Späth' ♀ ('Souvenir de Louis Spaeth'), one of the most popular garden lilacs, has single, wine-red flowers and is a reliable and excellent cultivar.

Syringa × prestoniae hybrids are vigorous, quickly attaining 2m (6ft). *Syringa × prestoniae* 'Elinor' is a superb choice, with dark purple-red buds opening to strong, upright, pinkish-lavender flower sprays.

Syringa vulgaris 'Madame Lemoine' ♀, a garden lilac, has creamy white, double flowers. The Lemoine family from Nancy, France, were responsible for the introduction of many cultivars in the 19th and 20th centuries.

Syringa pubescens subsp. *patula* 'Miss Kim' ♀ is a delightful selection of the Korean lilac, with purple buds opening to palest lilac. The flowers are very fragrant. Plant in a sheltered site – late frosts can damage the buds.

OTHER GOOD LILACS

Syringa × josiflexa 'Bellicent' ♀, very hardy, with huge loose plumes of scented, dusty pink flowers.

Syringa meyeri 'Palibin' ♀, lilac-pink; slowly reaches 1m (3ft) or so – ideal for small garden or container.

Syringa pubescens subsp. *microphylla* 'Superba' ♀, tiny leaves and dainty mauve-pink, fragrant flowers mainly in late spring but can continue until autumn.

Syringa vulgaris 'Charles Joly' ♀, gorgeous double, dark purple-red flowers.

Syringa vulgaris 'Firmament' ♀, single, lilac-coloured flowers.

Syringa vulgaris 'Katherine Havemeyer' ♀, double purple flowers, fading to lilac-pink.

Syringa vulgaris 'Vestale' ♀, single, pure white flowers.

Spiraea 'Arguta'

Viburnum × burkwoodii 'Anne Russell'

Viburnum 'Eskimo'

Spiraea 'Arguta' ♡, known as the bridal wreath or foam of May, is one of the most free-flowering of all deciduous shrubs. In mid- to late spring, the fine, arching stems are smothered with pure white flowers in flat clusters all along the top of the slender branches. After the flowers have finished, the narrow, oval, soft green leaves create a pleasing mound of summer foliage. This medium-sized plant does not have a long flowering season but it is an unmissable harbinger of summer.

Spiraea nipponica 'Snowmound' ♡ flowers after *Spiraea* 'Arguta', at the end of spring or in early summer. This is a small, dense mound of a shrub, not as graceful as *Spiraea* 'Arguta' but every bit as free-flowering. The white flowers smother the plant, making it worthy of its name.

These two spiraeas are easy to grow on any soil. Neither requires pruning, but if cutting back is essential to control size, it must be carried out immediately after flowering. Avoid trimming *Spiraea*

'Arguta' if possible, as it will rob the plant of its graceful arching habit.

Viburnums are such important plants in all seasons they feature throughout this book. In late spring, they excel both in flower spectacle and fragrance. *Viburnum × burkwoodii* is a broad evergreen shrub of open stature. The shiny leaves are well spaced on straight, light brown branches; waxy pink buds in rounded clusters open into white, pink-tinged flowers with the most delicious fragrance; *Viburnum × burkwoodii* 'Anne Russell' ♡ is a superb cultivar, with large flower clusters; *Viburnum × burkwoodii* 'Park Farm Hybrid' ♡ is vigorous and more spreading, with larger flowers, than *Viburnum × burkwoodii*.

Viburnum × carlcephalum ♡ is a more compact deciduous shrub growing to approximately 2m (6ft) high. The rounded flowerheads are pink in bud, opening white, and have a delicious fragrance. If sited in an open position, the leaves colour beautifully in autumn.

Viburnum carlesii is also deciduous. Compact and rigid in habit, with straight shoots and pale brown, downy shoots, it produces rounded heads of pink buds that open to white, richly fragrant flowers. The leaves are felty, greyish-green, and can display good autumn colour. *Viburnum carlesii* can suffer from aphid infestation, in which young leaves become distorted and crinkly. *Viburnum carlesii* 'Aurora' ♡ is a favourite variety, with salmon-red buds that open to flesh-pink, richly fragrant flowers. *Viburnum*

GOOD COMPANIONS

For an attractive grouping, plant *Olearia × scilloniensis* ♡ (1), *Elaeagnus* 'Quicksilver' ♡ (2) and *Ceanothus* 'Concha' ♡ (3).

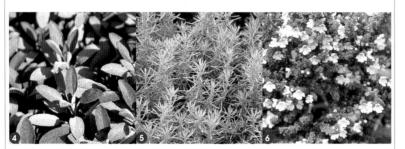

Plant *Salvia officinalis* 'Purpurascens' ♡ (4) and *Helichrysum* 'Korma' (5) with *Prostanthera cuneata* ♡ (6) for an attractive, aromatic combination.

carlesii 'Diana' is similar, but the young foliage is tinged purple. *Viburnum carlesii* cultivars are normally grafted, so watch out for and remove suckers: strong, upright-growing shoots, usually of the much more vigorous *Viburnum lantana*, which will take over if not removed from the base.

Viburnum 'Eskimo' is a small, compact hybrid, semi-evergreen with glossy, leathery leaves and exceptionally large, snowball-like flower clusters. The blooms are magnificent and scented, but not as wonderfully fragrant as *Viburnum carlesii*.

Viburnum × *hillieri* 'Winton' ♀ is a spreading, semi-evergreen shrub with oval leaves, which are copper when young and turn bronze-red in winter. The flowers, which resemble large flowering currant blossoms, are creamy white and followed by red fruits, which eventually turn black.

Viburnum × *juddii* ♀, a hybrid of *Viburnum carlesii*, is a small, bushy deciduous shrub with felty leaves and sweetly scented, pink-tinged flowers at the tips of the branches. It is less susceptible to aphids, but is not as popular as *Viburnum carlesii*.

The snowball bush, ***Viburnum opulus* 'Roseum' ('Sterile')** ♀, is one of the most familiar and also one of the

Viburnum plicatum f. *tomentosum* 'Mariesii'

Viburnum opulus 'Roseum' ('Sterile')

Viburnum sargentii 'Onondaga'

GOOD COMPANIONS

Viburnum plicatum f. *tomentosum* 'Mariesii' ♀ (1) is lovely with silver-variegated plants such as *Cornus alternifolia* 'Argentea' ♀ (2).

most spectacular deciduous flowering shrubs. Green flower clusters appear all along the branches in spring, gradually enlarging, turning to cream, then white and flushing pink. As they mature they hang like snowballs from the upright but arching branches. It is a very easy and tolerant shrub to grow.

Another glorious spring-flowering deciduous shrub is ***Viburnum plicatum* f. *tomentosum* 'Mariesii'** ♀, which is superb for specimen planting. It grows to 2m (6ft) or more, but the spreading horizontal branches create a shrub wider than it is high. The deeply veined leaves hang from the branches, and the lacecap hydrangea-like flowers are borne all along the top of the branches in late spring. More flowers sometimes appear

in autumn, before the leaves change colour. (See Good Companions, left.) ***Viburnum plicatum* f. *tomentosum* 'Pink Beauty'** ♀ has smaller blooms that turn pink as they mature, and the less spreading ***Viburnum plicatum* f. *tomentosum* 'Summer Snowflake'** flowers intermittently throughout the summer; although it produces a less spectacular display than the other cultivars, it is very useful for its long flowering period. *Viburnum plicatum* f. *tomentosum* cultivars should be given space and not pruned to control the size, as this spoils the shape.

***Viburnum sargentii* 'Onondaga'** ♀ is an upright deciduous shrub, prized for its purple foliage and pretty lacecap flowerheads (see page 54).

Summer

Summer is a season of richness in the garden: lush foliage, plentiful flowers and delicious scents. Summer-bloomers compete for the attention of pollinating insects with the colour and fragrance of their flowers. The deciduous shrubs take centre stage: against a backdrop of foliage at its most flamboyant, the performance of the flowers has to be strong.

The Red Border, Hadspen, Somerset.

In early summer, philadelphus, deutzia, weigela and cistus vie with roses, lilies and delphiniums for the leading role. Once the first flush of roses comes to an end, the competition is less intense; in this quieter season of late summer flowering shrubs prove their worth. Old garden favourites such as buddleia and hydrangea provide warm summer hues, whatever the weather, while caryopteris and perovskia supply that essential blue, regardless of the colour of the sky.

Most buddleias are very hardy, easy-to-grow shrubs. *Buddleja davidii*, the butterfly bush, is the best known and is widely naturalized in the UK. In summer its arching branches and long heads of lilac flowers are a familiar sight on wasteland and railway embankments. It thrives on poor soil in sunny, well-drained conditions. Frequently seen growing in crevices on old buildings, it has the ability to survive anywhere.

The cultivars of *Buddleja davidii* are popular, not only for the scent and colour of their flowers, but also for their unfailing ability to attract butterflies. They grow quickly to 2 or 3m (6–10ft)

with an elegant, arching habit. They give height and structure to herbaceous plantings, mix well with roses and extend the season of deciduous shrubs that flower early in the season.

Buddleja davidii 'Nanho Blue' is comparatively compact, suitable where space is limited. It has narrow panicles of violet-blue flowers with orange eyes. The *Buddleja davidii* 'Pixie' varieties **'Pixie Red'**, **'Pixie White'** and **'Pixie Blue'** are smaller, growing to about 1.5m (5ft). Other cultivars of *Buddleja davidii* include: **'Black Knight'** ♥, with long

Buddleja davidii 'Dartmoor'

Buddleja davidii 'Royal Red'

flowerheads of deep violet; **'Border Beauty'**, a compact variety with crimson flowers; **'Dartmoor'** ♀, large-branched panicles of magenta flowers; **'Empire Blue'** ♀, a beautiful buddleia with rich violet-blue, orange-eyed flowers; **'Royal Red'** ♀, massive red-purple flowerheads; **'White Profusion'** ♀, large, pure white flowers with yellow eyes.

Buddleja globosa

The best buddleia of all is the lovely **Buddleja 'Lochinch'** ♀, described in the 'Silver and grey' section. **Buddleja alternifolia** ♀ has a different habit, with graceful, arching branches and narrow leaves. (See page 74.)

Buddleja globosa ♀, the Chilean orange ball tree, is vigorous, with a more upright habit and broader foliage than

Buddleja davidii. Stiff clusters of orange, spherical flowers – quite unlike any other buddleia – appear in early summer.

Buddleias need no special attention, except pruning. Hard prune *Buddleja davidii* varieties in early spring, cutting back to 1m (3ft) or so in height. This may seem drastic but it keeps the plants young and vigorous. Dead-heading as the flowers fade helps to keep the plant looking good through late summer.

Buddleias work well when planted with screening shrubs; the latter provide the evergreen structure, the buddleia provides the summer colour (see Good Companions, below).

Caryopteris are valuable for colour in late summer and early autumn. Their aromatic foliage and shrubby habit suggest a Mediterranean origin but they hail from eastern Asia. They need well-drained soil and full sun, and thrive on chalk. The caryopteris grown in gardens are generally varieties of **Caryopteris × clandonensis.** Many are similar, which often leads to confusion over the true identity of a plant offered for sale (see box). All are small and compact, reaching

GOOD COMPANIONS

Buddleja 'Black Knight' ♀ (1) provides summer colour for evergreen shrubs such as *Elaeagnus × ebbingei* (2).

Caryopteris × clandonensis 'First Choice'

Caryopteris × clandonensis 'Summer Sorbet'

no more than 60–90cm (2–3ft). Cut all caryopteris back hard in late winter. By then new shoots are visible on the lower third of the plant and the top two thirds of the stems can be removed.

Probably the best-known cultivar of *Caryopteris × clandonensis* is **'Heavenly Blue'**, with clusters of sapphire blue

A TIP ON BUYING CARYOPTERIS

Because of the confusion between so many similar varieties, it is best to buy caryopteris while it is in flower so that you can see what you are getting.

flowers in the axils of the grey-green, willow-like leaves in late summer (see Good Companions, page 151). **'Arthur Simmonds'** ♀ is similar to, and often confused with, 'Heavenly Blue', but the flowers are a lighter colour. It is one of the most reliable. **'First Choice'** ♀ has large, deep blue flowers – a stunning colour – and excellent foliage. Full sun and good drainage are essential; it fails on damp sites in cold winter weather.

Other *Caryopteris × clandonensis* cultivars include: **'Kew Blue'**, a seedling of 'Arthur Simmonds', with slightly darker flowers; **'Summer Sorbet'**, with blue flowers and sage-green foliage edged soft yellow (this is an acquired taste); and **'Worcester Gold'** ♀, with soft gold foliage and bright blue flowers (see page 44).

Cistus

Cistus, the sun rose, is a plant that enjoys full sun, good drainage and poor soil – classic Mediterranean conditions. Many are surprisingly hardy, although some of the larger-leaved varieties need a sheltered site to thrive. They do well near the coast, like chalk soils and require little attention: no dead-heading and no pruning. They are also remarkably free from pest and disease problems.

Most cistus have large flowers, either white or shades of pink and red. The flowers are short-lived but are produced in rapid succession – as one flush fades, the next opens. Most flower in early to midsummer and deliver an outstanding performance, even if their season is not very long. Cistus are excellent plants to combine with silver foliage shrubs, lavenders and roses (see 'Hot, dry, sunny sites', pages 82–87; see Good Companions, page 151).

Some varieties of cistus take exception to pruning, others will withstand light trimming after flowering as long as this is done regularly from an early age. Ideally, young plants should be pinched back after flowering to encourage bushy growth. Never cut back into bare wood.

Container-grown cistus can suffer from instability and wind-rock after planting. A low stake is a good idea on windy sites, until the plants become established. Do not make the mistake of planting too deeply in an effort to overcome the problem.

Cistus × *dansereaui* 'Decumbens'♥ is low and spreading, 60cm (2ft) high but twice as broad. It has sticky, dark green leaves and large white flowers with crimson-blotched centres. *Cistus* '**Snow Fire**'♥ (left) is similar but makes a more rounded bush; a very good, reliable variety.

Cistus × *purpureus*♥ is a small shrub with narrow wavy leaves and large rosy-crimson flowers with deep maroon central blotches and yellow stamens.

Cistus × *pulverulentus* '**Sunset**'♥ has cerise flowers with yellow stamens. Its habit is open and upright; looks very good planted with silver foliage.

GOOD CISTUS

Large-flowered white cistus

Cistus × *aguilarii* 'Maculatus'♥, with bright green, wavy-edged foliage and very large white flowers with a central ring of crimson blotches.

Cistus × *dansereaui* 'Decumbens'♥.

Cistus 'Snow Fire'♥ (see left)

Cistus populifolius subsp. *major*♥, with wavy-edged leaves, red buds and white flowers; one of the hardiest.

Large-flowered pink cistus

Cistus × *argenteus* 'Peggy Sammons'♥, a vigorous, upright medium-sized shrub; grey-green foliage, purple-pink flowers with paler centres.

Cistus × *argenteus* 'Silver Pink' (right), a very hardy cultivar, with long clusters of satin, peach-pink flowers and grey-green foliage.

Cistus × *pulverulentus* 'Sunset'♥ (see left).

Cistus × *purpureus*♥ (see left and Good Companions, right).

Cistus × *rodiaei* 'Jessabel' has slightly sticky, dark green leaves; large, almost red flowers, maroon in the centre with yellow stamens.

Ceanothus thyrsiflorus 'Skylark'

Ceanothus thyrsiflorus 'Gloire de Versailles'

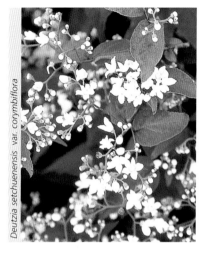

Deutzia setchuenensis var. corymbiflora

Ceanothus span the seasons. If you select the right varieties, it is possible to have a ceanothus in flower from mid-spring to the onset of winter. See pages 82–83, 118; Plant Profile page 140.

Ceanothus thyrsiflorus 'Skylark' ♀ follows the spring-flowering evergreen ceanothus into summer. Upright and bushy in habit, it grows quickly to 2m (6ft) or more. Its habit suits planting as a freestanding shrub for the centre of a border. The evergreen foliage is bright green and glossy, the perfect foil for the brilliant blue flowers that appear over several weeks in early summer.

The deciduous ceanothus are open, airy shrubs, producing their light, fluffy flowerheads through summer and into autumn. *Ceanothus × delileanus* varieties mostly grow to about 1.5m (5ft). 'Gloire de Versailles' ♀ is the most popular by far, with powder-blue flowers. 'Henri Desfossé', similar in habit and size, has deep violet-blue flowers. 'Topaze' ♀ has light indigo-blue flowers.

Pink ceanothus are not to everyone's taste. Think of them simply as pretty pink-flowering shrubs and they become useful additions to mixed planting. *Ceanothus × pallidus* 'Marie Simon' has light pink flowers. *Ceanothus × pallidus* 'Perle Rose' has bright rose-carmine smoky blooms.

Deciduous ceanothus flower on new growth, so should be lightly pruned and tidied in late winter. They like an open, sunny position and usually perform better than evergreen varieties on chalk.

Deutzias are rarely a first choice when it comes to selecting flowering shrubs. However, they are problem-free and easy to grow on any soil. *Deutzia scabra*, widely used as an amenity plant, has masses of white flowers in early summer on a large, upright woody bush that can reach 3m (10ft). Other

deutzias have exquisite flowers and are wonderfully refined deciduous garden shrubs, usually of medium size, growing to 1.2–2m (4–6ft). They flower best in early summer, in full sun. Many lovely hybrids originated in the Lemoine nursery, as did the best-known varieties of philadelphus and lilac (*syringa*).

Some of the best are: *Deutzia × elegantissima* 'Rosealind' ♀: a lovely plant with loose sprays of deep pink, fragrant flowers. *Deutzia × hybrida* Strawberry Fields' ♀ (× *magnifica*

GOOD COMPANIONS

For a colourful late-summer pairing, plant *Caryopteris × clandonensis* 'Heavenly Blue' (1) with the purple-red *Echinacea purpurea* (2).

Cistus × purpureus ♀ (3) is lovely with the grey foliage of *Lavandula stoechas* subsp. *pedunculata* ♀ ('Papillon') (4) and *Artemisia* 'Powis Castle' ♀ (5).

'Rubra'): free-flowering, with large mauve-pink flowers, edged white and tinged purple on the reverse. *Deutzia × hybrida* 'Mont Rose'♀: rose-pink flowers with darker tints, freely borne. *Deutzia longifolia* 'Veitchii'♀: long, narrow leaves and large clusters of rich lilac-pink flowers; the loveliest of the deutzias. *Deutzia × ningpoensis*♀: a very different flower form – reflexed petals, like the flowers of solanum, with yellow stamens; long sprays of flowers, pink or white all over the bush. *Deutzia setchuenensis* var. *corymbiflora*♀: small starry white flowers later than most deutzias; a lovely shrub, but not for cold areas (illus. page 151)

Prune deutzias immediately after flowering, cutting out some of the stems that have flowered. This results in graceful, arching growth that rises above other planting. Avoid snipping later in the season – this will ruin the effect.

Escallonia is much more than an excellent evergreen hedging shrub. Its glossy foliage and drought- and wind-resistance make the plant an excellent garden structure subject, with the added bonus of plentiful, pretty blossoms over a long period in summer.

Natives of South America, escallonias are not the hardiest evergreens. As with most flowering evergreens, those that have small leaves are hardier than those with larger leaves. Escallonias are not plants for cold sites but they can withstand coastal winds. Inland they are best planted with the protection of a wall or fence, or among other shrubs to provide shelter. They grow on any well-drained soil. Like many evergreens, they can be slow to grow in the first season after planting.

Escallonias are useful medium or tall shrubs to bring evergreen interest to plantings of roses and herbaceous plants: they prolong the interest, and the colour and character of the flowers sit well in mixed planting.

Escallonia 'Apple Blossom'

Escallonia 'Apple Blossom'♀ is the best-known hybrid, and the most widely planted. It is slow-growing and relatively compact compared to other escallonias, slowly reaching 1.5m (5ft). The dark green foliage is the perfect background to the pink-and-white flowers. See also pages 41, 122.

Prune escallonias immediately after flowering or the following spring. Cutting out the old flowered growth keeps the plant tidy and compact. Old, straggly specimens can be hard pruned at the same time. Escallonia regenerates well, even from older wood.

OTHER RECOMMENDED ESCALLONIA CULTIVARS

Escallonia 'C.F. Ball', a vigorous plant, growing to 3m (10ft) or more, with big aromatic leaves and crimson flowers.

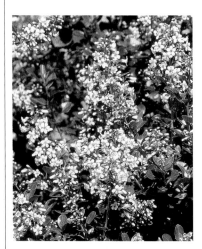

Escallonia 'Iveyi'♀, slightly more tender than some, with larger, very dark green leaves and large sprays of pure white flowers; a vigorous shrub, quickly reaching 2m (6ft) or more.

Escallonia 'Donard Radiance'♀, highly recommended, strong-growing, medium-sized shrub with large shiny dark green leaves and large bright, rose-red flowers.

Escallonia 'Langleyensis'♀, hardier than some cultivars, with smaller leaves, growing to 2.5m (8ft), with profuse rose-pink flowers on arching branches; a good choice for colder inland gardens.

Escallonia 'Peach Blossom'♀, similar to 'Apple Blossom' but with flowers of clear peach-pink.

Escallonia 'Pride of Donard'♀, large, bright pink bell-shaped flowers at the end of the branches throughout the summer and large glossy leaves.

Fuchsia is a favourite bedding plant, so it is not surprising that the hardier varieties are widely planted as flowering shrubs. Fuchsias originate from Central and South America, Tahiti and New Zealand. Some are hardier than others: as a rule, those with smaller leaves and flowers are hardier than those with larger leaves and flowers.

In colder areas fuchsias often die right back in winter, performing like a herbaceous plant. In mild localities they keep on growing and the more vigorous varieties, such as *Fuchsia* 'Riccartonii' and *Fuchsia magellanica* (see right and page 68), can make large shrubs up to 3m (10ft) in height.

Fuchsias are versatile plants and mix well with other shrubs and herbaceous perennials; they grow and flower in sun or shade. The fuchsia hedges of southwest England are a delight in summer when their arching branches hang with dainty red and purple flowers.

Because fuchsias are so popular there has been extensive hybridization and selection. There are numerous varieties. (See also pages 45, 68–69, illus. 42.)

Fuchsias should be pruned in early spring. Either cut them back hard to ground level or, if you want to preserve height, just give them a light trim.

FUCHSIA PESTS AND DISEASES

Pests and diseases can be a problem, especially where bedding fuchsias are grown in close proximity. Look out for rust, a fungal infection causing red-brown powdery spots on the leaves in late summer. Treat with a fungicide and repeat the following spring when new leaves appear.

Vine weevil may attack fuchsias grown in pots in a peat-based compost. Watch for notching on the edge of the leaves. Treat with a systemic pesticide or use biological controls.

A SMALL SELECTION OF FUCHSIA VARIETIES

Fuchsia 'Alice Hoffman' ♀, a compact variety, to 50cm (18in), with small purple-tinged leaves and flowers with a scarlet calyx and white petals.

Fuchsia 'Army Nurse' ♀, a vigorous, upright grower with carmine calyx and blue-violet petals.

Fuchsia 'Hawkshead' ♀, a lovely small variety, with deep green foliage and slender white flowers.

Fuchsia 'Lady Thumb' ♀, dwarf and bushy, with light red and white flowers.

Fuchsia 'Lena' ♀ (right): semi-double with pale pink calyx and purple petals flushed pink. Good for training.

Fuchsia magellanica var. *gracilis* ♀, a very graceful and pretty shrub, with slender, arching stems and numerous small, delicate flowers of scarlet and purple.

Fuchsia 'Mrs Popple' ♀ (below), an excellent small plant, with large flowers and a compact habit; scarlet calyx and violet petals.

Fuchsia 'Riccartonii' ♀, the best fuchsia for general planting where a tall shrub can be accommodated.

Fuchsia 'Snowcap' ♀, dwarf and compact but with large flowers; red calyx and white petals veined red.

Fuchsia 'Tom Thumb' ♀, a dwarf shrub, with masses of small freely produced flowers with scarlet calyx and violet petals.

Hebe 'Spender's Seedling'

Hebes, often referred to as veronicas, are favourite evergreen shrubs. The genus includes a number of our most popular variegated, silver-leaved and red-leaved shrubs. The dwarf green forms offer an alternative to box as compact, structural shrubs, while the larger hardy species are frequently used for structure and amenity planting. Nearly all flower in summer; the more flamboyant, larger-leaved varieties, with big, showy bottlebrush flowers, are attractive to bees and butterflies. (See Plant Profile, page 76.)

Many hebes have a long flowering season. They like well-drained soil and suit coastal situations. Those with lusher foliage do not suit cold exposed sites.

Pruning is not essential but may be necessary if growth becomes leggy or the bush falls open with age or if it is severely damaged by winter weather. If

HEBES TO GROW FOR FOLIAGE AND STRUCTURE (WITH THE BONUS OF SUMMER FLOWERS)

Hebe 'Emerald Gem' ♀ ('Emerald Green' or 'Green Globe'), a rounded bun-shaped bush, very dwarf and compact, with tiny green leaves packed on tight branches; white flowers in summer; a superb plant for a pot or for planting in gravel.

Hebe rakaiensis ♀, dwarf, compact and very hardy, forming dense mounds of bright green foliage; the leaves are tiny and crowd the stems, the white flowers frost the bush in early summer; a superb plant for fresh green foliage in full sun.

Hebe salicifolia, a medium-sized shrub reaching 2m (6ft); its willow-like foliage withstands most winters, the flowers are white or lilac in long, narrow, drooping spikes throughout the summer; an excellent choice in coastal or urban areas.

Hebe 'Spender's Seedling' (above left), a small, very hardy shrub with narrow foliage and plenty of fragrant, white, lilac-tinged flowers over a long period.

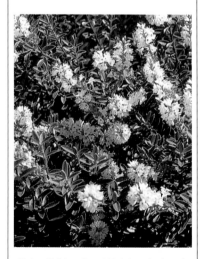

Hebe 'White Gem' ♀ (above): dwarf, compact and hardy with a profusion of white flowers in early summer.

GOOD COMPANIONS

The yellow flowers of *Hypericum* 'Hidcote' ♀ (1) are complemented by yellow-variegated *Euonymus* 'Emerald 'n' Gold' ♀ (2).

Indigofera potaninii (3) works well with *Nepeta* × *faassenii* ♀ or *Salvia* × *sylvestris* 'Mainacht' ♀ (4).

HEBES TO GROW FOR SUMMER FLOWERS (WITH THE BONUS OF GOOD FOLIAGE)

Hebe 'Autumn Glory', a small, open shrub with glossy green leaves tinged purple, and intense violet-blue flowers in short, dense spikes through summer and autumn.

Hebe 'Blue Clouds' ♀ (above), a small shrub with dark glossy-green leaves, purplish in winter; long spikes of blue flowers during summer and autumn.

Hebe × *franciscana* 'Blue Gem', a small, compact, dome-shaped shrub with dense spikes of bright blue flowers; one of the hardiest hebes, very resistant to salt spray; good for a low coastal hedge.

Hebe 'Great Orme' ♀ (above): a reasonably hardy, compact shrub growing to 1m (3ft); long, narrow leaves and bright pink flowers in long, tapering flowerheads; good with purple foliage plants such as *Physocarpus opulifolius* 'Diabolo'.

Hebe 'Marjorie' (above), one of the hardiest; neat and compact, growing to 1m (3ft) in height; spikes of light violet and white flowers through the summer.

Hebe 'Midsummer Beauty' ♀, a fairly hardy form with handsome foliage, and reddish undersides to the leaves; long spikes of lavender flowers throughout the summer.

Hebe 'Pink Paradise', very hardy and compact, with profuse pink flowers throughout the summer

Hebe 'Simon Délaux', a small, rounded shrub with rich crimson flowers in large bottlebrush spikes.

Hebe 'Youngii' ♀ ('Carl Teschner') (below), a hardy, dwarf shrub of spreading habit with small neat foliage and pretty violet flowers in summer; a good ground-cover plant.

you do prune, do so in spring, after the coldest weather has passed. Cut back to where new green shoots are appearing on the lower part of the stem; never cut back into old wood if there are no signs of growth shoots.

The more tender large-leaved hebe varieties can be prone to leaf-spot diseases after a damp winter. Treat with a fungicide. In severe cases cut back in spring and regrow.

Hoheria sexstylosa 'Stardust'

Hoherias originate from New Zealand and are not plants for cold, exposed gardens. The most widely grown species is *Hoheria sexstylosa*, a tall evergreen shrub of light and airy habit. The narrow leaves are often serrated and toothed and are shiny mid-green. The plant surprises in summer, with showers of starry white flowers like spring blossom – but at a time of year when few other trees and shrubs are blooming. *Hoheria sexstylosa* 'Stardust' ♀ is a very compact, upright form, with glossy foliage and clouds of flowers. The hybrid *Hoheria* 'Glory of Amlwch' ♀ keeps its leaves in mild winters. The flowers are much larger than those of *Hoheria sexstylosa*, 3cm (1in) across, crowded on the branches in midsummer.

Hydrangea arborescens 'Annabelle'

Hydrangea aspera Kawakamii Group

Hydrangea involucrata 'Hortensis'

Hydrangea conjures images of large mounds of foliage and heavy rounded flowerheads of pink, blue and white; a familiar sight in seaside towns. In fact, these 'mopheads' are only one part of this wonderful group of plants.

Two types of floret make up the flowerheads of hydrangeas: tiny, insignificant fertile florets, and showy sterile florets with conspicuous coloured sepals (which look like petals). In some cases, as with the mopheads, the flowerhead is almost entirely made up of sterile florets; in others, as with the lacecaps, it consists of a combination of the two types.

Hydrangeas are excellent shrubs for light shade. They also benefit from overhead shelter from trees. Although they are hardy, the new growth is often damaged by late frosts. All hydrangeas like a reasonably fertile soil and some moisture. Mulching and feeding in spring, with a slow-release fertilizer and some organic compost, improves the plants' performance.

Leave the dead flowerheads on the plants over winter. Remove them in early spring, cutting back to the first pair of fat buds behind the flowerhead. No other pruning is required, but older plants can be rejuvenated by selectively removing some of the oldest branches to ground level.

See right for the **Lacecap** and **Hortensia (mopheads)** groups.

See pages 167–68 for *Hydrangea paniculata*, **'Preziosa'** and *quercifolia*.

Hydrangea arborescens cultivars make a small, loose bush with upright stems, pale green serrated leaves and dense, domed flowerheads that are up to 15cm (6in) across. The blooms of *Hydrangea arborescens* 'Annabelle' ♛ start lime green and develop into huge clusters of small cream sterile florets. This is not a good plant for a windy site because of the weight of the flowers. It looks lovely in semi-shade with ferns and hostas. Prune in spring.

Hydrangea aspera is a very different animal – a medium-sized species, with velvety leaves and an open, branched habit. Semi-shade is preferred and fertile soil that does not dry out. The *Hydrangea aspera* Kawakamii Group is a very late-flowering form with deep violet flowerheads with white sterile florets, looking attractive against the exotic, luxuriant foliage. Prune selectively only to control size and shape. *Hydrangea aspera* 'Mauvette' has large flowerheads of sterile and fertile florets that start out mauve then gradually turn to grey-pink. *Hydrangea aspera* Villosa Group ♛ is one of the loveliest of the late summer-flowering hydrangeas, medium-sized, with a spreading habit and velvety stems and leaves. The huge flowerheads are lilac-blue with dainty serrated, sterile florets. *Hydrangea aspera* 'Velvet and Lace' is a particularly fine form, with superb foliage and flowerheads of purple-blue and mauve-pink.

A superb choice for a large tub in a shady spot is *Hydrangea involucrata* 'Hortensis' ♛. This glorious hydrangea is an upright suckering shrub with fresh green foliage and loose, creamy flowerheads of double, sterile florets in summer. The flowers open lime-cream and blush pink with age.

Hydrangea serrata is a dwarf shrub, rarely growing to more than 1m (3ft), with smaller foliage than most hydrangeas and pretty lacecap flowers. 'Bluebird' is the best known cultivar. Its blue fertile florets are surrounded by

Hydrangea macrophylla

The *Hydrangea macrophylla* group, familiar as garden shrubs and as pot plants, consists of the Hortensia group (mopheads) and the Lacecap group. Most grow to around 1.5m (5ft), but can get much larger in favoured locations. On shallow chalk soils the foliage becomes yellow and chlorotic; remedy this by mulching and feeding. Some pink varieties are blue on acid soils. On alkaline soils, blueing powder can be used to attempt to change the colour to blue, but in reality it is not worth the effort in the open ground. White varieties cannot be changed but will often blush pink as the flowers age in full sun. The Lacecap group, with their distinctive flowerheads of fertile florets surrounded by a ring of sterile florets, are lighter and prettier than the mopheads, more satisfactory in mixed planting.

The flowers of mophead hydrangeas can be dried for winter decoration. Cut them when fully mature and hang them upside down to dry.

Hydrangea macrophylla 'Ayesha', Hortensia group: a mophead but totally different from others in the group, with greyish-lilac flowers like those of a large syringa (lilac).

'Ami Pasquier' ♀ Hortensia group: a mophead with a dwarf habit; deep pink-red flowers.

Hydrangea macrophylla 'Mariesii Grandiflora' ♀ ('White Wave'), Lacecap group: a small shrub good for an open position, with blue to pink flowerheads surrounded by white ray-florets.

'Mariesii Perfecta' ♀ ('Blue Wave'), Lacecap group: a strong-growing shrub best in light shade; large heads varying from pink to deep gentian-blue.

OTHER GOOD MOPHEAD HYDRANGEAS

'Altona' ♀ (left), rose-coloured large florets, blues well; best in shade.

Japanese Lady group: white-edged flowers; several forms and colours.

'Madame Emile Mouillère' ♀, large serrated florets with blue or pink eyes; the best white.

'Maréchal Foch' (right), rich rosy-pink or purple to deep blue, free-flowering.

'Nigra' ♀, distinctive black stems and rose florets.

OTHER GOOD LACECAP HYDRANGEAS

'Lanarth White' ♀ (right), compact habit; flat heads of pink or blue surrounded by large white ray-florets.

'Lilacina' (below), broad heads of pink or blue flowers.

'Veitchii' ♀, medium-sized shrub with dark green foliage and white florets ageing to pink; best in semi-shade; lime tolerant.

Hydrangea serrata 'Bluebird'

Hydrangea serrata 'Tiara'

Hypericum 'Hidcote' can be pruned in early spring, before it makes the new growth that will flower next summer. Light trimming or harder pruning is possible. It is a wonderful planting partner for golden-variegated evergreens and for spiraeas with golden foliage (see Good Companions, page 154).

Hypericum 'Rowallane' ♀ is rarely seen but worth seeking out. It is a more tender form than 'Hidcote' and needs a warm sheltered garden to survive. The flowers are the largest of any hypericum: glorious golden saucers up to 7cm (3in) across, weighing down the branches. Good against a sheltered wall, it can reach 2m (6ft) and is a spectacular sight when in flower.

Indigofera heterantha ♀ is not an attractive shrub in the winter and is usually very late to break into leaf; when it does, it is a reliable performer. A medium-sized shrub, spreading and spiky in habit when not in leaf, it can be knocked back by cold winter weather. The new growth quickly emerges, fine, soft-green pinnate leaves on arching

Indigofera heterantha

branches and a flower cluster in every leaf axil. The pea-like, bright purple-pink blooms are carried in arching sprays.

Indigofera potaninii has clear pink flowers throughout the summer and early autumn. It is large enough to support a summer-blooming clematis, such as the pale blue **'Prince Charles'**, a delight with the indigofera's horizontal sprays of pink, vetch-like blooms.

Indigofera likes good drainage and full sun; it is an ideal partner for salvia or nepeta (see Good Companions, page 154). In spring cut dead wood back to the new shoots. Untidy plants can be cut back hard at the same time.

Kolkwitzia amabilis (beauty bush) is a lovely medium-sized shrub from western China. Graceful and arching in habit, it forms a dense, well-branched mound of soft green foliage. The branches are smothered with pink, bell-shaped flowers in early summer. *Kolkwitzia amabilis* 'Pink Cloud' ♀ is the best form, an aptly named plant.

Kolkwitzia is an easy shrub to grow in sun, or light shade, on any soil. Treat

Kolwitzia amabilis

as any other deciduous summer-flowering shrub: cut out some of the older stems when the flowers fade.

Lavandula, the lavenders, are such a feature of English summer gardens that it would be wrong not to mention them here. The best varieties are described in detail with the grey-foliage plants, on pages 72–73. New cultivars are being introduced all the time, particularly of *Lavandula stoechas*. Many are very decorative, for example *Lavandula stoechas* subsp. *sampaioana*, a selection of which is sold as **'Purple Emperor'**. With its soft purple-brown flowerheads and upright growth, it is an appealing creature, but only suits a well-drained sunny site in a mild area. However, lavenders of this type are useful container plants for sunny patios.

large ray florets, red-purple on alkaline soils and sea-blue on acid. Autumn colour is good. Other recommended cultivars of *Hydrangea serrata* include **'Grayswood'** (its white ray florets turn pink and finally crimson) and **'Tiara'** (with blue florets turning mauve-pink and foliage that colours well in autumn).

Hypericum 'Hidcote' ♀ has all the qualities we look for in a hardy shrub: it is easy to grow and free-flowering, and has a long flowering period throughout summer and autumn. It is semi-evergreen and left unpruned will reach 2m (6ft) or so. The large saucer-shaped flowers are a clear golden yellow, just like huge buttercups – pure summer sunshine. Their weight makes the branches arch gracefully. This wonderful shrub is thought to have originated at Hidcote Manor, Gloucestershire.

Until the 1990s the shrubby mallow, **Lavatera,** was generally offered for sale as a herbaceous plant and only a few small, soft specimens were sold each year. Since then its qualities have been recognized and it has now become a garden staple. It grows quickly, flowers for a long period and mixes well with herbaceous plants and other shrubs. Lavateras are good in hot, sunny sites, grow well on chalk and are excellent for seaside gardens.

The best lavateras to grow in gardens are cultivars of *Lavatera* × *clementii.* Once listed as either *Lavatera olbia* or *Lavatera thuringiaca,* they are in fact hybrids of the two. All are vigorous,

Lavatera × *clementii* 'Blushing Bride'

Lavatera maritima 'Princesse de Lignes'

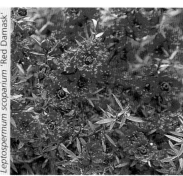

Leptospermum scoparium 'Red Damask'

LAVATERA TIPS

Lavateras are not long-lived plants. Expect to replace them after five or six years, and sooner on heavy clay soils.

They can be wobbly when first planted; a short stake to anchor unstable plants aids their establishment.

Tidy in autumn and hard prune, back to 30cm (1ft) or so, in early spring.

Lavatera × *clementii* 'Rosea'

medium-to-tall plants. The first cultivar to be grown was *Lavatera* × *clementii* 'Rosea' ♀ (*Lavatera olbia* 'Rosea'). This has large pink flowers all up the stems from early summer until late autumn. It resembles a hollyhock and combines superbly with nepeta and blue salvias.

Lavatera × *clementii* 'Barnsley' is now the best-known cultivar, a sport of 'Rosea', named after Rosemary Verey's garden in Gloucestershire. The flowers are palest pink with a red eye. It does tend to revert and shoots bearing clear pink flowers must be removed or they will quickly take over. **'Blushing Bride'** is very similar to 'Barnsley' but is more compact and less likely to revert. A more reliable plant, it is rapidly becoming the more popular choice. **'Burgundy Wine'** ♀ has deep purplish-pink flowers. It can look drab in the wrong setting, but is lovely with silver foliage and purple heucheras. Other × *clementii* cultivars include: **'Bredon Springs'** ♀, with wide-open funnel-shaped blooms of deep dusky-pink (a better choice than 'Rosea'); **'Candy Floss'** ♀, a pale pink option; and MEMORIES **('Stelav')**, whose pale pink buds open to white flowers with a pink eye.

Lavatera maritima 'Princesse de Lignes' is more tender than the × *clementii* cultivars, suitable only for a sunny sheltered spot. It is smaller-growing with greyish, downy leaves. The large flowers are saucer-shaped with elegantly turned back petals, a pale lilac with a dark eye and veins.

Leptospermum scoparium, the New Zealand tea-tree, is related to myrtle and is a native of New Zealand and Australia. A compact evergreen with wiry, arching stems and tiny leaves, it is an interesting contrast to broad-leaved shrubs. It is ideal against a sunny wall and looks good in pots. It suits Mediterranean-style planting and mixes well with silver-leaved subjects. This is a plant for warm seaside gardens and mild localities, needing full sun, good drainage and acid to neutral soil. It resents total desiccation, particularly in pots. Allowed to dry out, it sheds leaves and flowers.

There are numerous forms, with white, pink or deep red flowers. Best known is *Leptospermum scoparium* 'Red Damask' ♀, a medium-sized shrub with very double, deep red flowers and dark foliage. Similar in size, **var.** *incanum* 'Keatleyi' ♀ has large waxy-petalled, soft pink flowers; the young shoots are crimson and silky. Another medium plant, **'Nichollsii'** ♀ has carmine-red flowers and bronze foliage. **'Kiwi'** ♀ is dwarf, with pink flowers and bronze foliage.

Philadelphus

Philadelphus, the mock oranges, are often incorrectly known as syringas (lilacs), perhaps because they too are much-loved, easy-to-grow shrubs with heavily fragrant flowers. Most of the best-known hybrids were raised by the French nursery Lemoine in the early 1900s. This may also have led to the confusion over the name, as many of our most popular hybrid lilacs came out of the same stable, at the same time.

When selecting a philadelphus, make sure that it is a fragrant one. The scent is one of the great delights of the summer garden. A philadelphus that has no perfume is nothing more than an inferior deutzia. These are deciduous shrubs, ranging in height from dwarf to tall, with elegantly arching branches heavy with white, four-petalled single, semi-double or double flowers often with prominent yellow stamens.

Philadelphus grow on any soil and are particularly happy on chalk. Prune immediately after flowering, cutting out some of the older stems that have flowered, and allowing the new vigorous shoots to develop. Whatever its size, a philadelphus should be a graceful arching shrub, not a trimmed ball or mound.

Philadelphus coronarius is the most commonly cultivated species, especially in southern Europe. A medium-sized, vigorous, easy-to-grow shrub, very tolerant of dry conditions. The flowers are smaller than many of the hybrids, more bell-like, creamy white and wonderfully fragrant. The golden and variegated forms are seen more often (see pages 45, 69).

Philadelphus 'Belle Etoile' ♀ is one of the most beautiful philadelphus, with large, wonderfully fragrant, single creamy-white flowers, flushed maroon at the centre, on a fairly compact and upright, medium-sized shrub. Looks stunning planted with a purple-leaved cotinus or physocarpus.

Philadelphus 'Manteau d'Hermine' ♀ is the best choice for a small garden. A dwarf, compact plant, it reaches no more than 1m (3ft), with graceful, arching stems. The flowers are creamy white, double and fragrant. It is a lovely shrub to plant with silver foliage in a sunny position.

OTHER GOOD PHILADELPHUS

Philadelphus 'Beauclerk', a graceful, arching, medium-sized shrub, bears large open flowers, rounded white petals flushed pink towards the mass of stamens.

Philadelphus lewisii, is a tall, upright North American species. 'Snow Velvet' has huge fragrant, semi-double flowers.

Philadelphus microphyllus, a dwarf-grower with tiny sage-green leaves and starry, single, richly fragrant flowers.

Philadelpus 'Minnesota Snowflake', an American variety; its arching branches are weighed down with fragrant double flowers; medium and dwarf forms.

Philadelphus 'Virginal' is probably the best-known and most widely planted philadelphus. The large, double flowers are richly fragrant. Old plants left unpruned can grow to at least 3m (10ft), ideal to support a late-flowering *Clematis viticella*.

Perovskia 'Blue Spire'

Perovskia is a graceful, upright shrub, reaching no more than 1m (3ft) in height. The silvery-white stems carry soft, fern-like foliage and spikes of lavender-blue flowers in late summer. It is a plant for well-drained soil and full sun, where it associates well with silver-foliage plants and lavenders. **'Blue Spire'** ♔ is the best variety to grow and has the largest flower spikes. **'Filigran'** has even more finely cut foliage; in isolation this looks pretty but, as perovskia is a plant to mix with others, it is of secondary importance.

Perovskia has attractive white stems. Leave these in the border for winter interest and then cut back to 20cm (8in) before spring. The tops of the stems die back naturally and if left on the plant will become untidy and unsightly.

Potentillas belong to the rose family and include both herbaceous and woody plants. The shrubby ones are hardy, easy to grow and provide reliable summer colour. They grow in sun or semi-shade and perform on any soil, being particularly happy on chalk. A potentilla in winter is not a particularly pretty sight with its tangled brown stems and remains of last season's leaves and flowers. But, after a light trim in early spring, it soon bursts into life and begins its long succession of small, bright, single rose-like flowers.

The display starts in early summer and can easily extend into late autumn.

The white and yellow varieties are the best choice for full sun. Red, orange and pink varieties prefer semi-shade and more moisture; their colours bleach in strong sunlight.

Recommended cultivars of *Potentilla fruticosa* are described below. Most reach less than 1m (3ft) in height. They may be rounded or spreading in habit.

Tamarix, or tamarisk, is a large, light, feathery shrub, often untidy in habit, but nonetheless appealing. It is often planted near the sea as its supple branches withstand exposed conditions. The pale green, plume-like foliage is transformed when the fine, fluffy flowers appear, turning the whole shrub from green to pink for several weeks.

Tamarix ramosissima (*Tamarix pentandra*) has reddish-brown branches

---

RECOMMENDED *POTENTILLA FRUTICOSA* CULTIVARS

'Abbotswood' ♔, a favourite white-flowered variety with spreading growth and dark green leaves; the flowers are freely produced over a long period; good with silver-foliage and white-variegated shrubs.

'Elizabeth', an excellent plant raised by Hillier Nurseries, dome-shaped, over 1m (3ft) in height, with large canary-yellow flowers from spring to autumn.

'Hopley's Orange' ♔, dwarf and spreading, with bright green, fine foliage; flowers orange with a narrow yellow margin to the petals.

'Limelight' ♔ has soft yellow flowers with bright yellow centres set against bright green foliage.

'Pink Beauty' ♔ ('Lovely Pink'), dwarf, with bright green foliage, single and semi-double soft pink flowers.

'Manchu', dwarf and spreading, with grey foliage and white flowers; a good choice for planting in gravel or scree.

MARIAN RED ROBIN ('Marrob') ♔, low, compact and spreading with red flowers; a stronger colour than 'Red Ace' and less likely to fade.

'Medicine Wheel Mountain' ♔, compact, low and spreading, with red-flushed shoots and large yellow flowers.

'Primrose Beauty' ♔, this is one of the best; small, spreading and free-flowering,

with grey-green foliage and primrose-yellow flowers – a soft colour combination that mixes well in any planting scheme.

'Sunset', a small bushy shrub with light orange to brick-red flowers; looks pretty planted with *Spiraea* 'Firelight'.

'Vilmoriniana', a large one; upright growth to 2m (6ft), with silvery foliage and cream flowers.

Tamarix tetrandra

Weigela 'Bristol Ruby' with ceanothus

Weigela 'Majestueux'

and flowers in late summer on shoots produced earlier the same season. The whole shrub becomes a feathery mass of rose pink – which looks delightful in association with a purple-leaved sambucus (see page 54) or *Elaeagnus* 'Quicksilver' (see page 75). *Tamarix ramosissima* 'Rubra' ♀ is a particularly good form, with darker flowers.

Prune *Tamarix ramosissima* in early spring. Usually light pruning to tidy and control the shrub is all that is necessary. Maintain the light, open habit.

Tamarix tetrandra ♀ has dark branches and greener foliage. It flowers in late spring and early summer. These flowers are light pink, transforming the branches into long, waving plumes. Because this tamarisk flowers on the previous season's wood, it must be pruned straight after flowering, and never in spring.

Weigela is a good, solid flowering shrub that produces a splendid display of tubular flowers for a few weeks in early summer and, occasionally, another small flush in late summer or early autumn. Weigelas are tolerant creatures, growing well in town gardens and withstanding pollution. They suit clay soils and grow well on chalk. Most form a loose, rounded shrub 1.5–2m (5–6ft) tall.

Recommended varieties of weigela include the following. **'Abel Carrière'** is free-flowering with large, bright rose-carmine flowers, flecked gold in the throat. **'Bristol Ruby'** is a vigorous and upright bush, free-flowering with bright ruby-red blooms; it is excellent planted against purple cotinus or red berberis. CARNAVAL (**'Courtalor'**), a French hybrid, bears a mixture of pink and white bicoloured flowers and clear pink flowers on a small, compact shrub. An old favourite, **'Eva Rathke'**, is compact and slow-growing, with bright red flowers with straw-coloured anthers; it is a good choice for the smaller garden. **'Majestueux'** is upright-growing, with madder-pink, carmine-flushed flowers early in the season. **'Mont Blanc'** a vigorous shrub, has large white, fragrant flowers. See also pages 47, 54–55, 69.

Prune weigelas straight after flowering, cutting out some of the stems that have flowered so as to allow new shoots to grow through. It is not essential that this is done every year. Pruning in this way promotes arching sprays of flowers and an attractive habit.

Old weigelas are prone to thin foliage and growth of lichen on the branches; rejuvenate by hard pruning and feeding with a balanced, slow-release fertilizer.

MAINTAINING COLOUR

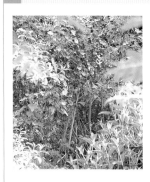

Continuity of interest throughout the long summer months is the ongoing quest in the garden. Use late-flowering summer shrubs such as buddleia and caryopteris to take over from early-flowering shrubs and herbaceous plants. *Buddleja* 'Lochinch' is a good planting partner for *Abutilon* 'Jermyns' (pictured left): when the abutilon has finished flowering, the buddleia is ready to bloom. *Caryopteris* × *clandonensis* 'Heavenly Blue' rekindles the sapphire hues of herbaceous geraniums that have been cut back after their early summer display.

Early-flowering shrubs such as philadelphus and deutzia can be given a new lease of life with the addition of a light-growing, late-flowering clematis such as a *Clematis texensis* or *viticella*.

Use the foliage backdrop of early shrubs to show off tall, later-blooming herbaceous plants such as veronicastrum, helenium and aster.

Plants for bees and butterflies

One of the greatest joys of the English garden in summer is the sight of butterflies flitting from bloom to bloom, while the buzzing of bees is surely one of the season's most evocative sounds. The summer garden, particularly in the latter part of the season, is rich in nectar-laden flowers. Shrubs and herbaceous perennials join forces to attract bees, butterflies and other beneficial insects.

There are numerous plants that attract insects. Favourites are those with flowerheads made up of hundreds of tiny flowers, such as: buddleia, sedum, caryopteris, hebe and verbena. These are easy-to-grow plants that thrive in an open, sunny position on any well-drained soil. All are excellent in a coastal garden, and will work their magic in attracting butterflies and bees in urban as well as rural situations.

Blue buddleias, such as the beautiful silver-leaved *Buddleja* 'Lochinch' ♇ combine well with the tall, airy *Verbena bonariensis* ♇. The latter has a longer flowering season than the buddleia and will continue into autumn with its vivid heads of bright purple flowers with orange stamens. Both are irresistible to butterflies.

A blue caryopteris such as *Caryopteris* × *clandonensis* 'First Choice' ♇ creates a classic, warm late-summer combination with the ever-popular *Sedum* 'Herbstfreude' ♇. The flat heads of sedums remain attractive to bees and butterflies for several weeks until they fade to the rich brown-pink of autumn.

Hebes, with their bottlebrush flowers, bloom for a long period. The purple-leaved, blue-flowered *Hebe* 'Caledonia' ♇, is the perfect planting partner for aromatic *Origanum laevigatum* 'Herrenhausen' ♇. Both grow well on chalk soils and the hebe provides evergreen interest when the origanum dies back to ground level in winter.

OTHER SHRUBS GOOD FOR BEES AND BUTTERFLIES

Amelanchier	Escallonia	Skimmia
Berberis	Helianthemum	Spiraea
Ceanothus	Hypericum	Syringa
Chaenomeles	Lavandula	Tamarix
Cistus	Nepeta	Thymus
Cotoneaster	Origanum	Weigela
Cytisus	Pyracantha	
Daphne	Ribes	
Elaeagnus	Rosmarinus	

Autumn

Autumn is such a long season. The first shades start to appear before the end of the summer holidays; the last leaves fall in midwinter. That's four months, one-third of a year! With a little planning, autumn can be a gloriously colourful time in the garden.

As the season progresses, the flat green of late summer is transformed into a rich backdrop for the blooms of dahlia, michaelmas daisy and nerine. Without any competition from their deciduous partners, the evergreens begin to shine out, ready to take on their role as stalwarts of the winter garden.

Fine days are spent gathering fallen leaves, consigning their glorious colours to the compost heap. Wet days are spent staring out of the window at the rain, lamenting the passing of another year. Suddenly some plants begin to come into their own in this more minimalist landscape. Falling leaves reveal the glories of the bark and berries that have developed under the heavy blanket of late-summer foliage.

It is trees that come to mind first for autumn colour: think of beech, acer, liquidambar. They provide the most obvious changes in the landscape. However, much of the best colour comes from shrubs. Even such British native plants as *Viburnum opulus, Cornus mas*, *Viburnum lantana* and *Euonymus europaeus* oblige with a rich display.

Adding to the spectacle are the ripening fruits of the late-summer and autumn months. Plants need to effect seed disposal and, by making their fruit appetizing and attractive, some plants persuade animals and birds to do the work of distributing the species. As hedgerows glow with shiny rose hips and sealing-wax red haws, so gardens glow with orange and scarlet berries of pyracantha and cotoneaster.

Some shrubs choose this season as their time to flower. Most start in late summer but continue through the mellow days of autumn; in some cases the flowers are enhanced by changing hues of foliage.

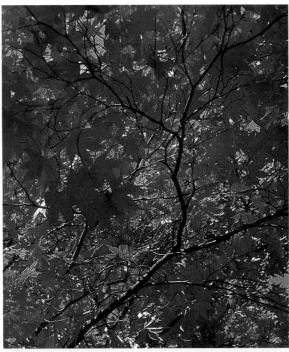

Acer palmatum 'Osakazuki'

THE CHEMISTRY OF AUTUMN COLOUR

Autumn colour occurs when the components of photosynthesis are broken down in the leaf and nutrients, particularly nitrogen and phosphorus, are reabsorbed for winter storage. In the case of trees and shrubs, the food is stored in the woody stems.

Different pigments are responsible for different colours. The bright yellow colours are caused by carotenoids. These are present in the leaf throughout the year, but their yellow colour becomes prevalent when chlorophyll, which is responsible for the green colour, breaks down and is reabsorbed into the plant during the autumn.

It is thought that the production of anthocyanins, responsible for the red shades of autumn, increases at this time. By screening the system from the effects of bright sunlight during the breakdown of photosynthetic compounds, anthocyanins enable a steady flow of energy to be maintained in the leaf, thus enabling complete breakdown and absorption.

While some evergreens do colour, displaying red and orange shades rather than yellow, the phenomenon of autumn colour mainly occurs in deciduous plants, which have a dormant season.

AUTUMN-FLOWERING SHRUBS

Abelia could never be described as our most popular genus of shrubs, but it has much to offer the gardener, not least its ability to perform in the autumn months. As young plants in pots, most varieties look ungainly and give little clue to the graceful, but robust, shrubs that they will make.

Abelia × grandiflora ♀ grows to a vigorous, arching, semi-evergreen shrub of medium size. The leaves are small, neat, dark and glossy. The flowers start to appear in midsummer and continue well into early autumn, white flushed pink with a pink calyx that persists after the flower has fallen. This hybrid, originally raised in Italy, has been in cultivation since 1866. The cultivar *Abelia × grandiflora* 'Francis Mason' has variegated leaves with a golden margin; this variegation needs full sun if it is to develop properly.

Abelia schumannii ♀ is a small, very hardy shrub. The lilac-pink flowers are blotched orange and slightly fragrant. They are produced over a long period, from late summer through the autumn.

Abelia 'Edward Goucher', a hybrid between *Abelia × grandiflora* and *Abelia parviflora*, was raised in the USA in 1911. It is a small evergreen shrub with bronze young foliage and profuse lilac-pink flowers in summer and autumn; excellent for a small garden.

Ceanothus 'Autumnal Blue'

With their graceful growth and pastel flowers, abelias make the perfect companion for some of our best autumn-flowering herbaceous plants, including echinacea, sedum, aster, as well as any purple-leaved shrubs, such as berberis and elder.

It is not necessary to prune abelias, but if you need to reduce the size of the plant, cut out whole stems selectively; trimming will only ruin the graceful character of the plant.

The glorious blues of **Ceanothus** are not confined to spring. The deciduous varieties perform in late summer and autumn, albeit in a more subtle way than their evergreen cousins.

A very popular deciduous ceanothus is *Ceanothus × delileanus* 'Gloire de Versailles' ♀, which has large panicles

Ceratostigma willmottianum

of powder-blue flowers. Its light and open habit is perfect with late-summer herbaceous plants and the last blooms of the roses. As its name suggests, the evergreen *Ceanothus* 'Autumnal Blue' ♀ performs now. It is one of the hardiest hybrids, with medium-sized, bright, glossy green leaves and sky-blue flowers in late summer and autumn. It often performs in spring, too.

Ceratostigma, the hardy plumbago, may well be regarded as a summer shrub because the most familiar form, *Ceratostigma willmottianum* ♀, starts to flower any time from midsummer.

Abelia 'Edward Goucher'

Hibiscus

Hibiscus syriacus, the hardy hibiscus or shrubby mallow, is so late to break into leaf in spring it is not surprising that it does not flower until late summer or autumn. It makes a very upright shrub, with ascending branches of ash grey, and most varieties grow to 2 or 3m (6–10ft). The leaves appear in late spring, pale yellow-green to start with, becoming mid-green. The flowers, which resemble individual hollyhock blossoms, appear from midsummer onwards, but are usually at their best during early and mid-autumn. Hibiscus thrive on well-drained soil and are good on chalk. Natives of eastern Asia, they are extremely hardy, but they do need full sun if they are to flower well.

Hibiscus syriacus was probably introduced to English gardens as early as the 16th century. Today, there are a surprising number of varieties, some with single flowers, others with double flowers, and in a range of colours from white through pink and red to almost blue. They are useful, structural deciduous shrubs for the back of the border. They combine well with herbaceous perennials that bring interest earlier in the season, including Japanese anemones, achillea and helenium. Hibiscus are often grown in pots, but because they are late to break into leaf and their season of interest is relatively short, their appeal as a permanent subject for a container is limited. There are other, better shrubs for pots.

Avoid pruning any hibiscus. They are not broad, spreading shrubs and if they are topped in order to control height their habit becomes ugly.

Hibiscus syriacus 'Oiseau Bleu' ♀ (left), better known as BLUE BIRD, is the best-known and most widely planted cultivar. The single, violet-blue flowers have a darker eye. 'Marina' is an improvement, with larger flowers of a clearer blue and a deep-red eye.

Hibiscus syriacus 'Red Heart' ♀ (left) has large white flowers with a deep red eye. The hybrid between this variety and BLUE BIRD, *Hibiscus syriacus* RUSSIAN VIOLET ('Floru') has lilac-pink flowers with a deep-red centre.

Hibiscus syriacus 'Hamabo' ♀, one of the most reliable and attractive cultivars, has pale pink flowers with a crimson eye, clean and clear, and without the tired colour of many varieties. 'Aphrodite' has much larger flowers (up to 13cm/5in across), deeper pink, with a red eye.

OTHER GOOD HIBISCUS

Hibiscus syriacus 'Diana' ♀, the best white, with large single flowers with crinkly petals.

Hibiscus syriacus PINK GIANT ('Flogi') ♀, large, feathered flowers, clear pink with a deep-red eye.

Hydrangea paniculata 'Unique'

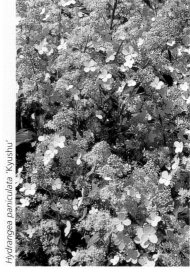

Hydrangea paniculata 'Kyushu'

Ceratostigma willmottianum grows to about 1m (3ft); wiry stems carry neat, dark green leaves that tint with dark mahogany and red as autumn progresses. This rich background is the perfect setting for the sapphire-blue flowers that stud the plant like jewels. This is indeed a gem, introduced by plant collector Ernest Wilson in 1908. *Ceratostigma griffithii* is another beautiful one, with deep blue flowers and foliage that turns particularly red in autumn and persists well into winter.

Treat ceratostigmas in a similar way to hardy fuchsias: trim, or cut back to ground level, in late winter. The latter will make a more lush shrub but of lesser stature. In hard winters these plants may be cut back to the ground by frost, unless they are in a sheltered spot.

Ceratostigmas like dry, well-drained soil, and flower and colour best in full sun. They are good plants for the base of a sunny wall and look stunning when planted with the sugar-pink *Nerine bowdenii*, which flowers when the ceratostigma is at its best.

Hydrangea is a feature of summer and the prevalent shrub of gardens in many coastal areas. The 'mophead' and 'lacecap' hydrangeas develop their greenish red, mature shades as summer turns to autumn (see pages 156–57). Others have their heyday in the autumn.

One of the most breathtaking and showiest of large shrubs, *Hydrangea paniculata* 'Grandiflora' ♀ cannot fail to grab attention as it erupts from the back of the border, with its large conical sprays of flowers resembling huge lilac blossoms. The flowers start in summer, pale green, then cream and, as they reach full size, pale cream strongly flushed pink in full sun.

There are many other cultivars of *Hydrangea paniculata*. 'Unique' ♀ is most spectacular, similar to 'Grandiflora' but with even larger flowerheads, 40cm (16in) or more in length. 'Tardiva' is a late-flowering type, again with large flowers. 'Kyushu' ♀ is upright in habit, and has dark glossy leaves and panicles of flowers with more, large ray florets. It is a native of Kyushu, Japan.

Hydrangea 'Preziosa' ♀, a mophead, is a hybrid between *Hydrangea*

GOOD COMPANIONS

The dark purple leaves of *Sambucus nigra* f. *porphyrophylla* 'Gerda' ('Black Beauty') (1) make it a good partner for *Abelia* × *grandiflora* ♀ (2).

A colourful autumn cameo: *Aster* × *frikartii* 'Mönch' ♀ (3) with *Clematis viticella* 'Royal Velours' ♀ (4) and *Hydrangea* 'Preziosa' ♀ (5).

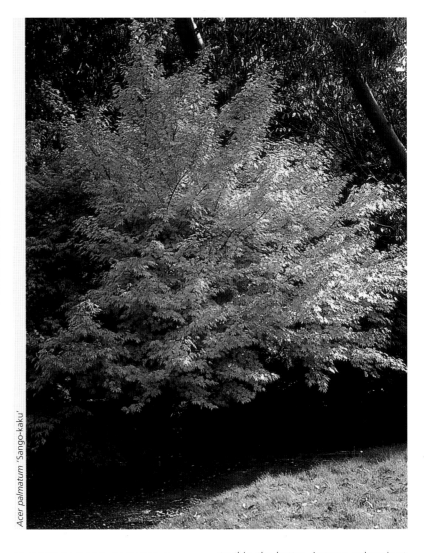

Acer palmatum 'Sango-kaku'

PRUNING HYDRANGEA PANICULATA

Most hydrangeas do not need pruning, but if *Hydrangea paniculata* are left unpruned, growth can be lax and weak – a habit displayed in young plants, and perhaps one that puts some people off them. To display the magnificent flower panicles, *Hydrangea paniculata* need strong upright branches. Once a strong base has been established, cut the plants back hard in late winter, to within 5cm (2 or 3in) of the previous season's growth, ideally 60cm (2ft) or so from the ground. This creates a pollarded effect.

---

macrophylla and *Hydrangea serrata*. Reaching 1.5m (5ft) in height, it has round heads of large rose-pink florets, contrasting with its purple-tinged young leaves and the purple-red stems. The flowers change to deep red-purple as autumn progresses, creating a bold, rich effect that suits the warm autumnal light. (See Good Companions, page 167.)

Hydrangea quercifolia ♀, the oak-leaved hydrangea, is one of the most underrated shrubs. Of medium size, it is an architectural plant with its bold lobed leaves that resemble those of oak. Throughout the year these are soft, felted green, turning magnificently in autumn to orange-red. Conical heads of large florets appear in late summer but these are of secondary importance to the foliage. A native of south-eastern USA, it was introduced to Britain in 1803. There are several named cultivars, all easy to grow and shade-tolerant. *Hydrangea quercifolia* 'Sike's Dwarf' is a very compact variety that makes a small shrub, wider than it is tall; this is a good choice for the small garden.

Hydrangea quercifolia requires no pruning and no maintenance once it is established; it can take two or three seasons to get going.

DECIDUOUS SHRUBS FOR AUTUMN COLOUR

Acer palmatum, the Japanese maples, are well known for their autumn colours. Versatile plants with numerous uses, they crop up in several sections of this book (see Plant Profile, pages 50–51). Their foliage is a feature throughout spring and summer, but the plants get a new lease of life with a glorious display of autumn colour.

For the finest display of autumn colour, plant acers in a sheltered spot, but one with good light and some direct sunshine; a woodland glade is the ideal, so the nearer the conditions are to this, the better. Autumn colour is at its best on neutral to acid soil rich in organic matter. It is essential the plants do not dry out in summer. Drought causes the leaves to brown and shrivel from the ends. They may fall or simply die on the plant without colouring.

Red varieties look spectacular when the light shines through the leaves; take this into account when planting. The yellow forms work well against a dark background of bold evergreens.

Acer palmatum 'Bloodgood' ♀ (see page 51) has deep reddish-purple foliage, which turns rich red in autumn. Mature plants produce attractive winged fruits to add to the effect.

Acer palmatum 'Seiryû'

Acer palmatum var. dissectum 'Inaba-shidare' ♀ is the best of the red Dissectum types for autumn colour. The strong, purple, finely cut foliage turns crimson in autumn. Its strong growth, and fine foliage, is less susceptible to summer drought than many of the varieties with finely cut leaves.

Acer palmatum 'Kamagata' is a smaller shrub, with bright green shoots and neat lobed leaves, red when young. The autumn colour is a mixture of brilliant yellow, orange and red.

Acer palmatum 'Ôsakazuki' ♀ is a green-leaved variety, with broader leaves than many. In autumn the foliage turns fiery scarlet. This is one of the most brilliant maples for autumn colour and is more scorch-resistant than most, being less susceptible to damage from wind and drought.

Acer palmatum 'Sango-kaku' ♀ ('Senkaki'), the coral bark maple, is best known for its coral-red young branches in winter. The habit is upright and when young the plant is easily mistaken for a bright Cornus alba. The leaves turn soft yellow in autumn, creating a most pleasing effect with the coral stems.

Acer palmatum var. dissectum 'Seiryû' ♀ is the best of the green Dissectum types for autumn colour, making a large, upright, graceful shrub.

The fresh green leaves are tinged red in summer, later turning orange-yellow splashed with crimson.

Acer palmatum 'Yezo-Nishiki' is fast-growing, vigorous, with upright growth becoming arching as the plant matures. The red-purple foliage becomes brilliant red in autumn.

Berberis may have declined in popularity, but it only takes the onset of autumn to remind us of their value. The cultivars of Berberis thunbergii reliably reward with a brilliant display of autumn colour on virtually any soil, regardless of the summer weather conditions. On a

dry site in full sun, their colour is simply unbeatable. Their other great attribute is the length of the display. Those tough, round leaves hang onto the stems for several weeks; the colour simply becomes more intense. Shining red berries are revealed by some varieties as their leaves thin. The species may be unprepossessing for most of the year but the display of orange-red from mid- to late autumn is sensational.

Most of the red-leaved varieties colour well. Of particular note are the fastigiate forms: Berberis thunbergii 'Helmond Pillar' and Berberis

Acer palmatum 'Yezo-Nishiki'

Callicarpa bodinieri var. giraldii 'Profusion'

Cotinus 'Grace'

Euonymus alatus

thunbergii 'Red Pillar'. Their bold upright form makes an unmissable statement as the red-purple foliage of summer turns to burgundy-scarlet in autumn. (See pages 52–53.)

Callicarpa conjures up an autumn cocktail of pastel colours. All summer the oval leaves are dull green, rather like those of a privet, then suddenly, as autumn comes upon us, they turn to amber flushed with bronze-purple, while pink and lilac-purple berries form clusters on the branches. The leaves exhaust their display and fall, leaving the berries: shining clusters of bright purple beads carried on fine straight branches, creating an almost molecular display that lasts well into winter. The most commonly grown callicarpa, *Callicarpa bodinieri* var. *giraldii* 'Profusion'♀, has bronze-purple young foliage. This is an upright, tall plant, ideal for a site where a green background shrub is needed behind herbaceous planting. In a more open situation, it is particularly effective underplanted with purple heucheras, such as *Heuchera* 'Amethyst Myst'. The fruit often shrivels before maturing on young plants. Be patient:

this shrub has to be firmly established before it performs well.

The virtues of **Cornus alba** are extolled in most parts of this book. Many cultivars of this versatile plant display superb autumn shades before they reveal their winter stems. They are a good choice for damp sites and clay, and for colour on neutral to alkaline soils. (See pages 177–79).

The colours of **Cotinus** 'Grace' intensify from soft red-brown summer hues to a climax of vivid scarlet by mid-autumn. The sun shining through the round, delicate leaves makes a truly wonderful sight – bear this in mind when positioning the plant.

A hybrid between *Cotinus obovatus* and *Cotinus coggygria* 'Velvet Cloak', *Cotinus* 'Grace' was raised by Hillier propagator Peter Dummer in 1979. A tall, vigorous shrub, it often reaches a surprising 3m (10ft) or more. It can be cut back hard in late winter and will reward with vigorous, graceful shoots carrying healthy foliage the next summer.

Cotinus 'Flame'♀ is another hybrid, between *Cotinus coggygria* and *Cotinus obovatus*. This is a large shrub, often tree-like, with big round green leaves. Huge smoky plumes of pink flowers in summer are followed by a spectacular display of autumn colour as the leaves turn brilliant orange-red.

The purple-leaved cotinus (see page 54) turn from purple to red as autumn progresses. **Cotinus** GOLDEN SPIRIT ('Ancot') colours extremely well, even in semi-shade. The coloured foliage, a wonderful shade of coral-orange, lasts well. (See page 45.)

Euonymus alatus♀ is the most surprising of all the shrubs grown for their autumn colour. A native of China

Cotinus GOLDEN SPIRIT ('Ancot')

and Japan, it is a dense, slow-growing shrub, often of horizontal habit, reaching a maximum height of 1.5m (5ft). This is an unassuming shrub; from the moment the leaves appear on the branches in mid-spring it is an unremarkable green, until one autumn day the bush is ablaze with colour. The vivid coral-red leaves last well, falling to show green-winged stems, attractive in their own right. A mature plant may produce purple fruits that split to reveal bright orange seeds.

Euonymus europaeus (spindle) is a European native. It sometimes makes a small tree with round green stems and good autumn colour. The twigs and branches are curiously straight and were once used as butchers' skewers, hence

so many of the shrubs that provide good autumn colour prefer acid soil.

Euonymus hamiltonianus is a larger-growing relative of *Euonymus europaeus*. **Euonymus hamiltonianus subsp. *sieboldianus* 'Coral Charm'** has pale pink fruits that split to reveal red seeds. **Euonymus hamiltonianus 'Red Elf'** has deep pink fruits and red seeds. If your garden is large enough to accommodate a big, green deciduous shrub that has a moment of glory in the autumn, consider one of these.

Parrotia persica ♀ (the iron tree) is a relative of hamamelis, resembling it in its growth habit, leaf shape, curious red flowers in winter and its sensational autumn colour. However, it differs from hamamelis in its tolerance of chalky soil,

Avoid pruning parrotias at all costs. This would rob them of their unique, open-centred and spreading shape. Do not underestimate the eventual size; in mixed planting, give them temporary partners that can be removed later.

Rhus typhina (stag's horn sumach) was an essential choice for gardens in the mid-20th century. Its reddish-brown felty stems and flocked brown seed-heads were widely seen, all the more noticeable in autumn with the onset of the fiery autumn tints of the foliage. This is a large suckering shrub that, once established, sends up offspring all over the garden, particularly if the roots are disturbed near to the parent plant. Suckers were passed on from gardener to gardener and so the plant spread. Its

Euonymus europaeus 'Red Cascade'

Parrotia persica

Rhus typhina 'Dissecta' ('Laciniata')

another common name, skewer wood. Masses of scarlet seed capsules split to reveal orange seeds.

A selected form with rich, scarlet autumn colour, **Euonymus europaeus 'Red Cascade'** ♀ is a large, light and airy shrub with masses of rosy-red fruits on elegantly arching branches. It works particularly well with white-variegated evergreens such as *Rhamnus alaternus* 'Argenteovariegata' and *Pittosporum* 'Garnettii'.

Euonymus alatus and *Euonymus europaeus* colour and thrive on chalk, making them especially useful when

on which it colours just as superbly as it does on acid soil. This is an excellent choice of large shrub for those who do not have lime-free soil and are looking for dramatic autumn effect.

Parrotias are superb shrubs either for specimen planting in a lawn, or as a striking backdrop for autumn-flowering herbaceous perennials such as helenium and rudbeckia. The growth habit is architectural and spreading, the foliage deep green and shiny on the upper surface. The autumn transformation is long-lasting, with shades of chestnut-brown, deep red, rich flame and gold.

invasive qualities and ability to sucker in the lawn has led to its demise from favour. Rhus look awkward as young plants; they are not appealing when offered for sale in pots in garden centres. However, they are interesting shrubs with architectural form and have the bonus of spectacular autumn display. *Rhus typhina* 'Dissecta' ♀ ('Laciniata') is an excellent form, with finely cut foliage, large brown seedheads and orange-yellow autumn colour.

Rhus copallina, the dwarf sumach, is a much more compact plant, from North America. The leaves are shinier than those of *Rhus typhina*. The seedheads are not as spectacular, but the autumn colour is rich red or purple. This plant is a good choice for the smaller garden.

Rhus × pulvinata Autumn Lace Group 'Red Autumn Lace' ♚ (*Rhus glabra* 'Laciniata') is a large shrub with bold fern-like leaves and deeply cut leaflets. The fruit clusters are red, set off superbly by the red, yellow and orange autumn tints. The shoots are green, only slightly hairy, and lacking the 'antler' bloom of the stag's horn sumach.

Viburnum opulus, the guelder rose, resembles a maple, with pretty, white flowers in spring that look like lacecap hydrangeas. In autumn the leaves turn rich and dark, plum-purple and flame scarlet. At the same time the fruits ripen, bunches of them, translucent and bright red, like the most luscious redcurrants. The fruits, delicate though they look, persist long into the winter. This is a familiar native plant of woods and hedgerows, and grows well in wet situations. It deserves wider use in the garden. In rural situations and open areas, *Viburnum opulus* can be planted as hedging whips in groups of three or five; producing large shrubs that sit well in the rural environment in an economic way. This is a good plant for wet sites with *Cornus alba* and species of willow (See Good Companions, page 173.)

Nyssa sylvatica 'Sheffield Park'

Viburnum opulus 'Compactum'

Viburnum opulus 'Compactum' ♚ flowers and fruits very freely and is a good cultivar for small gardens; sadly, it is hard to find. See page 147 for the snowball bush, *Viburnum opulus* 'Roseum' ♚ ('Sterile').

A number of other deciduous and semi-evergreen viburnums display good autumn colour, but they are rarely planted for this purpose. Our native *Viburnum lantana*, the wayfaring tree, turns a deep wine colour in autumn. The tiered horizontal branches of that frothy white beauty of the summer border *Viburnum plicatum* f. *tomentosum* 'Mariesii' ♚ colour well when the shrub is planted in good light. *Viburnum × carlcephalum* ♚ is a medium-sized, compact shrub with round heads of fragrant flowers in spring and leaves that often colour rich red-brown in autumn before they fall.

AUTUMN ON ACID SOIL

For those lucky owners of acid soil, **hamamelis** (see page 181) and **deciduous azaleas** (see page 104) are musts for autumn colour as well as for their respective winter and spring displays of flowers. Colours vary according to variety but rich bronze and orange reign supreme. These plants are not related but have much in common; with their elegant branch framework and noble stature, both are excellent as feature shrubs planted in grass. The close relative of hamamelis, *Fothergilla major* ♚, is another excellent choice for rich autumn shades (see page 111).

Eucryphia glutinosa ♚, *Enkianthus campanulatus* ♚ and *Enkianthus perulatus* ♚, described fully in the 'Acid soils' section of this book, pages 110–11, are among the most spectacular and reliable of autumn-colour shrubs.

Itea virginica 'Henry's Garnet' is a plant for neutral or acid soil originating from Pennsylvania, USA. It is a small, upright deciduous shrub, producing spikes of fragrant creamy flowers in July. The pointed leaves turn rich red-purple in autumn, lasting well into early winter.

Nyssa sylvatica ♚ is normally grown as a tree. Because it resents disturbance, it is transplanted when small and so is usually seen at garden centres in shrub-like proportions. On a moist, lime-free soil, the autumn colour is spectacular. *Nyssa sylvatica* 'Sheffield Park' is one of the best-known forms, with orange-red colour early in the season.

An increase in the popularity of blueberries has led to wider cultivation of the cultivars of the ericaceous shrub *Vaccinium corymbosum* ♚. These not

Leucothoe fontanesiana 'Rainbow'

Nandina domestica 'Fire Power'

only productive but also highly decorative shrubs, with arching stems and bright green leaves that turn scarlet and bronze in autumn. The summer fruits follow the clusters of pink and white flowers produced in May.

EVERGREENS THAT COLOUR IN AUTUMN

All evergreen shrubs and trees lose their leaves but the process is a gradual one that takes place throughout the year, and not all in one season. After a hot summer, and particularly after dry conditions, many evergreens show some autumn colour.

Leucothoe offer some attractive evergreen shrubs that are shade-tolerant but require lime-free soil. *Leucothoe fontanesiana* 'Rainbow', probably the best known, is a small spreading shrub with arching stems carrying leathery leaves variegated with cream, yellow, pink and burgundy. There is some intensification, and change, in foliage colour in autumn and winter. However, *Leucothoe fontanesiana* LOVITA ('Zebonard') and SCARLETTA ('Zeblid') are at their best during the autumn and winter months. Raised in Ohio, USA, they are extremely hardy and have become popular in Europe for their winter hardiness and suitability for pots. LOVITA is a compact, low-growing shrub with arching stems and slender, bright green, pointed leaves, flushed

red when young. In autumn and winter leaves colour rich reddish purple. SCARLETTA is similar but with finer, shorter stems and a more clump-forming habit. With the onset of cold weather, the foliage develops deep red shades, scarlet at the leaf tips.

Both plants make excellent ground cover in shade or semi-shade on acid soils. They are excellent for seasonal or permanent planting in containers. Because they survive in shade, they can bring colour to areas where other winter container plants fail. For the best results, pot them in lime-free, loam-based compost .

The light airy structure of *Nandina domestica* ♀, the sacred bamboo, is

unlike that of any other broad-leaved evergreen. As the common name suggests, it resembles a bamboo, but it is in fact related to berberis. This is a medium-sized shrub with erect stems like canes, and large, spreading, fern-like, leaves consisting of numerous leaflets. A native of China and Japan, it is hardy in most areas and grows on virtually any well-drained soil. After a hot summer, the small creamy white flowers turn into loose clusters of shining red berries at the top of the stems. The little pointed leaflets are tinged purplish red at the edges when the shrub is planted in sun. In spring and autumn the leaves become much more purplish-red. On less fertile soils and in full sun this colouring can include shades of copper-orange and red.

Nandina domestica is a useful shrub for specimen planting in gravel, staying upright and neat. It looks attractive in a big oriental-style pot. In mixed planting, it contributes the lightness and grace of a grass and the permanence and structure of an evergreen.

Nandina domestica 'Fire Power' ♀ is smaller, with a compact, rounded

---

GOOD COMPANIONS

Nandina domestica (1) is a striking evergreen to plant with *Cornus sanguinea* 'Winter Beauty' (2), grown for winter stems.

An excellent group for a damp site: *Viburnum opulus* (3) with *Cornus alba* 'Elegantissima' ♀ (4) and *Salix alba* subsp. *vitellina* ♀ (5).

Hypericum × inodorum 'Rheingold'

Pyracantha 'Orange Glow'

habit. The foliage is an unusual yellowish green in summer, turning orange-red in autumn and winter. (See Good Companions, page 173.)

AUTUMN BERRIES

Varieties of ***Hypericum × inodorum*** are now popular for floral decoration – not for their flowers but for their long-lasting autumn fruits. An upright shrub, *Hypericum × inodorum* flowers on wood produced the same season. The small yellow flowers are followed by conical, orange-red or sometimes chestnut brown berries, trimmed with the neat green frill of the calyx. *Hypericum × inodorum* 'Rheingold' is an excellent cultivar that stays free of the rust and mildew that plague other varieties. To encourage long stems for cutting, prune hard at the end of winter. Strong

174

> ### BERRIES FOR BIRDS
>
> A plant produces berries as one way of getting its seeds dispersed – via birds and other animals that eat them. Plant berry-bearing shrubs and you will attract birds, surely the greatest joy of the winter garden!

new shoots follow during spring and summer that will carry flowers and, in autumn, fruit.

Pyracantha (firethorn) is a member of the rose family and a close relative of cotoneaster. It has a mass of hawthorn-like flowers in spring and colourful berries in autumn. Most commonly grown as wall shrubs, many pyracanthas make excellent freestanding shrubs of loose, spreading habit. They are very hardy, evergreen and easy to grow on almost any soil. Their drawback is their suscepti-bility to disease, in particular fireblight and canker. It is best to choose one of the disease-resistant varieties.

Pyracantha 'Teton' ♀ is a hybrid between 'Orange Glow' and the yellow-berried *Pyracantha rogersiana* 'Flava' ♀. This also fruits freely, with orange-yellow berries, and is very resistant to fireblight. The Saphyr varieties are all very disease-resistant. SAPHYR ROUGE ('Cadrou') ♀, with red berries, ripening to orange, is a particularly good one for hedging. **Pyracantha 'Rosedale'** is another red-fruited variety resistant to fireblight.

Whatever new varieties come along, **Pyracantha 'Orange Glow'** ♀ remains popular. A vigorous shrub that makes a large dense mound, it is exceptionally free-flowering and fruiting, with bright

orange-red berries that hang on the branches well into winter. The once-popular cultivar **'Mohave'** is rarely seen now because of its susceptibility to scab, an increasingly serious problem in the mild, damp English winters.

Pyracanthas grown as wall shrubs should be trimmed after flowering. Cut the new growth back to the flower clusters so the autumn berries are not hidden by leaves. Apply the same technique to freestanding shrubs.

Pyracanthas are useful shrubs for bringing autumn colour to plantings of plain evergreens. They also combine well with all the yellow-variegated shrubs, such as *Elaeagnus pungens* 'Maculata'.

Rosa rugosa is probably the easiest rose to grow. Large suckering shrubs, they require no pruning, apart from an occasional tidy-up in spring. They are very disease-resistant, with healthy apple-green foliage, and grow on almost any soil, including the poor sandy soils disliked by most roses. The season of flowering is one of the longest of any rose: from early summer to late autumn. The flowers are mostly wonderfully fragrant, and the big tomato-like hips persist after the yellow-gold autumn leaves have fallen. Single-flowered varieties are best for fruit: *Rosa rugosa* 'Alba' ♀ is a vigorous cultivar with fragrant, silky, white, single flowers and exceptional fruits. *Rosa rugosa* 'Rubra' ♀ has wine-crimson flowers and large, showy hips. For hips, do not dead-head *Rosa rugosa*.

Rosa rugosa

Cotoneaster

Cotoneaster is an essential genus in the garden. It includes shrubs of all proportions, from prostrate creepers to medium-sized and large shrubs or small trees. They are generally easy to grow on any soil. Some are evergreen and some deciduous, but all have at least two seasons of interest and are much appreciated by wildlife. The profuse, small, pink or white flowers in early summer are attractive to bees, and the berries, produced in autumn, are attractive to birds.

The large cotoneasters are always loaded with clusters of autumn fruit weighing down the arching branches. Often semi-evergreen, these varieties have a much longer season of interest than do many small trees, such as prunus or malus varieties, and may well be worth considering as an alternative.

Many cotoneasters are invaluable for poor soil and difficult sites. Of the medium-sized shrubs, *Cotoneaster franchetii* and *Cotoneaster lacteus* ♲ are both easy and effective structure shrubs that thrive almost anywhere.

The ground-cover cotoneasters, such as *Cotoneaster dammeri* ♲, are excellent on banks or under other shrubs. Traditionally planted against a sunless wall of the house under a window, *Cotoneaster horizontalis* ♲ is a low-growing, spreading shrub, with characteristic herringbone branches. Do not prune as this robs the plant of the dramatic effect of its branch formation.

There are numerous other cotoneasters, some with yellow, cream or salmon fruits, but the red-berried varieties are the showiest and the ones that best compete with the autumn colours of foliage.

Cotoneaster × *watereri* 'John Waterer' ♲ (left) and *Cotoneaster frigidus* 'Cornubia' ♲ are large, semi-evergreen shrubs or small trees with arching branches and heavy clusters of red fruits.

The tiny, shiny green leaves of *Cotoneaster horizontalis* ♲ are deciduous but colour well before they fall, leaving the bright red berries that persist on the herringbone branches well into winter.

Cotoneaster franchetii (left) is a graceful, medium-sized, semi-evergreen shrub with sage-green leaves and orange-scarlet berries, larger and more oval than most. The small red berries of *Cotoneaster lacteus* ♲, an evergreen, colour late but last until midwinter.

In autumn sealing-wax berries stud the shiny evergreen foliage of *Cotoneaster dammeri* ♲ (left) and *Cotoneaster procumbens* 'Queen of Carpets'. Both are very good for ground cover and are also suitable for training over a frame.

Winter

Winter should on no account be regarded as a dead time in the garden. The lush green landscape and burgeoning borders that we associate with the traditional English garden take on a different persona during the coldest months. The low-level light and the lack of competing colour alter the character of plants, even those that do not undergo a radical seasonal change.

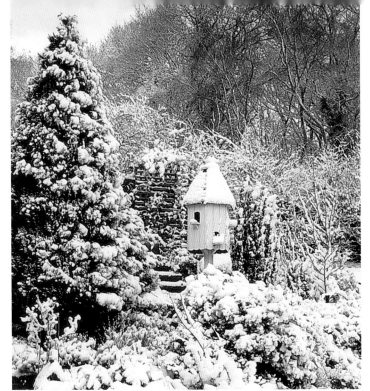

A fall of snow transforms the garden scene, emphasizing shape and structure.

Woody plants can contribute to the winter garden in many ways: through their flowers and foliage, of course, but also through the colour and texture of their stems and the framework of their branches. As the days become shorter and leaves fall, so deciduous trees and shrubs reveal hidden assets and take on a different dimension.

The blossoms of those plants that do flower during this season may not be the most spectacular in terms of size and colour, but the majority of them are deliciously fragrant as they work hard to attract the few insects that are around on cold winter days.

Some winter-flowering shrubs make perfect subjects to plant near the house. There they can enjoy some shelter, and their beauty can easily be appreciated at a time of year when we may only rarely venture out into the garden. Many winter performers thrive happily in shade or semi-shade, situations where shrubs that bloom in summer so often struggle.

Abeliophyllum distichum is a hardy shrub from Korea, a member of the olive family and related to forsythia. It is sometimes called white forsythia, for the sake of giving it a common name, but it is more graceful and delicate than its yellow-flowered cousin. Although it is hardy, it needs a warm, sunny position to ripen the wood if it is to flower well. It is slow-growing and produces thin branches of dark purplish wood that lose their leaves after some display of autumn colour. The fragrant, fragile, pearl-white flowers open on the bare branches in February. In the wild, this plant is now rare and in danger of extinction. Hardly spectacular, it does have a delicate beauty, and is well worth preserving in our gardens.

Chimonanthus praecox, known commonly as wintersweet, lives up to its name when it comes to fragrance. This is not a conspicuous plant but, in flower, it cannot go unnoticed as it fills the garden with its delicious fragrance.

Abeliophyllum distichum

Chimonanthus praecox

Chimonanthus praecox (*praecox* means early) is a native of China and is a very hardy plant. It is an easy plant to grow, but needs a sunny spot to ripen the growth for flowering; it is often grown against a sunny wall. This would not be the best choice of plant for a key position as it is not particularly attractive: the foliage is ordinary – long, narrow, pointed leaves of mid-green. It likes good drainage and is excellent on chalk.

The species produces waxy, pale, translucent flowers stained purple in the centre, carried on the bare branches in late winter. The form *Chimonanthus praecox* 'Grandiflorus' ♀ has larger flowers than the species, stained red, while those of *Chimonanthus praecox var. luteus* ♀ are clear, waxy yellow.

Long shoots can be cut back immediately after flowering, but any pruning later in the year reduces flowering potential. Flowers are rarely produced on young plants, so patience may be needed – but the winter fragrance is worth waiting for.

Cornus alba, red-barked dogwood, boasts many cultivars that are very useful foliage plants in the summer garden. However, it is for the beauty of the winter stems that the plant is best known. *Cornus alba* makes a large shrub, a thicket of stems that layer themselves where they touch the ground. The winter stems of the species, exposed when the leaves fall after a fine display of autumn colour, are rich red.

Cornus alba is one of the easiest shrubs to grow and succeeds on any soil, from dry to waterlogged. It grows in shade, but the stems need a bit of winter sun to show off their colour. Originating in Siberia, Manchuria and North Korea, it is extremely hardy. Its tough character and easy cultivation have led to it being used widely by commercial landscapers for amenity planting. This makes it no less valuable as a garden plant.

Left unpruned, the more vigorous varieties of cornus make effective screening plants. They are useful on banks and sloping ground where their suckering, layering habit successfully stabilizes the ground. For a particularly dramatic grouping, mix red- and yellow-stemmed varieties of winter dogwoods. They combine well with bold evergreens such as hollies and *Viburnum tinus* (see Good Companions, page 184).

The cultivar *Cornus alba* 'Sibirica' ♀ (also known as 'Atrosanguinea' or 'Westonbirt') is less robust than the species but it displays very brilliant, crimson-red winter shoots. *Cornus alba* 'Sibirica Variegata', the variegated form, is an excellent deciduous shrub and is suited to gardens of all sizes. The leaves, margined with creamy white and often flushed with pink, colour superbly in the autumn, and the winter stems are no less vivid than those of the green-leaved form.

Cornus alba 'Kesselringii' has unusual black-purple stems. This is a subject for creative planting: put it where the stems show against paving or a light background. It combines very well with the arching, white stems of *Rubus cockburnianus* 'Goldenvale' ♀.

Cornus alba 'Kesselringii'

GOOD COMPANIONS

For year-round interest, underplant *Corylus avellana* 'Contorta' (1) with *Ajuga reptans* 'Atropurpurea' (2) and *Hedera helix* 'Glacier' ♀ (3).

The dark plum-purple flowers of *Vinca minor* 'Atropurpurea' (4) provide interest after *Daphne odora* 'Aureomarginata' ♀ (5) has finished flowering.

Cornus sanguinea 'Winter Beauty'

Cornus alba 'Sibirica'

PRUNING CORNUS FOR WINTER STEMS

The secret of success with cornus grown for their winter stems is correct pruning. After the end of winter selectively cut back at least half the stems to ground level. Leave the others to provide structure through the following season, then cut them back at the end of the following winter. By that time, new shoots will have grown from the base to take their place. It is these new shoots, one year old, that display the best stem colour. Light trimming will produce unattractive twiggy growth with poor colour.

Alternatively, where space allows, plant winter dogwoods in groups and cut half the plants right back to ground level every winter, leaving the others to provide height through the summer months.

Cornus alba 'Elegantissima' ♀ is the widely grown white-variegated form, with pale green leaves margined and mottled white. This is a vigorous grower, and is excellent where a large, light shrub is required. Slightly more upright in character and often less vigorous than *Cornus alba* 'Elegantissima', **Cornus alba** 'Spaethii' ♀ has golden-variegated leaves, frequently flushed red when the shrub is grown in full sun. *Cornus alba* 'Gouchaultii' is similar in habit to 'Spaethii' but its leaves are flushed pink. *Cornus alba* 'Aurea' ♀ deserves much wider planting. The leaves are a soft yellow (yellow-lime when grown in shade) and the habit light and airy. It is one of the more subtle yellow-foliage shrubs and has the bonus of the winter interest of the stems.

Cornus sanguinea is the British native common dogwood: green red-flushed stems with small white flowers followed by black fruits. This is not a noticeable plant for most of the year, but in autumn is outstanding for its rich purple-red leaf colour. Various Dutch selections of this plant have become very popular for their outstanding stem colour. *Cornus sanguinea* 'Midwinter Fire' and *Cornus sanguinea* 'Winter Beauty' have bright orange-yellow stems that turn orange-red in winter. The leaves are pale green in summer, turning orange-yellow in autumn. This is a striking plant. On the nursery, the stock beds of container-grown plants positively glow in the winter sun.

All *Cornus sanguinea* cultivars can be more difficult to establish than other cornus ('Midwinter Fire' is the most vigorous). The roots are susceptible to frost damage in containers, so early winter planting is recommended.

Cornus sericea (previously better known as *Cornus stolonifera*) is similar

Cornus sericea 'Flaviramea'

CORNUS IN THE HOUSE

The stems are attractive when cut and used for decoration in the house. A vaseful of brightly coloured stems brings a surprisingly long-lasting touch of winter cheer. Long, flexible stems can be used to make wreaths and garlands for Christmas decorations.

to *Cornus alba*; a rampant suckering shrub that grows up to 2.5m (8ft) high. It is a native of North America, so equally hardy and just as easy to grow. The best-known cultivar is **Cornus sericea 'Flaviramea'** ♕, whose yellow-green shoots combine well with the red-stemmed varieties of cornus. It thrives on wet sites. **Cornus sericea 'Budd's Yellow'** has bright yellow young shoots and is considered an improvement on 'Flaviramea'. **Cornus sericea 'Cardinal'** has scarlet shoots tipped orange, and makes a rather more vigorous alternative to *Cornus sanguinea* 'Midwinter Fire'.

Corylus avellana 'Contorta' is a form of the native hazel originally discovered growing wild in a hedgerow in Gloucestershire. Its greatest attribute is its extraordinarily twisted stems, which have given it the common name corkscrew hazel or Harry Lauder's walking stick. These are concealed in summer by a mass of green foliage that shares this distorted habit. It has to be said that in leaf this is not the most attractive plant; it could easily be mistaken for one suffering from disease or pest infestation. However, when the leaves fall, it is a most strikingly architectural shrub. What's more, the stems are adorned in late winter with long, yellow lambs' tails.

Corylus avellana 'Contorta' are propagated by grafting on to rootstocks of the common hazel, *Corylus avellana*. Suckering from the rootstock can occur; remove suckers as they appear, before the more vigorous rootstock takes over. This is a very easy plant to grow and thrives on any soil in sun or shade.

Growing *Corylus avellana* 'Contorta' in a container allows it to show off the branch structure and the catkins to advantage. The plant also looks good when grown as a specimen rising above low ground cover, such as hedera or ajuga, or when grown against a light fence or stone wall. (See Good Companions, page 177.)

Daphnes have been some of the most sought-after shrubs for many years. The genus contains around 50 species, both evergreen and deciduous, natives of Europe, Asia and North Africa. Many are quite small, though some make substantial shrubs. The flowers are not spectacular, in some cases even insignificant, but many possess the most divine fragrance and it is for this quality that they are cherished.

Daphnes are poisonous plants, and are left alone by rabbits and deer; for

Corylus avellana 'Contorta'

Daphne odora 'Aureomarginata'

Daphne bholua 'Jacqueline Postill'

this reason, they are excellent subjects for the country garden.

Daphne mezereum is a deciduous, small shrub with upright branches. It produces masses of purplish-red flowers on the previous year's shoots in February and March; red berries often follow. The one-time popularity of this plant has diminished owing to a viral infection of stock. Affected plants will still flower, but look very poor in the garden for the rest of the year and grow reluctantly.

Daphne odora is a small rounded, evergreen shrub with glossy, dark green leaves. The hardier form, and the most frequently grown, is **Daphne odora** '**Aureomarginata**' ♥, which has a narrow, creamy yellow margin around the leaves. The starry, mauve-purple flowers are carried in clusters and are wonderfully fragrant. This plant does well in semi-shade and is an excellent choice to plant near the house, where its fragrance can be appreciated. It can be propagated from cuttings, which are best taken in late summer.

Daphne bholua is a much taller species, originating in the Himalayas. It

---

DAPHNES IN THE HOUSE

Daphne flowers do not last well indoors if you pick the woody stems. The trick is to pick only the flower clusters, with a few leaves, and place them in water up to their necks.

PLANTING AND CARING FOR DAPHNES

Daphnes like good loamy soil; they like moisture but must have good drainage. They do well on chalk soils as long as the other parameters are met. They are not ideal subjects for pots, and always thrive better in the open ground.

Many daphnes are reluctant rooters and difficult to propagate. They are often grafted and therefore more expensive than many other garden shrubs. On grafted daphnes such as *Daphne bholua* 'Jacqueline Postill', look out for vigorous suckers coming from the rootstock. Left alone, these can take over the plant.

Daphnes are not long-lived plants and often deteriorate after 10 or 15 years. *Daphne mezereum* and *Daphne odora*, in particular, manifest their decline by shedding leaves while still producing a few flowers. This means the virus has taken its toll and it is time to buy a new plant.

---

grows a bit like a leggy teenager, up to a height of 2m (6ft). It is best described as a semi-evergreen, but the amount of leaf retention depends on the exposure of the site. It is narrow in habit and is ideal to plant close to the house, perhaps at the base of a climber that provides interest later in the year.

In 1982 Alan Postill, propagator at Hillier Nurseries, raised the cultivar

Daphne bholua '**Jacqueline Postill**' ♥. This is an excellent, very hardy form and one that no winter garden should be without. The flowers are large and showy for a daphne, purplish-pink in clusters and freely produced. Their powerful fragrance carries widely on the cold winter air.

Garryas are inconspicuous plants for much of the year, with tough dark leathery leaves. They are excellent to grow on a shady wall, tolerant of urban pollution and resistant to maritime exposure. Originating from the south-western USA, Mexico and the West Indies, garryas are used to warmer climes and can be hit by severe cold, despite the tough appearance, so they are not for exposed sites.

The main attribute of garryas is their catkins, which are produced during the winter months. These are most spectacular on the male. In fact, female plants are not worth growing, and it is essential to acquire a named male clone if you are to be certain of the performance of the plant.

Garrya elliptica '**James Roof**' ♥ (illus. page 182) is the best known and deservedly the most popular choice. The plant is draped with long, silvery grey-green catkins from early to late winter. As a relatively upright shrub, it lends itself to being grown against a wall, where it will also benefit from the extra protection. *(Continued on page 182.)*

Hamamelis

The genus Hamamelis is a small one, with a handful of species, but they are remarkably beautiful trees and shrubs, natives of North America, Japan and China. As well as their strangely delicate flowers produced in the depths of winter, witch hazels contribute some of the best autumn foliage colour in the garden.

Ideal as freestanding small trees or large shrubs, hamamelis make architecturally beautiful specimens, with a spreading, irregular branch pattern and bowl-like form. Avoid pruning; these plants should be free spirits! All like a good, but not heavy, soil with plenty of organic matter. They colour better on acid soils and the cultivars of *Hamamelis mollis* prefer a low pH. They do not enjoy drought, and careful watering during establishment is essential. Hamamelis are perfectly hardy but enjoy the shelter of neighbouring trees.

Site these plants so as to show off the wonderful flowers. Those with pale yellow flowers look better against a dark background; red-flowering cultivars should catch the low winter light. Buy witch hazels when they are in flower, so you can see what you are buying. Even the youngest shrub will flower, as most are grafted.

Hamamelis look stunning against the intense blue of a winter sky.

Hamamelis virginiana, the Virginian witch hazel (whose branches early settlers in Virginia used as divining rods – a 'magical' property that gave this plant the name witch hazel), is the commercial source of witch hazel lotion.

The Sir Harold Hillier Gardens and Arboretum near Winchester, in southern England, is a wonderful place to see witch hazels. Here you will find the National Collection of the genus Hamamelis. The guided 'Witch Hazel Walks' in January are some of the most popular events in the gardens, a reflection of how passionately people feel about these extraordinary, delectable plants.

Hamamelis x *intermedia* 'Pallida' ♀ is the most popular of the named x *intermedia* clones. Sulphur-yellow flowers cover the naked branches in midwinter. The autumn foliage colour is yellow.

Hamamelis x *intermedia* 'Jelena' ♀ is one of the best-loved of the exotic, red- and orange-flowered witch hazels. Autumn colour is a late-season echo of the colour of the blooms

Hamamelis x *intermedia* 'Diane' ♀ is truly red, perhaps the best of the red-flowering hamamelis, with autumn foliage shades to match.

Hamamelis mollis ♀ (Chinese witch hazel) is the most popular variety. Its large flowers are sweetly fragrant, with broader ribbon-petals than on many witch hazels. The species is an excellent plant but, like all seed-raised plants, can be variable in flower quality.

Garrya elliptica 'James Roof'

Garrya × issaquahensis 'Glasnevin Wine'

Garrya × issaquahensis 'Glasnevin Wine' is a broader shrub than *Garrya elliptica* but has the same undulating, leathery foliage. The shoots are a more reddish purple, as are the long catkins; the total effect is most attractive.

Garryas benefit from pruning during their early years. Do this after the catkins fall. This creates a plant that is bushy at the base rather than one that becomes top heavy.

Positioning garryas alongside light-variegated evergreens can lighten their heavy appearance, particularly after the catkins are over. *Pittosporum* 'Garnettii' (see page 64) is ideal for this purpose; the silvery quality of the foliage is the perfect complement to the pewter catkins of the garrya.

Lonicera × purpusii is one of the shrubby honeysuckles, a vigorous shrub, a hybrid between *Lonicera fragrantissima* and *Lonicera standishii*, both of which are winter-flowering, semi-evergreen species.

It has to be said that the plant is ordinary for most of the year, looking not unlike a privet with its plain, dark green foliage. The stems are arching and often layer themselves. This enlarges the overall bulk of the shrub. Its appearance as a young container plant is deceiving; growth is initially weak and lax and belies its potential. It is an excellent subject for the back of a border where the vigorous stems can be allowed to grow. This is an easy shrub to grow, tolerant of any soil or aspect.

Any pruning is done immediately after flowering, usually in late March. Ideally whole stems that have flowered should be cut back hard to allow new shoots to grow through and flower the following midwinter.

The flowers are creamy white with cream stamens, carried in pairs at the leaf nodes. They are wonderfully fragrant, and the cultivar *Lonicera × purpusii* 'Winter Beauty' produces them freely over a long period. It was raised in 1966 by Hillier foreman Alf Alford from a backcross of *Lonicera × purpusii* with *Lonicera standishii*.

Today's milder winters mean that this plant retains some of its foliage. This is an advantage to some degree, but the leaves tend to obscure the flowers. If you bring stems into the house to enjoy the fragrance, remove the leaves.

Mahonias have long been some of our most popular winter-flowering evergreens. With their stiff stems and strange leaf arrangement, they are awkward as young plants but acquire grace with maturity. Their leathery texture belies their delicate beauty and the delicious fragrance of the flowers, borne on long, spreading racemes.

Mahonia aquifolium See page 90.

Mahonia japonica ♀ is the best-known and arguably most beautiful species. This is a tolerant plant, grows on virtually any soil – even chalk – and succeeds in shade. Although it is evergreen, on poor shallow soils some leaves display rich scarlet and red shades that last well into the winter.

Lonicera × purpusii 'Winter Beauty'

Mahonia japonica

Mahonia × media 'Underway'

PRUNING MAHONIA

Mahonias pose a pruning problem: if you cut the stem below the whorls of leaves, where will new growth emerge? Clad in small spiny leaflets, the stems do not look as if they will produce new shoots. In fact, mahonias have plenty of dormant buds and respond well to pruning.

Mahonia japonica has a more relaxed habit than many other mahonias.

Normally the foliage is a deep, shiny green, with holly-like leaflets arranged opposite each other down both sides of a rigid leaf stalk. These large, compound leaves are held in whorls on tough upright stems. Like its cousin the berberis, this is a plant with armour; never pleasant to handle, it makes a good boundary plant where intruders are to be deterred. *Mahonia japonica* is one of the most fragrant mahonias. In midwinter the terminal rosettes of foliage produce a delightful posy of flowers that resemble lily-of-the-valley; the colour is soft primrose yellow and the fragrance delicious.

Mahonia lomariifolia ♀ is an imposing, upright creature from Burma and western China. The leaves have more leaflets, of a narrower shape, than *Mahonia japonica*, and the magnificent sprays of showy yellow flowers are carried upright. However, outside the mildest localities, this plant can be hit by frost. Not only are the flowers affected, the desiccating effect of freezing wind can cause extensive leaf fall.

The hybrid **Mahonia × media** combines attributes of both species and has given rise to some of our most popular garden cultivars. These can reach a height of 3m (6ft) and have a strong architectural quality, with racemes of bright yellow flowers. They may be an excellent alternative to a small tree in a limited space, particularly in shade.

There are several well-known named clones of *Mahonia × media*, including 'Lionel Fortescue' ♀ (named after the gentleman who raised it), which has upright racemes, and **'Buckland'** ♀, named after the village where both were raised. Another × *media* clone, **'Charity'** has become very popular because of its robust nature and long

Mahonia × media 'Winter Sun'

flowering period but, sadly, it is not especially fragrant; like 'Buckland', its racemes are long and spreading. More compact forms of *Mahonia × media* include **'Underway'** ♀, with upright racemes, and **'Winter Sun'** ♀, which excels with its erect racemes of very fragrant flowers.

Sarcococcas (Christmas box) are charming dwarf evergreen shrubs. There are several popular species, all good on any fertile soil and especially happy on chalk. They are slow-growing, rarely reach over 1m (3ft) in height, and are remarkably tolerant, succeeding well in shade and under trees.

The evergreen foliage is valuable in its own right but the delightful surprise comes in midwinter, when the tiny white, thread-like flowers open. Not conspicuous in colour or showiness, the blooms cannot escape attention because of their wonderful fragrance.

PLANTING PARTNERS FOR MAHONIA

Mahonias are plants with strong, bold form; clever planting with yellow-variegated partners highlights their yellow flowers. The golden-variegated *Euonymus japonicus* 'Aureus' is an easy-to-grow plant that thrives in the same conditions as mahonias. For ground cover, choose the ever-popular *Euonymus fortunei* 'Emerald 'n' Gold'; its small leaves lighten those of the mahonia. Where space allows, grow a large-leaved hedera as ground cover; *Hedera colchica* 'Sulphur Heart' is particularly effective. Nowadays mahonias start to flower early, often at the beginning of winter. Extend the season of interest by planting yellow narcissi alongside; the mahonia's bold green foliage makes the perfect backdrop.

Sarcococcas are very useful garden plants. There are few other hardy, dwarf evergreens that are as accommodating. They are superb for filling in at ground level under taller subjects. Their glossy, rich green foliage is an excellent background for early spring-flowering bulbs. Plant them beside a path and near the entrance of the house, where their scent can be enjoyed even on cold winter days. They are good for cutting, both for the quality of the foliage and the fragrance of their flowers.

Sarcococca confusa ♀ has especially good glossy, rich green foliage and a graceful spreading habit. Once the plant becomes established, it tends to sucker and spread – not invasively but densely. Black berries follow the fragrant creamy flowers.

Sarcococca confusa

Sarcococca hookeriana var. **digyna** ♀ is a more upright shrub than *Sarcococca confusa*, with narrow leaves and a more open habit. The flowers appear thinner and sparser but are no less fragrant. **Sarcococca hookeriana** var. **digyna 'Purple Stem'** is attractive for its young stems and leaf stems, which are flushed purple. This is a good plant to provide

Sarcococca hookeriana var. digyna

a backdrop for the red and purple *Helleborus orientalis* hybrids.

Sarcococca orientalis is upright and vigorous, with strong green stems. The leaves are larger than those of *Sarcococca confusa*, up to 9cm (7in) long, and the flowers are tinged pink. **Sarcococca ruscifolia** is uncommon in cultivation but is often confused with *Sarcococca confusa*. Look out for **Sarcococca ruscifolia** var. **chinensis** ♀; the rich green foliage is the perfect setting for dark red berries. This is a most attractive plant, forming a dense clump similar in appearance to butcher's broom, *Ruscus aculeatus* (see page 90).

Skimmias are shrubs that come to the fore as the days shorten and winter approaches. However, they look good all year round in the right situation. For many years their decorative qualities have been recognized by Europeans; frost hardy, they withstand the freezing conditions of the Continental winter.

Skimmias bring colour and interest to winter containers and their dark green cut foliage, colourful flower buds or shiny red berries are used in seasonal flower decorations. But skimmias are more than seasonal decorations. Hailing from the Himalayas and eastern Asia, these excellent evergreen shrubs tolerate shade, maritime conditions and urban pollution. They have a compact bushy habit and dark green, glossy evergreen foliage. The leaves appear to be arranged in rosettes; they make an excellent background for the showy

GOOD COMPANIONS

For a striking winter grouping, plant *Viburnum tinus* (1) with red-stemmed *Cornus alba* 'Sibirica' ♀ (2) and a silvery *Ilex aquifolium* 'Ferox Argentea' ♀ (3).

Viburnum × *bodnantense* 'Dawn' (4) makes a good partner for the evergreen *Pittosporum* 'Garnettii' (5).

Underplant *Mahonia* × *media* 'Charity' (6) with *Hedera colchica* 'Sulphur Heart' (7); the ivy's yellow leaves set off the mahonia's flowers.

Skimmia japonica 'Rubella'

Skimmia japonica subsp. reevesiana

GETTING THE BEST OUT OF YOUR SKIMMIAS

Skimmias are plants for shade on well-drained soil. They enjoy a soil rich in organic matter and establish better when plenty of good garden compost or well-rotted manure is incorporated at the time of planting. The fibrous root system must be kept well watered until the plant is established. Skimmia is an easy shrub to grow and requires no special care and no pruning.

Planted in the open ground in full sun, Skimmia has a tendency to go yellow, often leading to the conclusion that this plant is a lime-hater, and that this yellowing is a reaction to alkaline soil. Most skimmias are in fact happy on chalk soils as well as acid, as long as they are planted in shade or semi-shade. In a hot sunny position the yellowing can also be due to an infestation of red spider mite; use a biological control or a drench of systemic pest-killer.

If a plant fails to perform, does not flower and refuses to berry, it is nearly always because it has been planted too deeply. Never plant deeper than the level of compost in the pot, otherwise the plant will sulk.

clusters of flowers and prominent berries produced by some varieties. Because of the fruiting season, they are sometimes used as a substitute for holly. Those that produce red flower buds in the winter are equally decorative.

Skimmia is a member of the family Rutaceae (other members include citrus and choisya), hence its aromatic foliage and fragrant flowers.

Skimmia japonica 'Rubella' ♥ is the best-known cultivar. This is a male clone, so does not produce berries. However, it is very free-flowering and compensates with a profusion of red flower buds through autumn into winter. In spring these open as clusters of fragrant creamy flowers. This is an ideal subject for winter containers and temporary decoration, as well as for permanent planting.

Skimmia japonica **susp.** *reevesiana* produces both male and female flowers. Self-pollinating, it produces sealing-wax red berries on dwarf plants that rarely grow to over 60cm (2ft). The white flowers are sweetly fragrant. This plant is not good on chalk. In fact, it is one of the more difficult skimmias to establish in the garden and is popular only because it berries as a young plant in a pot.

A female clone, *Skimmia japonica* 'Veitchii' ('Foremanii') produces berries of excellent quality if it has a male pollinator such as *Skimmia* × *confusa* 'Kew Green' ♥ to set the fruit. The male clones should never be regarded as inferior because of their lack of berries; the flowers are just as much of an attribute. 'Kew Green' is a superb cultivar, with glossy apple-green foliage and large panicles of white, lily-of-the-valley scented flowers. As its name implies, *Skimmia japonica* 'Fragrans' ♥ is also fragrant.

WINTER-FLOWERING BULBS TO PLANT UNDER WINTER SHRUBS

Crocus tommasinianus ♥
Cyclamen coum ♥
Eranthis hyemalis ♥
Galanthus nivalis ♥
Iris reticulata ♥
Puschkinia scilloides

SKIMMIAS IN POTS

Because of their compact habit, skimmias make excellent shrubs for containers. Planted in a sensibly sized pot, in excess of 35cm (14in) in diameter, a skimmia can be regarded as a permanent subject that will give years of pleasure in any situation out of full sun. Use loam-based compost for potting, and ensure that the container has good drainage.

The bold form and strong foliage of skimmia contrasts well with ferns and hostas, also good subjects for pots.

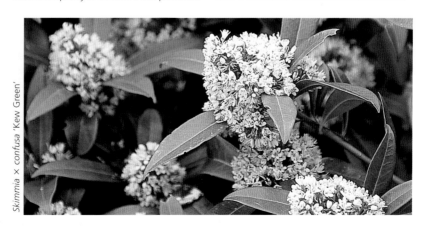

Skimmia × *confusa* 'Kew Green'

Viburnum

Viburnum tinus etched with frost.

Of the 150 or more species of evergreen or deciduous viburnums, several are highly valued for their winter flowers. All are easy shrubs to grow on any soil, succeed in sun or shade, are frost-hardy, and make excellent structure plants.

Viburnum tinus originally known as *Laurustinus*, was introduced to our gardens in the 16th century from the Mediterranean region. Like many Mediterranean plants, it is a survivor, tolerant not only of inhospitable conditions and poor soil, but, surprisingly, of the cold and wet of the British winter. It has all the sought-after qualities: low-maintenance, evergreen, free-flowering over a long period, responsive to trimming. It copes well on the coast and seems resistant to urban pollution.

The species is a medium to large shrub, of dense and bushy habit, with masses of dark green, glossy oval leaves. The flattened heads of pink buds, opening to white flowers, are produced continuously from autumn through to late spring. Blue-black fruits often follow the flowers and are usually still present when the following season's flower buds are emerging.

With its evergreen mass, *Viburnum tinus* contributes bold, all-year-round form to any planting scheme. Its robust foliage and free-flowering habit make it easily compatible with any planting scheme, formal or informal.

Viburnum tinus survives in dry shade, even under oak trees. However, despite this, it has to get properly established before it can flourish. The secret of success is good soil preparation and watering – even in winter if it is dry.

Viburnum × *bodnantense* is one of the best-known winter-flowering shrubs. It has strong upright growth and clusters of deep pink buds, opening to pale pink, sweetly scented flowers. Usually unaffected by frost, these are produced freely from mid-autumn onwards.

A hybrid between two winter-flowering species, *Viburnum farreri* ♀ (often known as *Viburnum fragrans*)

and *Viburnum grandiflorum*, *Viburnum* × *bodnantense* was raised at the Royal Botanic Garden, Edinburgh and later at Bodnant, in Wales, after which it was named.

Viburnum × *bodnantense* makes a tall shrub, often in excess of 3m (10ft), and is an excellent structure shrub for the back of the border, where it can be allowed to reach its potential. However, its eventual size is often underestimated and it outgrows its allotted space. When grown in a sheltered position, *Viburnum* × *bodnantense* has a tendency to hang onto its foliage in winter, which spoils the effect of the flowers. For best effect, plant it in an open position .

TRIMMING AND TRAINING VIBURNUMS

All cultivars of *Viburnum tinus* respond well to trimming. Do this immediately after flowering in early spring, to give the plant time to produce mature growth on which to flower next winter. Pruning is necessary only to control size and shape; it is not essential. *Viburnum tinus* makes an excellent informal hedge or screen and is an interesting subject to train as a standard, cone or ball – a softer and prettier alternative to the more traditional bay and box.

Because of the upright growth of *Viburnum* × *bodnantense*, poor pruning often spoils the shape and habit. Partially cutting back shoots, to reduce height, results in vigorous ugly growth at the top of the plant. Pruning is not essential; where it is necessary to control size, selectively remove whole branches to ground level, allowing new wood to come from the base.

Viburnum tinus SPIRIT ('Anvi') produces profuse white flowers, pink in bud, over a long period. Blue-black fruits follow reliably after the flowers. The foliage is excellent, lush and dark green, carried on deep red stems that add considerably to the overall effect of the plant. This will make a large shrub over 2m (6ft) in height if left unpruned.

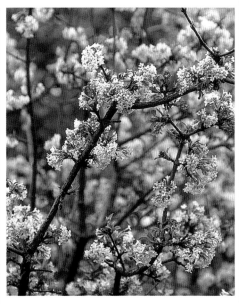

Viburnum × *bodnantense* 'Dawn' ♀ (above) was the first named form of the × *bodnantense* cross and still the most widely grown. It is vigorous and hardy with dark, pleated foliage often flushed red-brown later in the year. The cultivar *Viburnum* × *bodnantense* 'Deben' ♀ has paler flowers.

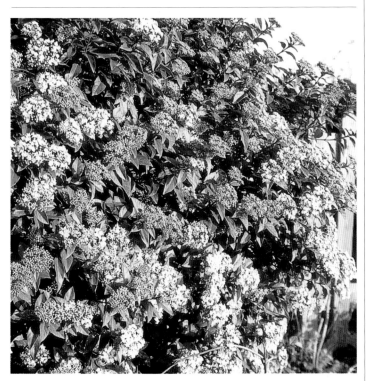

Viburnum tinus 'French White' ♀ (above) is similar in stature to *Viburnum tinus* SPIRIT ('Anvi') and is one of the most widely planted forms. 'Purpureum' is a selection with darker foliage and bronze-tinged young growth. It has a looser habit than most viburnums, making it rather less solid – a useful attribute in mixed planting.

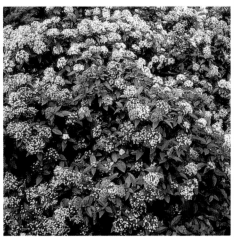

Viburnum tinus 'Eve Price' ♀ (above) is the most compact form, growing slowly to 1.5m (5ft). The leaves are smaller than the type, and closer together. It produces masses of deep pink buds and pink-tinged flowers. It survives out of full sun and is a good evergreen for a large pot. 'Gwenllian' is another compact grower, with whiter, larger, flowers.

Author's choice: top 20 performance shrubs

From the large selection of ornamental shrubs described in this book I have chosen 20 I consider to be excellent, easy-to-grow garden plants that have a long season of interest and will succeed on virtually any soil of reasonable fertility.

I have put these plants into four groups, two suitable for sun and two for shade. Between them, the plants in each combination give a pleasing variation in colour, form and texture, and achieve all-year-round appeal. All are tried and tested.

TALL SELECTION FOR A SUNNY POSITION – MAXIMUM HEIGHT 3M (10FT)

 ***Buddleja* 'Lochinch'** ♔ (page 74) Silver foliage; lilac-blue, fragrant flowers in summer

 ***Ceanothus* 'Concha'** ♔ (page 140) Evergreen; fast-growing; blue flowers in late spring

 ***Choisya* 'Aztec Pearl'** ♔ (page 139) Evergreen; fragrant white flowers in late spring

 Sambucus nigra* f. *porphyrophylla ('Black Lace') ♔ (page 54)

 ***Weigela* 'Florida Variegata'** ♔ (page 69) Variegated foliage; pink flowers in late spring

TALL SELECTION FOR SEMI-SHADE – MAXIMUM HEIGHT 2M (6FT)

 ***Euonymus japonicus* 'Chollipo'** ♔ (page 59) Evergreen, gold-and-green variegated foliage

 Fatsia japonica ♔ (page 89) Evergreen, bold leaves; white flowers in early winter

 ***Hypericum* 'Hidcote'** ♔ (page 158) Golden-yellow flowers through summer and autumn

 ***Osmanthus heterophyllus* 'Goshiki'** (page 43) Evergreen, golden-bronze variegated foliage

 ***Philadelphus coronarius* 'Aureus'** ♔ (page 45) Golden-yellow foliage; fragrant white flowers in early summer

SHORT SELECTION FOR A SUNNY POSITION – MAXIMUM HEIGHT 1M (3FT)

 ***Cistus* ×*obtusifolius* 'Thrive'** (page 83) Evergreen; white flowers in summer

 ***Hebe* 'Red Edge'** ♔ (page 76) Evergreen, grey-green foliage, red-edged in winter

 Lavandula stoechas* subsp. *pedunculata ♔ (page 73) Grey-green aromatic leaves; mauve-blue flowers in summer

 ***Rosmarinus officinalis* 'Miss Jessopp's Upright'** ♔ (page 86) Evergreen, aromatic, culinary foliage; blue flowers in early spring

 ***Salvia officinalis* 'Purpurascens'** ♔ (page 49) Evergreen, purple-grey, aromatic, culinary foliage; blue flowers in summer

SHORT SELECTION FOR SHADE – MAXIMUM HEIGHT 1M (3FT)

 ***Cornus alba* 'Sibirica Variegata'** (page 177) White-and-green variegated leaves; red winter stems

 ***Euonymus fortunei* 'Silver Queen'** (page 59) Evergreen, cream-and-green variegated foliage

 Sarcococca confusa ♔ (page 90) Evergreen; fragrant white flowers in winter

 Viburnum davidii ♔ (page 37) Evergreen, bold foliage; small white flowers in summer

 ***Viburnum tinus* 'Eve Price'** ♔ (page 187) Evergreen; pink buds and white flowers in winter

Index

The letter *i* following a page number (for example 165*i*) refers to an illustration. A page number in **bold** type refers to a Plant Profile.

INDEX